Bible

Crosswords

101

Vol. 2

ISBN 978-1-60260-878-8

Crosswords were created using licensed Crossword Weaver software (www.crosswordweaver.com).

Puzzles were prepared by Patricia Mitchell, Laura Lisle, Vicki J. Kuyper, and Tonya Vilhauer in association with Snapdragon Group℠, Tulsa, Oklahoma, USA.

All scripture quotations, unless otherwise noted, are taken from the King James Version of the Bible.

Published by Barbour Publishing, Inc., P.O. Box 719, Uhrichsville, Ohio 44683, www.barbourbooks.com

Our mission is to publish and distribute inspirational products offering exceptional value and biblical encouragement to the masses.

Printed in the United States of America.

Bible
Crosswords
101

Vol. 2

BARBOUR
PUBLISHING

1 AARON'S ERRANDS
by Patricia Mitchell

• • • • • •

ACROSS

1 Prejudice
5 Aaron stretched his hand over this (Ex. 7:19) (Sp.)
9 Summer stinger
13 "Ye are ___" (Ex. 5:17)
14 Seventh commandment no-no
15 '80s shampoo brand for highlighting hair
16 "Gather a certain ___ every day" (Ex. 16:4)
17 "They shall ___ their swords into plowshares" (Isa. 2:4)
18 Flippered mammal
19 Front of church
21 Harvard's rival
23 Aaron died here (Num. 20:27–28)
24 Anointing element
25 Aaron's sister (Ex. 15:20)
29 U.K. time zone
30 Matron
32 Compass point
33 Dispute
36 Epics
37 Potter's vessel
38 Peter compares the devil to one (1 Peter 5:8)
39 Priestly fabric
40 Nail
41 Tire measurement
42 Bluish-white metals
43 Psalms, e.g.
44 "A ___ gathereth her chickens" (Matt. 23:37)
45 Egyptians would ___ the Israelites to leave (Ex. 12:33)
46 Jacob or Laban, e.g.
47 Very soft fur
49 Energy measurements
50 Wing

53 "He called for Moses and Aaron by night, and said, ___ up" (Ex. 12:31)
55 Navies
57 Jacob's father (Gen. 25:26)
60 "Keep it up until the fourteenth day of the ___ month" (Ex. 12:6)
62 "Hail smote. . .___ man and beast" (Ex. 9:25)
63 Mooring
64 "Whereby we cry, ___, Father" (Rom. 8:15)
65 Canal
66 "No more give the people straw to ___ brick" (Ex. 5:7)
67 Sacred lot carried by Aaron (Exod. 28:30)
68 Eyeglass part

DOWN

1 White-barked tree
2 American state
3 Aaron ministered at one (Ex. 28:43)
4 "I have surely ___ the affliction of my people" (Ex. 3:7)
5 "The LORD saith it; ___ I have not spoken" (Ezek. 13:7)
6 Squelch
7 Uncle Sam's place
8 Lawyer (abbr.)
9 "This is the ___ of Meribah" (Num. 20:13)
10 Something else (abbr.)
11 Nazareth to Jericho (dir.)
12 Golfer's goal
15 Holy of ___
20 "And it shall ___ to pass" (Ex. 4:8)
22 Jordanian capital

26 Accustom
27 Sarai's spouse
28 God does this to broken spirits
29 Weapon
30 One was performed by 25 Across (Ex. 15:20)
31 Genesis 5 data
33 "I am ___ and Omega" (Rev. 1:8)
34 "He is ___" (Matt. 28:6)
35 Moses' "hands were steady until the ___ down of the sun" (Ex. 17:12)
36 "I will ___ unto the Lord" (Ex. 15:1)
39 Italian currency
40 Pharaoh's daughter found one (Ex. 2:5–6)

42 Swiss city
43 Prune beginnings
46 The Jordan, in places
48 Aaron did this better than his brother (Ex. 4:14)
49 Disney deer
50 Worship fervently
51 Language of the Vulgate
52 Burnt offering remains
54 Jacob's twin (Gen. 25:25–26)
56 First murder victim (Gen. 4:8)
57 Computer makers
58 God's people were led through the Red ___ (Ex. 13:18)
59 ___ of the covenant
61 Reduced (abbr.)

2 AMAZING ABIGAIL
by Patricia Mitchell

• • • • • •

ACROSS
1 Abigail's husband (1 Sam. 25:3)
6 Measurement replaced by hertz
9 Apt description of Abigail's husband
13 "Horns of ivory and ___" (Ezek. 27:15)
14 According to song, Jesus slept on it
15 "And ye have done ___ than your fathers" (Jer. 16:12)
16 "Thou art God ___" (Ps. 86:10)
17 "The birds of the ___ have nests" (Matt. 8:20)
18 Jesus does this
19 Bag
20 "An angry man stirreth up ___" (Prov. 29:22)
22 His wife was salty (Gen. 19: 23–26)
23 Maybe Adam used one in Eden to till the earth
24 Distress call
25 Ark builder
27 Coarse
29 Slain with a sling
33 Spy org.
34 Abigail's servants ___ the way (1 Sam. 25:19)
35 Abigail's husband's party attitude (1 Sam. 25:36)
36 "All we like ___ have gone astray" (Isa. 53:6)
39 Noah, Jacob, Joseph, e.g.
40 What shepherds do
41 Tyre or Sidon, e.g.
42 Kitten's cry
43 "I ___ no pleasant bread" (Dan. 10:3)
44 Some say it was what Eve picked
46 Also known as Myanmar

49 Abigail gave David five measures of it (1 Sam. 25:18)
50 Recede
51 Flightless bird
53 Typing rate
56 "The tongue. . .is. . .full of ___ poison" (James 3:8)
58 Where Abigail and her husband lived (1 Sam. 25:2–3)
59 David, upon hearing Abigail's husband's message (1 Sam. 25:13)
61 Cow sound
62 Doctrine
63 "Noah ___ grace in the eyes of the Lord" (Gen. 6:8)
64 Prophetic gift
65 Excuse
66 Shine
67 "I was blind, now I ___" (John 9:25)
68 Perfect

DOWN
1 Under, (poet.)
2 Like Eden
3 Infant's sock
4 Mary's mother, traditionally (var.)
5 Caustic substance
6 Talks with
7 Set of ark animals
8 Medicine deliverers
9 David was one to Abigail's husband (1 Sam. 25:13)
10 Voiced
11 Norwegian capital
12 "Shall bear thee up. . .___ thou dash thy foot" (Ps. 91:12)
15 Wale
20 Member of the legume family
21 Abigail's husband refused this to David's men (1 Sam. 25:11)

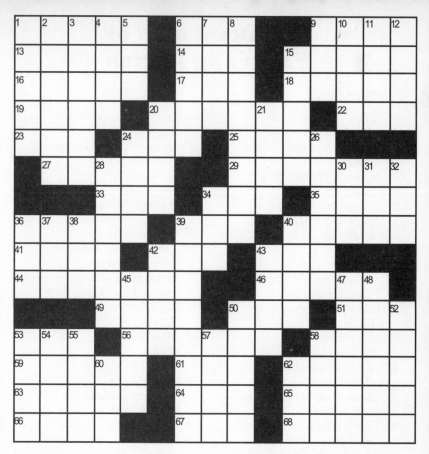

24 "My feet did not ___" (2 Sam. 22:37)
26 "Friend, go up ___" (Luke 14:10)
28 Vinegar's acid
30 Abigail's husband had too much of this, perhaps (1 Sam. 25:36)
31 Herbal beverage
32 Abigail "bowed herself on ___ face" (1 Sam. 25:41)
34 The Ten Commandments, e.g.
36 Place of ahhhs
37 Jump
38 Make a mistake
39 Affectionate monikers (2 wds.)
40 Hurt one's toe
42 Abigail "told him nothing, less or ___, until the morning light" (1 Sam. 25:36)

43 Subject of this puzzle, familiarly
45 Encrypted
47 Someone not nice
48 One-celled water creature
50 To escape secretly to marry
52 "Wait upon the LORD our God, ___ that he have mercy" (Ps. 123:2)
53 Abigail became David's ___ (1 Sam. 25:39)
54 High school event
55 Aloha place
57 Medicine amount
58 Blend
60 Dynamite
62 ___ chi

ABRAHAM: MAN OF FAITH AND ACTION

by Patricia Mitchell

• • • • • •

ACROSS

1 Six-pack muscles (abbr.)
4 Walk on Mt. Sinai, perhaps
8 Lease giver
14 It's put in a horse's mouth (James 3:3)
15 Eve's garden
16 Take a deep breath, then ___
17 "Deliver thyself as a ___" (Prov. 6:5)
18 God promised it to Abraham
19 The Israelites ___ Egypt
20 Progressive decline
22 Ishmael to Abraham (Gen. 17:23)
23 1960's skirt
24 Did Noah use these?
27 Abraham's grandfather (Gen. 11:24–26)
31 Abraham received one from God
33 Pixie
35 Flightless bird
36 Greek goddess of dawn
38 ___ Schwarz, NY toy store
39 Hagar was one (Gen. 16:1)
40 Describes the rock in the wilderness struck by Moses (Num. 20:11)
44 Chemist's tube
46 James the ___, son of Alphaeus (Mark 15:40)
47 Conger
49 What Israelites were with God's Commandments
50 Unrefined metal
51 "Ye shall not surely ___" (Gen. 3:4)
52 Huff
55 "Offer him there for a ___ offering" (Gen. 22:2)
58 Jerusalem to Babylon (dir.)
61 Marrow
63 Lord's Prayer opener
65 Neglected
67 Abraham was rich in these (Gen. 13:2)
70 Condiment
71 Flavor enhancer
72 "I lift up my hands toward thy holy ___" (Ps. 28:2)
73 Swiss mountains
74 A Pharisee might consider himself this in religious law
75 Abraham built an altar between here and Hai (Gen. 12:8)
76 Prophecy is not this (2 Peter 1:21)
77 "Arise, lift up the ___" (Gen. 21:18)

DOWN

1 Abraham's former name
2 Relating to life
3 Relating to Eve's origins
4 "He is our ___ and our shield" (Ps. 33:20)
5 Gem State
6 African nation
7 "The ___ of all flesh is come before me" (Gen. 6:13)
8 "Moab. . .hath settled on his ___" (Jer. 48:11)
9 Gas company
10 Indo-Aryan language
11 "She ___ over against him, and. . . wept" (Gen. 21:16)
12 Grand ___ Opry
13 Israelites crossed the ___ Sea
21 Lubricators
25 The Lord acted as one between Laban and Jacob (Gen. 31:49)
26 Portion of meat
28 "Cold and ___. . .day and night shall not cease" (Gen. 8:22)

29 We may not ___ any part of God's Word (Rev. 22:19)
30 Describes Nabal (1 Sam. 25:3)
32 Abraham's nephew (Gen. 11:27)
34 "My face is ___ with weeping" (Job 16:16)
37 "Unto thy ___ will I give this land" (Gen. 12:7)
39 Tijuana's country
40 Slovenly person
41 South American country
42 Exploiter
43 Tack
45 Sacrificed instead of Isaac (Gen. 22:13)
48 Downwind
53 Ceremonious

54 Soft drink brand
56 Tally marker
57 Net fabric
59 Onion roll (var.)
60 Famine drove Abraham here (Gen. 12:10)
62 "Sharper than any two-___ sword" (Heb. 4:12)
64 Peter fished with a net instead of this
66 Eat
67 Male swan
68 "___ sure that thou art that Christ" (John 6:69)
69 Make lace
70 Form of address (var.)

ABRAHAM: KEEPER OF THE PROMISE

4

by Patricia Mitchell

• • • • • • •

ACROSS

1 Composer Johann Sebastian
5 Temple leaders brought Jesus to one
10 Powder
14 Surrounded Jesus at His transfiguration (Matt. 17:2)
15 Cringe
16 Describes the blackish streams in Job 6:16
17 Abraham's seed would number as these (Gen. 22:17) (4 wds.)
20 Canaan flowed with this (Ex. 3:8)
21 British W.C.
22 Caps
23 Sinai to Syria (dir.)
25 Lyons affirmative
27 "Kings of armies did flee ___" (Ps. 68:12)
30 Fool does this (Prov. 14:9)
35 Actor Alda
36 Jesus of many carols
40 Fanfare
41 Abraham's seed would number as these (Gen. 22:17) (4 wds.)
44 "Herd ran violently down a ___ place" (Mark 5:13)
45 Clump
46 "Take of the ram the fat and the ___" (Ex. 29:22)
47 TV sitcom family
49 Tricksters Jacob and Laban
51 *Missouri* is one
53 Vigor
54 "A wise son heareth his father's instruction" without this (Prov. 13:1)
57 Ice skater Babilonia
59 Part of Ahasuerus' kingdom (Est. 1:1)

64 Abraham's promised position (Gen. 17:4) (3 wds.)
67 Choir section certainly in the king's house (1 Kings 10:12)
68 Ahasuerus would ___ a decree that wives shall honor their husbands (Est. 1:20)
69 Snack on manna, maybe?
70 Laodiceans may have had a salve for this
71 Genesis section, e.g.
72 Might describe a Hobby Lobby customer

DOWN

1 Nabal's feast, e.g.
2 Not what Abram used in Gen. 15:11
3 Berry start
4 Unclean animal (Lev. 11:6)
5 Ark number
6 Burglars might do this
7 Lazarus was carried "___ Abraham's bosom" (Luke 16:22)
8 Cold sound
9 Downwind
10 Kon ___, Heyerdahl ship
11 Phenol
12 "A feast of wines on the ___" (Isa. 25:6)
13 Recording medium
18 We desire to act in ___ with God's will
19 Thin cuts
24 Moab mount (Deut. 32:49)
26 "Lead ___ not into temptation" (Matt. 6:13)
27 Like the dove in Ps. 55:6
28 Jury
29 Chilean mountain range
31 Yellow pigment

32 Unleavened Exodus staple
33 Cain does this
34 "But a ___ between me and death" (1 Sam. 20:3)
35 Business group (abbr.)
37 Fore companion
38 Energy measurement
39 Radio band
42 Sarah to Abraham
43 Fancy case
48 Canadian prov.
50 "They ___ upon" Jesus (Matt. 27:30)
52 God could use this to raise up a child for Abraham (Luke 3:8)
53 Bluish-white metals
54 ___ Sea, biblical site

55 Courtroom figure (abbr.)
56 Abram wouldn't take a lachet of one of these (Gen. 14:23)
58 "Abraham. . .saw the place ___ off" (Gen. 22:4)
60 Little girl (Sp.)
61 Abraham "sat in the tent ___ in the heat of the day" (Gen. 18:1)
62 Smithsonian ___ (abbr.)
63 Sodom and Gomorrah the day after
64 USDA global group
65 Church leader, familiarly
66 Abraham and his visitors did this (Gen. 18:5)

5. ABSALOM: A MONARCH WANNA-BE
by Patricia Mitchell

● ● ● ● ● ●

ACROSS

1 Bilhah or Zilpah (Gen. 30:7, 9)
5 Tamar's appearance (2 Sam. 13:1)
9 Antitraditional artistic movement
13 "Bless me, even me ___, O my father" (Gen. 27:34)
14 "It is a ___ thing that the king requireth" (Dan. 2:11)
15 Absalom felt this way toward his brother (2 Sam. 13:22)
16 It went away and left Absalom hanging (2 Sam. 18:9)
17 Baruch needed these (Jer. 36:18)
18 There were six of these during creation (poet.)
19 "He would not go, but ___ him" (2 Sam. 13:25)
21 Native of former Siam
23 Cereal
24 Qumran to Jerusalem (dir.)
25 ___ of Israel, Absalom's supporters (2 Sam. 17:4)
29 Possible descriptor of Absalom
30 Bible pronoun
32 Jericho's walls fell amid one (Josh. 6:20)
33 Descendants of Benammi (Gen. 19:38)
36 Absalom's servants set Joab's on fire (2 Sam. 14:30)
37 The fool's problem (Prov. 12:15)
38 Descriptor of Absalom
39 Absalom's princely friends
40 Arab leader
41 ___ Baba
42 An angel's trumpet might do this
43 Forest clearing
44 "O Absalom, my ___, my son!" (2 Sam. 19:4)
45 RR org.
46 The kind of tree that held Absalom (2 Sam. 18:9)

47 Pasty in color
49 Choose
50 Colorado winter time zone
53 Tub spread
55 Describes Esau's arms (Gen. 27:11)
57 "Let him turn to his own ___" (2 Sam. 14:24)
60 El ___, TX
62 An earthly disaster could be this (Luke 21:11)
63 Went gently
64 Shield of Zeus (var.)
65 Infant Moses might have held one
66 Doctor's picture
67 "I will put my hook in thy ___" (2 Kings 19:28)
68 Chewy candies

DOWN

1 Cuban dance
2 Bird's "bastard" wing
3 Tiny offshore landform
4 Acts
5 "What a ___ We Have in Jesus"
6 Root beer brand (3 wds.)
7 Annoy
8 "Arise, O LORD, into thy ___" (Ps. 132:8)
9 Absalom's father (2 Sam. 13:1)
10 Jesus and disciples did this in the Upper Room
11 Daniel and lions sat together in this (Dan. 6:16)
12 Commercials, for short
15 Jesus did this often
20 Thames bird
22 Tilts
26 Water retention
27 Taut
28 Saw logs

29 Against
30 Hanging Gardens of Babylon had these
31 Not there
33 Commander of Absalom's rebel army (2 Sam 17:25)
34 Fruit
35 Northeastern state
36 "Smite Amnon; then kill him, ___ not" (2 Sam. 13:28)
39 Set
40 Antlered animal
42 Paul and shipmates no doubt did this (Acts 27:15)
43 Absalom stood here to greet men (2 Sam. 15:2)
46 Absalom would do this to his father

48 Stroll
49 Water in the wilderness of Zin, e.g. (Num. 27:14)
50 Old timer's office copy, for short
51 Form of trapshooting
52 Leans
54 "Encamped in the ___ fields" (2 Sam. 11:11)
56 Absalom "vowed unto the ___" (2 Sam. 15:7)
57 Balak wanted Balaam to put one on the Israelites (Num. 22:6)
58 "All that handle the ___, the mariners" (Ezek. 27:29)
59 Stars and stripes nation
61 Long ___

ADAM:
THE FIRST DUDE
6
by Patricia Mitchell

• • • • • •

ACROSS

1 British cop
6 Wound healer
10 UAE native
14 "Oh, come, let us ___ Him!" Christmas refrain
15 Knitting stitch
16 Painter of melting clocks
17 "This is now bone of my ___" (Gen. 2:23)
18 One of the Great Lakes
19 "Grievous words ___ up anger" (Prov. 15:1)
20 Space
21 Adam felt this when hiding from God
23 "With you. . .unto the ___ of the world" (Matt. 28:20)
24 Adam was to do this to the garden
26 Makes noise during sleep
28 Delineated
31 God gave Adam "every herb bearing ___" (Gen. 1:29)
32 There you are!
33 They of Tyre did this (1 Chron. 22:4)
36 Jacob's description of Leah, maybe (Gen. 29:17)
40 Soda
42 God "drove ___ the man" (Gen. 3:24)
43 "Man became a living ___" (Gen. 2:7)
44 Maybe part of Noah's ark
45 What broke out when Samson brought the house down
48 When Eve offered, Adam did this
49 Adam's second son (Gen 4:1–2)
51 Herb
53 "___ is the ground for thy sake" (Gen. 3:17)

56 Half
57 Adam's helpmeet
58 You can tiptoe through them
61 "Male and female created he ___" (Gen. 1:27)
65 "God formed man of the ___ of the ground" (Gen. 2:7)
67 "The LORD is on my ___" (Ps. 118:6)
68 Leather
69 Choir member
70 "Been faithful over ___ things" (Matt. 25:21) (2 wds.)
71 Small knife
72 Grate upon
73 "Fill the waters in the ___" (Gen. 1:22)
74 "Not good that the man should be ___" (Gen. 2:18)

DOWN

1 Ali ___
2 Isaac was fooled with this (Gen. 27:27)
3 God used one of Adam's
4 God gave Adam the ___ of life (Gen. 2:7)
5 Adam did not say this to God's question (Gen. 3:11)
6 What a foolish man will do with his treasure (Prov. 21:20)
7 Jesus is the ___ for Adam's sin
8 Opera solo
9 "Created he them; and ___ them" (Gen. 5:2)
10 Spots
11 A judgmental Pharisee is one
12 Dress style (2 wds.)
13 Adam named these
21 "I will ___ all that afflict thee" (Zeph. 3:19)
22 Egypt to Canaan (dir.)

25 Snakelike fish
27 Chances of winning
28 Tongues of fire "sat upon ___ of them" (Acts 2:3)
29 "Where art ___?" (Gen. 3:9)
30 "To see what he would ___ them" (Gen. 2:19)
31 Adam's third son (Gen. 4:25)
34 Paul had one (Phil. 3:14)
35 Adam, e.g.
37 "The young lions ___ after their prey" (Ps. 104:21)
38 Accord not meant in Acts 1:14
39 "After one day the south wind ___" (Acts 28:13)
41 Alack's partner
45 Snake-haired women
46 Forbidden fruit was pleasant to these (Gen.3:6)

47 Member of Mayan people
50 Wager
52 Jewish ceremonial law directed this
53 Solomon's Temple wood (1 Kings 5:10)
54 Throat dangler
55 God does this on the seventh day
56 What God does to the lukewarm (Rev. 3:16. var.)
59 Tree of ___, the other tree in the garden (Gen. 2:9)
60 Adam's bite of the fruit was a bad one
62 Abel is a ___ of the faith (Heb. 11)
63 Adam called this home
64 Scant
66 A tower "whose ___ may reach unto heaven" (Gen. 11:4)
68 Relaxing tub

7

AMOS SPEAKS GOD'S WORD
by Patricia Mitchell

• • • • • •

ACROSS

1 Math sign
5 The captives were taken here (Amos 1:6)
9 Soft white cheese
13 Wise men's home
14 No need to take this, according to Matthew 10:10
15 Modern-day Elam
16 "He kept his wrath for ___" (Amos 1:11)
17 Rebekah's ride (Gen. 24:64)
18 "I will ___ the house of Israel among all nations" (Amos 9:9)
19 "The houses of ivory shall ___" (Amos 3:15)
21 Amos was one
23 "They sold. . .the ___ for a pair of shoes" (Amos 2:6)
25 "She is not afraid of the ___ for her household" (Prov. 31:21)
26 Rainbow shape
29 "The LORD will ___ from Zion" (Amos 1:2)
31 "Flight shall perish from the ___" (Amos 2:14)
34 Bambi's mom
35 Santa's helpers
37 Amos's prophecy (Amos 1:4, e.g.)
39 Slitherer
41 Before, (poet.)
42 Alamo location
43 Zarephath widow had a handful of it (1 Kings 17:12)
44 Rebekah's accompanied her (Gen. 24:59)
46 Seers have this
47 Black and white snacks
50 Dent
51 Bashful
52 Cocoon inhabitant

54 The "swift of ___ shall not deliver himself" (Amos 2:15)
56 Attain
59 Paul and Silas' keeper, e.g. (Acts 16:27)
63 Opera solo
64 Mount Everest site
66 Writer Bombeck
67 Look over
68 God put Adam "into the garden of Eden to ___ it" (Gen. 2:15)
69 Highway sight
70 "Their tongue is as an arrow ___ out" (Jer. 9:8)
71 "If my ___ hath turned out of the way" (Job 31:7)
72 Beautiful bird

DOWN

1 "Seek. . .unto wizards that ___" (Isa. 8:19)
2 Wash
3 Consumer
4 "Shall also ___ thee out of thy clothes" (Ezek. 23:26)
5 Airport info
6 Gideon's fleece was this (Judg. 6:38)
7 Beyond the limit (pl.)
8 Fondly remembered fruits (Num. 11:5)
9 Coarse woman nickname
10 Pennsylvania city
11 U.S. president
12 Sluggard's role model (Prov. 6:6)
14 Paul disputed "daily in the ___ of one Tyrannus" (Acts 19:9)
20 "Of how much ___ punishment" (Heb. 10:29)
22 Gun noise
24 Elijah's server (1 Kings 17:6)

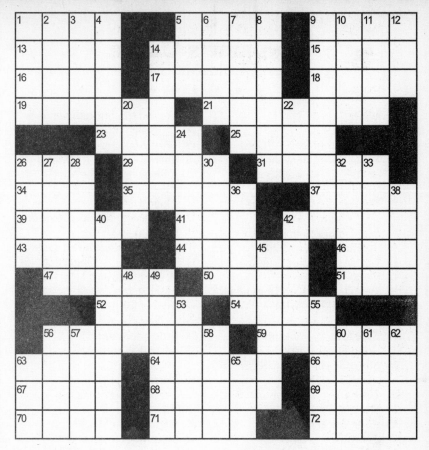

26 First name
27 Cowboy show
28 Amorites compared to this tree (Amos 2:9)
30 Summer TV offering
32 God does this to the heart (Ps. 57:7)
33 To Paul, anything other than Christ (Phil. 3:8)
36 Lettering stroke
38 Moses sent Caleb to ___ out Canaan (Josh. 14:7)
40 Memorable animal
42 Amos's town
45 Frowns angrily
48 Parisian's vote
49 The foolish man does this (Prov. 21:20)

53 Israel could not ___ Amos's prophecies
55 One of Samson's seven (Judg. 16:19)
56 Constantine is one in Rome
57 See ya! (It.)
58 Type of what God placed east of Eden
60 Jesus did this on the ground (John 8:6)
61 Austin title
62 "I have withholden the ___ from you" (Amos 4:7)
63 Jesus' ride (John 12:14)
65 It caused Cleopatra's demise

ANDREW'S CATCH
by Patricia Mitchell

• • • • • •

ACROSS

1 ___ Kong
5 Venomous snake
10 Philip told Andrew the Greeks said, "___, we would see Jesus" (John 12:21)
13 "Man shall not live by bread ___" (Matt. 4:4)
15 Some things do this on Day 6 of creation (Genesis 1:24)
16 "All ye ___ brethren" (Matt. 23:8)
17 He called out to Andrew and his brother (Matt. 4:18)
18 Poem division
19 "The herd ___ violently down a steep place" (Mark 5:13)
20 Son of Rachel, familiarly (Gen. 35:24)
21 Door grip
23 Writing tablet
25 Mote size in brother's eye (Matt. 7:3)
26 With Andrew in upper room (Acts 1:13)
28 "In the ___ of the book it is written" (Ps. 40:7)
31 Plant seen at Easter
32 Idealized mental image
33 Probable author of Acts
34 Lingerie item
37 Today's chariots
38 Description of Andrew's catch
40 "The First ___," carol
41 "He that endureth to the ___ shall be saved" (Matt. 10:22)
42 Parent groups
43 He's blessed who does this in Rev. 1:3
44 St. Andrew's ___, an X
45 Forbidden in Lev. 19:28
46 "A good tree bringeth not forth ___ fruit" (Luke 6:43)
49 Tasks
50 Architect Frank ___ Wright
51 Andrew heard John say, "Behold the ___ of God!" (John 1:36, 40)
52 Rotational speed measurement
55 Mil. rank
56 Religion of those on a 1 Down
59 Ahab's house (1 Kings 22:39)
61 "I was blind, now I ___" (John 9:25)
62 Kind of fish
63 Andrew's brother (Matt. 4:18)
64 Expert, for short
65 Adam does this when God calls (Gen. 3:8)
66 Plateau

DOWN

1 Pilgrimage to Mecca
2 Margarine
3 "The smell of thy ___ like apples" (Song 7:8)
4 African antelope
5 50s TV family name
6 Many adherents of 56 Across
7 Jesus told Andrew, "I will make you fishers of ___" (Matt. 4:19)
8 Wager
9 Andrew became one
10 Abraham's wife (Gen. 17:15)
11 How Jonah felt when God spared Nineveh (Jonah 4:1)
12 What the Holy Ghost does in Titus 3:5
14 Igloo dweller
22 Jerusalem to Damascus (dir.)
24 Conservation group
25 Pulls

26 He who bears false witness in Prov. 25:18
27 Relating to alkali (abbr.)
28 Sin
29 Muscat's site
30 Fat
31 Grade
34 Vessel of Andrew's trade
35 Make again
36 If you forgive, God "will ___ forgive you" (Matt. 6:14)
38 "No man shall ___ me of this boasting" (2 Cor. 11:10)
39 Andrew did this (Mark 1:16)
40 What Andrew left to follow Jesus (Matt. 4:20)
42 Prissy
43 Masters in John 1:38

44 "At midnight there was a ___ made" (Matt. 25:6)
45 Doubting disciple, familiarly
46 You ___ your hands in prayer, maybe
47 Esau in relation to Jacob
48 Juliet's boyfriend
49 Son of Zebedee (Matt. 10:2)
51 Foolish virgins were this to the wedding (Matt. 25:10–11)
52 City of Paul's captivity
53 Not cons
54 Starling
57 Slide on snow
58 Andrew said, "There is a ___ here" (John 6:9)
60 Vitality

ANNA THE PROPHETESS
by Patricia Mitchell

● ● ● ● ● ●

ACROSS

1 City in Judah (Josh. 15:26)
5 One who builds a house on sand, e.g.
10 What the Gardener will do with non-fruitful branches
13 Kind of woman Anna was
14 ___ protector
15 State of unconsciousness
16 Final word in prayer
17 Agitator does this to crowd, as at Jesus' trial (Mark 15:11–13)
18 Feature of God's sign to Noah after the Flood (Gen. 9:16)
19 Winglike part
21 The Garden of Gethsemane and the Temple in Jerusalem, e.g.
23 Anna "served God. . .night and ___" (Luke 2:37)
26 Conger
28 Fish tank growth
29 ___ steroids
32 Ranch guy
33 Man with unclean spirit (Mark 5:4–5) (Coll., Sp.)
34 Anna's piety, perhaps
36 Murky
37 Holy ___, source of Anna's inspiration
38 Bearer of the ark of the covenant (2 Sam. 6:3)
42 Hanger-on-er, e.g.
43 Certain idol in Sinai
44 String section instrument
46 Cloth put over Jesus' face in the tomb (John 20:7)
49 Sew with a gathering stitch
51 How you might get across the Sea of Galilee
52 Format for delivering web content
53 Sign shoppers love to see
57 Sock
59 It's often upped
60 San ___, CA
62 Prophet from Tekoa (Amos 1:1)
66 "Play skilfully with a ___ noise" (Ps. 33:3)
67 Genesis 1:1 gives this of life as we know it
68 Promissory notes
69 What Job's comforters do
70 What God does on the seventh day
71 It happens to manna kept overnight (Ex. 16:20)

DOWN

1 When Anna saw Jesus, it was this kind of moment (Luke 2:38)
2 Mary was one
3 The glutton's partner has too much of this (Prov. 23:21)
4 Chatty bird
5 Anna and Simeon waited "for the consolation of ___" (Luke 2:25)
6 Paul and Silas, e.g.
7 Flower with a beard, often
8 David did this when he saw Bathsheba bathing (2 Sam. 11:2)
9 What a God-sent challenge might be
10 Settee
11 "I am Alpha and ___" (Rev. 1:8)
12 So yesterday
15 One presented to the Lord (Luke 2:21–22)
20 Name for tamed beast in Isa. 11:6
22 Tight
23 Painter of melting clocks
24 "And ___ they tell him of her" (Mark 1:30)
25 We should not do this when we pray (Matt. 6:7)

27 Supple
30 One called holy to the Lord (Luke 2:23)
31 Story from Job's comforters, e.g.
32 Morse code element
35 Anna's tribe (Luke 2:36) (var.)
37 Harden
38 Exclamation in Munich
39 Samson was not to cut this (Judg. 13:5)
40 French islands
41 David ___ Goliath with a stone (1 Sam. 17:49, coll.)
42 Anna "gave thanks. . .unto the ___" (Luke 2:38)
44 Anna's faithfulness was one
45 Saul felt this way when the women praised David (1 Sam. 18:7–8)
47 Mechanical agents

48 Top-ranking corporate webmaster
49 "They had a few ___ fishes" (Mark 8:7)
50 Vietnam capital
54 Jacob fooled Isaac with this (Gen. 27:27)
55 Last Supper beverage
56 Loch ___ monster
58 "___ of turtledoves," sacrifice choice (Luke 2:24)
61 "___ thee behind me, Satan" (Luke 4:8)
63 Pasture sound
64 "Gracious words which proceeded ___ of his mouth" (Luke 4:22)
65 Sound from the tree in the midst of Eden, perhaps (Gen. 3:1–4)

10 BARNABAS: BEARER OF GOD'S WORD

by Patricia Mitchell

• • • • •

ACROSS

1 Barnabas treated people with this
4 "Like ___ that find no pasture" (Lam. 1:6)
9 Jostle
14 Slithery fish
15 God set ___ Barnabas for His work (Acts 13:2)
16 Theologians do this to Bible phrases
17 ___ Maria
18 Barnabas laid this at the apostles' feet (Acts 4:37)
19 Paul and Barnabas discussed these with the apostolic council (Acts 15:20)
20 "Unworthy of everlasting ___" (Acts 13:46)
22 Braces oneself
24 Barnabas was not one of these
25 Prime Meridian clock reading
27 ___ a small world!
29 "Barnabas. . .___ go as far as Antioch" (Acts 11:22)
32 Barnabas took this to Christians in Judea (Acts 11:29–30)
35 Spy org.
36 After a stoning, Paul went here with Barnabas (Acts 14:20)
38 North Pole workshop workers
40 "Hold up my goings. . .that my footsteps ___ not" (Ps. 17:5)
42 24 Across had too much of this
44 "I will perform the ___ which I sware" (Gen. 26:3)
45 Barnabas ___ Mark when Paul refuses (Acts 15:39)
47 Rebekah's husband (Gen. 24:67)
49 "I am ready. . .to ___ at Jerusalem" (Acts 21:13)
50 Grand Turk
52 The disciples did this, then ordained Barnabas as a missionary (Acts 13:3)
54 Farm org.
55 Before (prefix)
56 What Saul hoped to do to David with his javelin (1 Sam. 18:11)
59 Barnabas went to one in Antioch (Acts11:26)
63 Paul's former name
67 In a tilted position
69 Athenian lawmaker and poet
71 Campus ministry org.
72 "Ye are of more ___ than many sparrows" (Matt. 10:31)
73 The Colosseum in Rome was one
74 ___ Baba
75 Because of Barnabas, "much people was ___ unto the Lord" (Acts 11:24)
76 Old ___ (stubbornly old-fashioned person)
77 Hip

DOWN

1 Greenish blue
2 Barnabas' tribe (Acts 4:36)
3 Notation in music
4 Noah's son (Gen. 5:32)
5 Those who named Barnabas (Acts 4:36)
6 Jeremiah's preaching, to a scorner
7 Mid-Eden feature
8 Eye infection
9 Barnabas took one to Antioch (Acts 15:30)
10 Bearer of barley loaves and fish (John 6:9)
11 James and John, e.g. (Matt. 4:21) (abbr.)
12 Capital of Norway
13 Wild ___
21 Self
23 Ananias and Sapphira told one (Acts 5:3, 8)
26 Wet dirt
28 What a foolish man would fill with grain (Luke 12:16–20)

29 A man chosen along with Barnabas (Acts 15:22)
30 17-syllable poem
31 Run off
32 Summary
33 Jesus did this to those wanting to make Him king (John 6:15)
34 Manna would be this if kept overnight (Ex. 16:20)
35 Kansas City winter hours
37 Vehicle
39 Mourners showed Peter garments Dorcas had made "while ___ was with them" (Acts 9:39)
41 You can't serve God and this
43 Radio receiver
46 Joshua did this with 12 stones in the Jordan (Josh. 4:9)
48 Vehicle

51 It became a boil on man and beast (Ex. 9:10)
53 Barnabas said this to God's call
56 Morning beverage
57 School (abbr.)
58 "Paul and Barnabas waxed ___" (Acts 13:46)
60 Mil. branch
61 Vehicle-accommodating ship
62 Horsefly
64 "All that are ___ off" (Acts 2:39)
65 CA university
66 They "___ their hands on" Paul and Barnabas (Acts 13:3)
68 Jewish opposition was Barnabas and Paul's ___ to preach to the Gentiles
70 "By what law? of works? __: but by the law of faith" (Rom. 3:27)

11 BATHSHEBA THE BEAUTIFUL

by Patricia Mitchell

• • • • • •

ACROSS

1 "He . . .put them under___" (2 Sam. 12:31)
5 Black
9 Samson's riddle was this (Judg. 14:12–13)
14 Noted persecutor of early Christians
15 Opera solo
16 David and Bathsheba found they were not ___ God's law
17 Mil. branch
18 Careen
19 Bathsheba bore Solomon, "and the LORD ___ him" (2 Sam. 12:24)
20 Terra-___ (type of clay)
22 "___, thou desirest truth" (Ps. 51:6)
24 U.K. driver's concern
25 Beetle
27 Time periods
31 Opposite of David and Bathsheba's attitude when accused of sin
32 Zero
34 A psalm, perhaps
35 A prophet accused David of this (2 Sam. 12:9)
38 Movie bio with Will Smith
40 Israel's enemy (2 Sam. 11:1)
42 Uriah ___ his life in battle (2 Sam. 11:17)
44 "Little ___ lamb" (2 Sam. 12:3)
46 "A thousand ___ in thy sight are but as yesterday" (Ps. 90:4)
47 David was this while his men went off to war (2 Sam. 11:1)
48 The rich man had many, the poor man had ___ (2 Sam. 12:3)
50 Prophetess at the Temple (Luke 2:36) (var.)
51 Pseudonym
52 Roman trio
55 Adultery is this
57 Bathsheba to Solomon (2 Sam. 12:24)
59 Metal
61 Corn holder
64 Relating to the brain
66 Bathsheba's baby would ___ her guilt
68 Joab would ___ the men to put Uriah up front (2 Sam. 11:15–16)
71 Sinai's Peninsula
73 Musical composition
74 Cabled
75 Nathan's story had David on the ___ of his seat
76 ___ Accords, 1993 agreement
77 David ___ as Bathsheba bathes
78 David tried to cover up his guilt, so he did this (2 Sam. 11:25)
79 David to Uriah: "Go. . .wash thy ___" (2 Sam. 11:8)

DOWN

1 David and Bathsheba had done this while Uriah was gone
2 "Ant and Grasshopper" author
3 David and Bathsheba brought about God's ___ (2 Sam. 11:27; 2 Sam 12:7–12)
4 David's accuser was not this (2 Sam. 12:1–7)
5 David would not do this while Bathsheba's son lay dying (2 Sam. 12:17)
6 Joab knew the truth, but was probably this
7 Tanker
8 Accused David (2 Sam. 12:1)
9 "They would shoot from the ___?" (2 Sam. 11:20)
10 "Uriah ___ in Jerusalem that day" (2 Sam. 11:12)
11 State official (abbr.)
12 She talked to a serpent
13 David's face may have been this when he recognized his sin

21 Communication method

23 Kimono sash

26 Spy org.

28 Paul's citizenship (Acts 22:25)

29 A bride may ___ herself with jewels (Isa. 61:10)

30 "They read. . .distinctly, and gave the ___" (Neh. 8:8)

31 Gaiety

33 David took Bathsheba, and "he ___ with her" (2 Sam. 11:4)

35 Bathsheba's dad (2 Sam. 11:3)

36 Popular spirit in Russia

37 Religion promulgated in the 7th century

39 ___ Jima

41 David prepared this for Uriah (2 Sam. 11:8)

43 ___ Lanka

45 Preservation by silo storage

49 Flightless bird

53 Rich man could give one of these to poor man (2 Sam. 12:4)

54 Uriah said: "___, and Judah, abide in tents" (2 Sam. 11:11)

56 Referee

58 "David's ___ was greatly kindled" (2 Sam. 12:5)

60 ___ Gras

61 Thicket

62 Plant seed

63 Bathsheba's beauty would do this to David (2 Sam. 11:2)

65 Tails

67 Where Bathsheba bathed

68 Punching tool

69 Uriah would not ___ with his wife (2 Sam. 11:11)

70 David's feelings for the rich man (2 Sam. 12:5)

72 "David arose from off his ___" (2 Sam. 11:2)

12 BENJAMIN: THE YOUNGER BROTHER
by Patricia Mitchell

• • • • • •

ACROSS

1 Panicked, Benjamin's brothers needed to send this signal
4 Ziti
9 Pharisees and Sadducees, e.g.
14 Item found in Benjamin's bag (Gen. 44:12)
15 "My lovers and my friends stand ___" (Ps. 38:11)
16 Benjamin couldn't use this to send a message from Egypt
17 What Benjamin and brothers did at Joseph's (Gen. 43:16)
18 God made Joseph "a ___ throughout all the land of Egypt" (Gen. 45:8)
19 "God Almighty give you ___ before the man" (Gen. 43:14)
20 This existed between Hebrews and Samaritans
22 Jacob believed Benjamin's trip was ___ to death (Gen. 43:14)
24 Stand, and have on this (Eph. 6:14) (var.)
25 Off-Broadway award
27 As Isaac ages, his eyesight does this (Gen. 27:1)
31 Huldah was one (2 Kings 22:14)
32 Herodias' daughter's costume, perhaps (Matt. 14:6)
33 If Benjamin "should leave his father, his father would ___" (Gen. 44:22)
34 There was little of this among Jacob's sons
36 Maine sighting
38 Jesus ___ lepers (Luke 7:22)
40 You may find them on the seashore
42 Joseph's brothers expressed this when asked to bring Benjamin (Gen. 42:21)
43 Turn over
44 Son of Benjamin (Gen. 46:21)
45 Epistle of sorts

47 Roman worship service
51 Sometimes it's more
53 Bearing
54 The unjust steward must give this to his master (Luke 16:1) (abbr.)
55 Prominent N.T. member of the tribe of Benjamin (Rom. 11:1)
57 Joseph harbored none toward his brothers (Gen. 50:20)
59 Rain falls mainly on the plain here
62 Messages from Isaiah, e.g.
65 Bard's "before"
66 Rainbows are this
67 Nebuchadnezzar's order to worship an idol, e.g.
68 "___ of thy youth" (Ps. 110:3)
69 Joseph's brothers' dilemma was this
70 Used to hold Simeon, perhaps (Gen. 42:24)
71 White-tailed sea eagle (var.)

DOWN

1 Benjamin's leaving with his brothers ___ his father
2 Interruption of power
3 Coins the brothers used to pay for food, e.g.
4 Standard golf scores
5 Univ. graduate
6 Roman deity
7 Part iron, part clay digit in the king's dream (Dan. 2:42)
8 Benjamin must have felt this when searched (Gen. 44:12)
9 It might be a Mack
10 Make corrections to
11 Jaguar, e.g.
12 Involuntary movement
13 Crafty
21 Jacob's God-given name (Gen. 32:28)
23 "The ___ of the house of David" (Isa. 22:22)
25 Horse food

26 Jacob said, "Go again, ___ us a little food" (Gen. 43:2)
28 Baal, e.g.
29 Overlook
30 "Your eyes ___, and the eyes of my brother Benjamin" (Gen. 45:12)
32 Card game
35 Found at many doors
36 Joseph saw Benjamin and said, "Bring these ___ home" (Gen. 43:16)
37 "We have a father, an ___ ___" (Gen. 44:20) (2 wds.)
38 Jesus would do this often
39 Caps
40 Bridge
41 ___ you!
42 Guy's partner
43 "When ye pray, ___ not vain repetitions" (Matt. 6:7)

45 Flightless bird
46 Kind of cup found in Benjamin's bag (Gen. 44:2)
48 Jacob would reluctantly do this, to Benjamin's journey
49 Goal maker
50 The sower in Jesus' parable had done this to his seeds (Luke 8:5)
52 Joseph accused his brothers of being these (Gen. 42:9)
56 One of Jesus' disciples, familiarly
57 Japanese staple
58 N.T. book
59 O.T. priest, for short
60 Often goes before
61 Health org.
63 How about: "Why make ye this ___, and weep?" (Mark 5:39)
64 Moses put blood on the ___ of Aaron's right ear (Lev. 8:23)

13 CAIN: FIRST BORN
by Patricia Mitchell

• • • • • •

ACROSS

1 "Began ___ to call upon the name of the LORD" (Gen. 4:26)
4 Cain did not feel this as a vagabond (Gen. 4:14)
8 Meat stew
14 Battle tool in 1 Sam. 13:20 (var.)
15 Off-Broadway award
16 Acceptance of Abel's gift would do this to Cain (Gen. 4:5)
17 Owner of the Technicolor Dreamcoat, familiarly
18 "If haply they might ___ after him" (Acts 17:27)
19 First name in mysteries
20 Cain may have felt like one among other men
22 God ___ Cain live
23 God told Cain to "___ over" temptation (Gen. 4:7)
24 Cain was banished east of here (Gen. 4:16)
27 Files
31 Peasant
33 Distress call
35 Forbidden to a Nazarite (Judg. 13:7)
36 God said to Cain's father, "In the sweat of thy face shalt thou ___ bread" (Gen. 3:19)
38 Long time
39 What a student might do the night before a test
40 Adam ___ the blame to Eve for their sin
44 An Iraqi's southern neighbor
46 Wise men came from this direction (Matt. 2:1)
47 Cain's dwelling place (Gen. 4:16)
49 Oxygen
50 Form of communication
51 ___ Giovanni, Mozart opera

52 Dish at many Thanksgiving feasts
55 Cain's brother kept these (Gen. 4:2)
58 "The ___ is not to the swift" (Eccl. 9:11)
61 "There was a swarm of ___ and honey" (Judg. 14:8)
63 ___ Lanka
65 Italian dish
67 Eli was this to Samuel
70 Wrap a flag, e.g.
71 Pastor, familiarly
72 One-celled water creature
73 Soft white cheese
74 Winter hazard
75 God said to Cain, "Now art thou ___ from the earth" (Gen. 4:11)
76 What Gomorrah might have looked like
77 Eve said of Cain, "I have gotten a ___ from the LORD" (Gen. 4:1)

DOWN

1 Isaiah is considered a ___ prophet
2 Second book of the Bible
3 "Eye of a ___" (Mark 10:25)
4 Living room furniture piece
5 White poplar
6 Site of Abel's death (Gen. 4:8)
7 Conger
8 Cain's fear of God's punishment was this
9 God expressed this toward Cain (Gen. 4:10)
10 Persona non ___
11 Horse morsel
12 Good reaction to sin
13 Can be made with a bag
21 Cain felt ___ of hope (Gen. 4:14)
25 Tel Aviv to Jerusalem (dir.)
26 Cranny partner

28 Eastern garment
29 Perhaps what Cain farmed
30 Very large truck
32 Abel gave his best beast "and of the ___ thereof" (Gen. 4:4)
34 How a bug in a rug feels
37 Cain would to this to his crops
39 Sweet melon
40 "Waters called he ___" (Gen. 1:10)
41 Discuss with, over
42 Paphos is on one
43 God warned Cain, "sin lieth at the ___" (Gen. 4:7)
45 Woe to those who "have gone in the ___ of Cain" (Jude 1:11)
48 Genetic code
53 Dizziness
54 Roman statesman
56 ___ Park, Colorado destination

57 God would do this to Cain concerning Abel (Gen. 4:9)
59 There are these on this page
60 Cain said, "Thou hast driven me out. . .from the face of the ___" (Gen. 4:14)
62 Multiple of punishment due a killer of Cain (Gen. 4:15)
64 Cain's grandson (Gen. 4:18)
66 "Every one that findeth me shall ___ me" (Gen. 4:14)
67 Apple computer
68 Flightless bird
69 "Remember not the sins. . .___ my transgressions" (Ps. 25:7)
70 Org. of aspiring tillers of the field

DANIEL: THE LION TAMER

14

by Patricia Mitchell

• • • • • •

ACROSS

1 Daniel chose the ___ of righteousness
5 What Daniel heard as the door to the lions' den closed, maybe
9 Daniel's face was not this after refusing the king's food
13 Great lake
14 "Take thee a ___, and lay it before thee" (Ezek. 4:1)
15 Painting prop
16 Daniel was given a new one of these (Dan. 1:7)
17 "___, Father" (Mark 14:36)
18 Plant part
19 Daniel and his friends "had ___ in them" (Dan. 1:4)
21 Subject of Nebuchadnezzar's dream (Dan. 4:10)
23 Hallucinogen
24 Spy guys' org.
25 Daniel would do this from the lions' den
29 Luke for short (Col. 4:14)
30 Nick
32 "Do they not ___ that devise evil?" (Prov. 14:22)
33 Adam and Eve each made one (Gen. 3:7)
36 Nathan may have done this as he said, "Thou art the man" (2 Sam. 12:7)
37 Man has dominion "over the fowl of the ___" (Gen. 1:26)
38 Subject of Daniel's vision (Dan. 8:5)
39 "He sent divers ___ of flies among them" (Ps. 78:45)
40 Dog food brand
41 Actress MacGraw
42 Daniel's pussycats
43 Marcel Marceau, for one
44 "Prove thy servants. . .___ days" (Dan. 1:12)
45 Sight the king expected would be left in the fiery furnace
46 Where Nebuchadnezzar dreamed (Dan 2:29)
47 Compositions
49 Beige
50 Tweak
53 "___ of the kingdom" (Matt. 16:19)
55 Daniel could not have this on him (Dan. 1:4)
57 Burnt color
60 Asian country
62 For sure, Daniel was not this (Dan. 1:4)
63 Wall word (Dan. 5:28)
64 Volcano
65 Guards probably did this to the lions' den
66 Psalmist's bed did this (Ps. 6:6)
67 Daniel would ___ it wrong to eat the king's food (Dan. 1:8)
68 Humorist Bombeck

DOWN

1 Inability to interpret the king's dreams was a ___ offense (Dan. 2:5)
2 Persians' neighbors
3 Stepping forward to interpret the king's dreams, Daniel was not this (Dan. 5:17)
4 "Thou shalt bruise his ___" (Gen. 3:15)
5 Lions were this with Daniel
6 African nation
7 Clerical garment
8 "In it was ___ for all" (Dan. 4:12)
9 Recipient
10 Form of communication
11 Downwind
12 Idols were worshipped under this (Hos. 4:13)

15 Daniel was not ___ from the king's decree (Dan. 6:13)
20 Saintly image of sorts
22 "Try my ___" (Ps. 26:2)
26 Darius set Daniel "over the whole ___" (Dan. 6:3)
27 Even Job did this at times
28 Concerning Daniel, there wasn't "any ___ or fault found in him" (Dan. 6:4)
29 Morse code mark
30 Kansas in August descriptor, according to song
31 Wallops
33 Syrian merchandise (Ezek. 27:16)
34 Sticks
35 Blessings are like these in Ezek. 34:26
36 What Daniel could have said to the king's magicians

39 No one could call Daniel this
40 Assist
42 Tiers
43 Wall word (Dan. 5:25)
46 Ointment
48 '80s pro-wrestler, ___ the African Dream
49 Steak
50 African country
51 Muslim religion
52 Animal kingdom division
54 Snow vehicle
56 "I ___ on the work of thy hands" (Ps. 143:5)
57 Down's partner
58 What the lions may have said to Daniel
59 Undergarment
61 Daniel never ___ the king's food

DAVID: THE GREAT KING

15

by Patricia Mitchell

● ● ● ● ● ●

ACROSS

1 Javelin's results, if David hadn't ducked (1 Sam. 18:11)
6 Essence
10 Saul was more than a ___ jealous of David (1 Sam. 18:8)
13 Balloon filler, often
15 Scandinavian capital
16 See 42 Across
17 Saul's changing moods made him one to David
18 "They. . . burn incense unto their ___" (Hab. 1:16)
19 Might accompany "snow, and vapours," as in Ps. 148:8
20 David's strings (1 Sam. 16:23)
22 David's son (2 Sam. 13:37)
24 Describes the scope of David's experiences
26 "Moab. . .hath settled on his ___" (Jer. 48:11)
28 Jonathan's feelings toward David (1 Sam. 18:1)
29 "Fiddlesticks!"
30 David's popularity was ___ for Saul's jealousy
31 Nathan ___ David's guilt (2 Sam. 12:7)
32 Samuel anointed David with it (1 Sam. 16:13)
33 Absalom gathered one to run ahead of him (2 Sam. 15:1)
34 Min. part
35 Shelve again
37 A hose with a hole is ___
41 Gardener's tool
42 Beverage in the hand of a drunkard, perhaps (Prov. 26:9)
43 Snaky scarf
44 The rich man "___ sumptuously every day" (Luke 16:19)
47 "The Philistines. . .___" (1 Sam. 17:51)
48 Because of David and Bathsheba's sin, "the child ___" (2 Sam. 12:18)
49 Greek god of war

50 Campus military org.
51 David's dad, for short (Ruth 4:17)
52 Saul's jealousy would ___ David's life (1 Sam. 18:11)
54 Joseph's coat had many (Gen. 37:3)
56 Battle with no winner
57 Opposing (dial.)
59 Absalom set himself up as a ___ ruler (2 Sam. 15:2–4)
63 "As a ___ doth gather her brood" (Luke 13:34)
64 "Git!"
65 Web cruiser
66 Booming transport
67 Battlefield casualty, often
68 David's weapon (1 Sam. 17:49)

DOWN

1 Referring to Michal (1 Sam. 14:49)
2 "Ascribed unto David ___ thousands" (1 Sam. 18:8)
3 ___ Baba
4 David was one with the crowds (2 wds.) (1 Sam. 18:8)
5 "Berried shrub, often poisonous
6 "Defy the armies of the living ___?" (1 Sam. 17:26)
7 "Established him king over ___" (2 Sam. 5:12)
8 Thick slices
9 Jonathan gave David his (1 Sam. 18:4)
10 Dorcas was one (Acts 9:39)
11 Shelf for a religious object, perhaps
12 Saul ___ David too young to challenge Goliath (1 Sam. 17:33)
14 Priests' advice: "Make. . .images of your mice that ___ the land" (1 Sam. 6:5)
21 Sound of Goliath when he fell, maybe (1 Sam. 17:49)
23 Alas! partner
24 Great Lakes city
25 Describes David and Jonathan (1 Sam. 18:1)
27 Brain wave tracker

29 Conquered by Joshua (Josh. 12:23)
30 David's plea to God: "Hide thy ___ from my sins" (Ps. 51:9)
31 "Thy servant kept his father's sheep" from one (1 Sam. 17:34)
33 "He hath requited me evil for ___" (1 Sam. 25:21)
34 Jonathan to David: "The LORD be between me and thee, and between my ___ and thy seed for ever" (1 Sam. 20:42)
36 "David laid up ___ words in his heart" (1 Sam. 21:12)
37 Hanger-on
38 Wading bird
39 Responses to Saul's order to kill David (1 Sam. 19:1-2)
40 David's seer's name (2 Sam. 24:11)
42 Bacon-lettuce-tomato sandwich
44 In Athens, Paul found many (Acts 17:22-23)

45 "The God of the ___ of Israel" (1 Sam. 17:45)
46 What Nathan's story led David to do (2 Sam. 12:13)
47 Folded sheets of paper
48 David's cry: "Render to them their ___" (Ps. 28:4)
50 "David did that which was ___ in the eyes of the LORD" (1 Kings 15:5)
51 David's kingly descendent (Matt. 1:1)
53 Grating sound
55 FedEx competitor
58 East of Eden land (Gen. 4:16)
60 Suspicious aircraft
61 Where Daniel spent time with lions (Dan. 6:16)
62 Silver or gold, e.g.

16 DEBORAH: THE JUDGE

by Patricia Mitchell

• • • • • •

ACROSS

1 Queen of ___, Solomon's visitor (1 Kings 10:1)
6 Abel's portions offered to the Lord (Gen. 4:4)
10 Deborah's song: "They rehearse the righteous ___ of the LORD" (Judg. 5:11)
14 "Blessed above ___ shall Jael. . . be" (Judg. 5:24)
15 Off-Broadway award
16 "Shall ye not eat of them that ___ the cud" (Lev. 11:4)
17 This does not exist between Deborah and Sisera (Judg. 4:11–17)
18 Cincinnati baseball team
19 Companion of harp, viol, tabret and wine (Isa. 5:12)
20 The Baptizer's mom, familiarly
21 Barak's response to Deborah would ___ to his fear (Judg. 4:8)
23 Pan mate
24 Jael would go out of her tent and ___ Sisera (Judg. 4:18)
26 Iodine compound
28 Succoth shelters (Gen. 33:17)
31 Barak would not go unless Deborah did this (Judg. 4:8)
32 "They chose new gods; then was ___ in the gates" (Judg. 5:8)
33 Noble's attendant
36 Dutch cheese
40 Highest point
42 "They that handle the ___ of the writer" (Judg. 5:14)
43 God to Gideon: "The people are yet too ___" (Judg. 7:4)
44 Children's love
45 Jael covered Sisera with this (Judg. 4:18)
48 Deborah to Barak: "Take with thee ___ thousand men" (Judg. 4:6)
49 Herod's brother, familiarly (Matt. 14:3)

51 Capital of Canada
53 Jael to Sisera: "___ ___, my lord" (Judg. 4:18) (2 wds.)
56 God will be there you when your hair turns this (Ps. 71:18) (var.)
57 ___ Maria
58 Matthew thru Acts, e.g.
61 Food for your printer
65 Adam and Eve, originally
67 "Out of Ephraim was there a ___ of them" (Judg. 5:14)
68 Priest in Toledo
69 Margarine
70 Wager
71 "Curse ye Meroz, said the ___ of the LORD" (Judg. 5:23)
72 A woman of Deborah's wisdom and courage is this
73 Jabin king of Canaan suffered this (Judg. 4:24)
74 Jesus stood in yours

DOWN

1 You might do it to the deck
2 "That disciple took her unto his own ___" (John 19:27)
3 Give off
4 Deborah dwelt "between Ramah and ___" (Judg. 4:5)
5 "Is there ___ man here?" (Judg. 4:20)
6 "Shield or spear seen among ___ thousand in Israel?" (Judg. 5:8)
7 Sisera hoped Jael would ___ his escape (Judg. 4:18)
8 Wave word
9 Meeting
10 Med. org.
11 Hot stuff
12 Barak was this about fighting Sisera (Judg. 4:8)
13 Scandinavian
21 Sanctuary section
22 Doubting disciple, familiarly
25 Jael was this with Sisera (Judg. 4:17–21)

27 Deborah would ___ Barak's request with disfavor (Judg. 4:9)
28 Jael did more than this to Sisera
29 Folded Mexican sandwich
30 Sisera, captain of Jabin's ___ (Judg. 4:7)
31 Barak basically said to Deborah, "I ___!" (Judg. 4:8)
34 October birthstone
35 Deborah and Jael outshine these in this story
37 Book of Numbers contains these
38 After victory, Israel had peace ___ (Judg. 5:31)
39 Loud bird
41 Sports channel
45 Lot's wife turned to one (Gen. 19:26)
46 "The children of Israel again did evil in the sight of the ___" (Judg. 4:1)

47 LAX info
50 Deborah and Jael were this
52 Herod the Great was this
53 "Go and draw toward mount ___" (Judg. 4:6)
54 Screamer's throat dangler
55 Deborah's song would ___ to the Israelite's victory
56 People of the LORD go down to the ___" (Judg. 5:11)
59 A commandment might be this
60 Jesus welcomed them (Matt. 19:14)
62 Sisera's soldiers "fell upon the ___ of the sword" (Judg. 4:16)
63 Israel is one
64 Israelites were not to do this with heathen peoples
66 Sisera was Deborah's (Judg. 4:14)
68 Abraham, Isaac, and Jacob, for short

DORCAS: FULL OF GOOD WORKS
by Patricia Mitchell

17

• • • • • • •

ACROSS

1 Flightless birds
5 Corp. ending, often
10 Genetic code
13 Parrot
15 With alms, Dorcas would ___ out to the poor (Acts 9:36)
16 Dorcas did this before her death (Acts 9:37)
17 Many, as the garments Dorcas had made
18 Dorcas' creation, in Spain (Acts 9:39)
19 Card game
20 ___ ___ carte, menu choice (2 wds.)
21 Dorcas' sources of colors for clothing
23 Adar, e.g.
25 Peter took one to reach Joppa
26 Dorcas' Hebrew name (Acts 9:36)
28 Hair style
31 Lox mate
32 Pressing items for Dorcas?
33 Ruler
34 Peter showed this toward Dorcas (Acts 9:41)
37 Dorcas had this in herself (Mark 9:50)
38 One without Christ (Eph. 2:12)
40 Peter's prayer would ___ Dorcas (Acts 9:40)
41 Herod was this, according to Jesus (Luke 13:32)
42 Salvation is God's gift, so we should not do this (Eph. 2:8–9)
43 "Lydda was nigh to Joppa," so Peter didn't have ___ ___ go (Acts 9:38) (2 wds.)
44 Peter presented Dorcas this way (Acts 9:41)
45 Put on something Dorcas made
46 Build up to a level
49 Because of Dorcas, "many believed in the ___" (Acts 9:42)
50 Dorcas' creations (Acts 9:39)
51 Dorcas "was ___, and died" (Acts 9:37)
52 ___ Dolorosa, Jerusalem pilgrimage site
55 Focal point
56 The Apostles' Creed, e.g.
59 Hearers must not do this to God's prophecies (Rev. 22:18)
61 See 59 Across: Anyone who does this surely has a big one
62 New Testament period, e.g.
63 Where the blind leading the blind end up (Matt. 15:14)
64 Where Daniel and the lions spent time together (Dan. 6:16)
65 "Inferno" author
66 Jesus' is light (Matt. 11:30)

DOWN

1 Austin title
2 A tale-bearer is one (Prov. 25:18)
3 West Coast educ. inst.
4 When Dorcas "saw Peter, she ___ up" (Acts 9:40)
5 "A strong man ___" (Luke 11:21)
6 "Waters called he ___" (Gen. 1:10)
7 ___ Francisco
8 Mo. Martin Luther posted *Theses*
9 Dorcas was laid "in an upper ___" (Acts 9:37)
10 Dorcas' condition didn't ___ Peter
11 Topaz was the city walls' ___ foundation (Rev. 21:20)
12 Island "hi"
14 Dorcas' mourners (Acts 9:39)
22 Chat
24 Silly virgins had none (Matt. 25:3)
25 Mockers regarded the disciples' words at Pentecost as this (Acts 2:13)

26 "The tongue can no man ___"
(James 3:8)

27 In opposition (dial.)

28 Mourners would ___ Dorcas, a
godly woman

29 Peter's words to Dorcas, e.g.
(Acts 9:40)

30 Churches received "the comfort
of the ___ Ghost" (Acts 9:31)

31 Natural color of Dorcas' fabrics

34 Marine bird

35 "To sit up ___" (Ps. 127:2)

36 Boor

38 Wilderness of Sin, e.g. (Ex. 17:1)

39 Bathe

40 Peter "gave her his ___, and lifted
her up" (Acts 9:41)

42 Nabal's condition at his feast
(1 Sam. 25:36)

43 A deacon's tongue should not be
this (1 Tim. 3:8)

44 KJV verb

45 Luke's profession, for short
(Col. 4:14)

46 Dorcas' body may have done this
(Acts 9:37)

47 Philistines would ___ out
Samson's eyes (Judg. 16:21)

48 Libreville's location

49 Beloved must have been this
(Song 2:8–9)

51 Sadducees (Acts 5:17)

52 Peter gave death one, so to speak
(Acts 9:40–41)

53 South American empire

54 Developmental diagnosis

57 Regulatory organization

58 Paris negative

60 Cubic measure (abbr.)

ELI:
THE GREAT PRIEST
by Patricia Mitchell

• • • • • •

ACROSS

1 Sheep's clothing wearer
5 Nebuchadnezzar's nail resembled this (Dan. 4:33)
9 You can chart Paul's missionary journeys on these
13 The ark sat on the "great stone of ___" (1 Sam. 6:18)
14 Fruit
15 Upon
16 "Hannah ___ up after they had eaten" (1 Sam. 1:9)
17 Blend
18 "Hophni and Phinehas, are ___" (1 Sam. 4:17)
19 Eli, Hophni, Phinehas, and Samuel, e.g. (abbr.)
21 18 Across to Eli (2 wds.)
23 Arizona Indian
25 Needs of the "ready writer" in Psalm 45:1
26 What the messenger may have put on himself (1 Sam. 4:12)
29 Part of offering Eli's sons took for themselves (1 Sam. 2:15)
31 Eli's sons' behavior did not ___ God's will for priests
34 Officer in U.S. Armed Forces (abbr.)
35 Gem State
37 Asian country
39 As priest, Eli wore this
41 Shape of God's sign to Noah
42 IHOP condiment
43 "Eli. . . sat ___ a seat by a post of the temple." (1 Sam. 1:9)
44 Terra-___ (type of clay)
46 Tire wall letters
47 Altar builders do this
50 "Spear was like a weaver's ___" (1 Sam. 17:7)
51 Philistines took the ark "and ___ it by Dagon" (1 Sam. 5:2)
52 Eli ___ his sons' disobedience (1 Sam. 23–24)
54 In a parade, but not the Bible
56 Man with the unclean spirit, e.g. (Mark 5:2)
59 Gomer's appearance, perhaps (Hos. 1:2–3)
63 Soft drink
64 Most of the Bible is written in this
66 Eli presided over the Temple ___
67 Stave
68 Jael ___ ___ Sisera (Judg. 4:18) (2 wds.)
69 European river
70 No one could do this to 56 Across (Mark 5:4)
71 Biblical paradise
72 Sunday song

DOWN

1 "How can one be ___ alone?" (Eccl. 4:11)
2 In orchestra, but not the Bible
3 "Knew nothing of all this, ___ or more" (1 Sam. 22:15)
4 "Give ___ to roast for the priest" (1 Sam. 2:15)
5 "Whatsoever. . .cheweth the ___" (Lev. 11:3)
6 Samuel's offering (1 Sam. 7:9)
7 20 Down descriptor
8 Eli's "eyes began to ___ ___" (1 Sam. 3:2) (2 wds.)
9 Eli's sons did not behave this way
10 The Holy Spirit makes hearts ___
11 Parents' school groups
12 Third day creation (Gen. 1:11)
14 At first, Eli ___ to see Hannah (1 Sam. 1:13–14)
20 Fifth day creation (Gen. 1:20)
22 Basketball assoc.
24 Almost sacrificed (Gen. 22:9–12)

26 National rights org.
27 Eli's sons would ___ what they wanted (1 Sam. 2:16)
28 Eli gave more ___ to his sons than to God (1 Sam. 2:29)
30 Heart's motion
32 See 20 Down
33 Eli served in the Lord's ___
36 Musical group, perhaps
38 "Then did they ___ in his face" (Matt. 26:67)
40 Eli's sons were this
42 Dance
45 To make firm
48 Eli took a ___ from Hannah's behavior (1 Sam. 1:13)
49 "The lamp of God went out in the ___" (1 Sam. 3:3)
53 Eli's sons ___ dishonor the Lord

55 Hannah was ___ in grief (1 Sam. 1:7)
56 Fizzy beverage
57 Christ was the second (1 Cor. 15:22)
58 Eli's life ends on a sad ___
60 Hauling cart
61 Printer need
62 "Solomon had horses. . .and linen __" (1 Kings 10:28)
63 Sound-barrier breaker
65 "If a man ___ against the LORD, who shall intreat for him?" (1 Sam. 2:25)

19 ELIJAH HEARD IT

by Patricia Mitchell

● ● ● ● ● ●

ACROSS

1 Elijah's disciple (1 Kings 19:19)
7 Elijah "___ slain all the prophets" (1 Kings 19:1)
10 Abba (familiarly)
14 Cowboy shows
15 Lyric poem
16 Actor Alda
17 Elijah suggested the prophets' idol was this (1 Kings 18:27)
18 Associated with 17 Across
19 Ding's partner
20 "A rod out of the ___ of Jesse" (Isa. 11:1)
21 Singing cowboy Autry
22 "Who may stand. . .when ___ thou art angry?" (Ps. 76:7)
23 Elijah's nemesis
25 Moray
26 Sound from bird Noah sent out (Gen. 8:8)
29 Elijah was not this to Jezebel
30 Popular tape
34 Asian plum
36 Many boomers now
39 Where Elijah discovered God (1 Kings19:12) (3 wds.)
42 Least fresh
43 The widow's never emptied (1 Kings 17:16)
44 Elijah would do this from Jezebel (1 Kings 19:3)
45 Sports org.
46 Thanks to Elijah, the widow and her son did this (1 Kings 17:15)
47 Place of ahhhs
50 "All the ___ of the earth shall fear him" (Ps. 67:7)
51 God's Commandments are one of these to us
53 George Bernard ___
55 Girl

59 Opera offering
60 The God that sends fire, "___ him be God" (1 Kings 18:24)
61 Highest
63 Plateau
64 "Dress it first; for ye ___ many" (1 Kings 18:25)
65 "O LORD, ___ ___" (1 Kings 18:37) (2 wds.)
66 Rind
67 Yearning
68 Elijah and the heathen prophets ___ to a contest (1 Kings 18:24)

DOWN

1 Time periods
2 The prodigal son was this
3 The heathen prophets' idol was this
4 "If it ___ good to thee, I will give" (1 Kings 21:2)
5 Used by Cain, perhaps
6 Forbidden fruit offerer
7 Elijah went "unto ___ the mount of God" (1 Kings 19:8)
8 Yemini city
9 Districts of ancient Attica
10 Pedestal part
11 Elijah felt this way (1 Kings 19:10)
12 Herodias' daughter did one (Matt. 14:6)
13 Who told Elijah, "Arise and eat" (1 Kings 19:5)
21 Guy's partner
23 Roman god
24 Gretel's friend
26 Bank products
27 Horse chow
28 Leave out
30 Eastern state (abbr.)
31 Disarm a gun

32 Social science
33 Pliers, e.g.
35 Part of Elijah's and the prophets' altars
36 Elijah "came and ___ down under a juniper" (1 Kings 19:4)
37 Omani town
38 Beat it!
40 Colorado Springs zone
41 Before (poet.)
45 Mt. Carmel to Zarephath (dir.)
47 Classic comics pooch
48 Mash
49 God to Elijah: "___, get thee to Zarephath" (1 Kings 17:9)
50 Man of God had done this, and he shouldn't have (1 Kings 13:22)

52 He had no ability to send fire to his altar
53 Widow to Elijah: "Art thou come. . .to ___ my son?" (1 Kings 17:18)
54 "God Was ___," title for 39 Across
55 When he spoke, Elijah was not one of these
56 Land for the two altars, perhaps
57 Elijah proved God was not the ___ as a heathen idol
58 Snow goer
61 Elijah's response to 39 Across?
62 Place to hang Elijah's mantle

20 ELISHA: MAN OF GOD
by Patricia Mitchell

● ● ● ● ● ●

ACROSS

1 "___ of lions" (Dan. 6:16)
4 Moses' burning sight (Ex. 3:2)
9 Pump
14 Cain's mom
15 Naaman "stood at the door of the ___ of Elisha" (2 Kings 5:9)
16 Gehazi made a serious one (2 Kings 5:20)
17 Fluffy's doc
18 Naaman's letter caused the king of Israel this (2 Kings 5:7)
19 Elisha to Gehazi: "Is it a time to receive ___?" (2 Kings 5:26)
20 God is always this (Heb. 10:37) (2 wds.)
22 Candy bar choice
24 Elisha healed many of these
25 Ahaz worshipped "under every green ___" (2 Kings 17:10)
27 Community org.
31 Lydia needed one (Acts 16:14)
32 A "corruptible crown," perhaps (1 Cor. 9:25)
33 A long time
34 Fabled fabler
36 Epistle of Paul, in a way
38 They go along with a Day 3 creation (Gen. 1:10)
40 Gehazi did not tell Naaman the ___ story (2 Kings 5:22)
42 Stones of the altar will become like this (Isa. 27:9)
43 Relating to what Peter cut off Malchus' head (John 18:10)
44 Charged particle
45 Gehazi could have used one to haul his loot (2 Kings 5:23)
47 Elisha's question proved one to Gehazi (2 Kings 5:25)
51 Naaman does this to Gehazi's request (2 Kings 5:23)
53 Gehazi's was a bad one (2 Kings 5:20)
54 Hearing what Elisha said, Naaman "went away in a ___" (2 Kings 5:12)
55 Dueling sword
57 Legendary lady of soul
59 Tylenol's competitor
62 Part of Gehazi's loot (2 Kings 5:26)
65 Conversational computer of film
66 Naaman was one (2 Kings 5:1)
67 Lover's voice was like this (Song 2:14)
68 Samaria to Gilgal (dir.)
69 Bingo
70 How Naaman felt when he heard Elisha's orders (2 Kings 5:12)
71 Business org. ending

DOWN

1 The slothful man is ___ of understanding (Prov. 24:30)
2 Smoothly
3 You'll find one in 1 Down's field (Prov. 24:31)
4 Gehazi's story to Naaman was this (2 Kings 5:22)
5 Under Elijah, Elisha could ___ his skills
6 On the floor of a Syrian's tent, perhaps (2 Kings 7:8)
7 *Missouri* letters
8 "___ than all the waters of Israel?" (2 Kings 5:12)
9 Interstate sight
10 Elisha sent one to Naaman (2 Kings 5:10)
11 The widow may have borrowed one (2 Kings 4:3)
12 "Beloved is like a ___" (Song 2:9)
13 Naaman's servants wanted him to ___ Elisha's instructions (2 Kings 5:13)
21 Where Naaman's wife's maid came from (2 Kings 5:2)
23 The couple in Cana did this (John 2:1)
25 Numbers in which Naaman measured payment (2 Kings 5:23)

26 Music style

28 Costa ___, CA

29 One was kindled by God's fire (2 Sam. 22:9)

30 Widow to Elisha: "Thine handmaid hath not ___ thing in the house" (2 Kings 4:2)

32 Handy communication

35 Deer cousin

36 La Guardia message (abbr.)

37 Summer in Samaria, sometimes

38 "___ thee with badgers' skin" (Ezek. 16:10)

39 Naaman thought Elisha should "strike his ___ over" his scars (2 Kings 5:11)

40 Manner

41 The widow would do this to Elisha (2 Kings 4:1)

42 Hush-hush org.

43 Elisha: "They that be with us ___ more than they that be with them" (2 Kings 6:16)

45 Elisha heard one (2 Kings 5:25)

46 Ukrainian city

48 Wept for her kids (Matt. 2:18)

49 How Syrians felt to hear "noise of a great host" (2 Kings 7:6)

50 Pared

52 How many times the child sneezed (2 Kings 4:35)

56 Caffeine-free beverage brand

57 Fruit

58 Elisha was this until his death (2 Kings 13:19–20)

59 Church garb

60 Downwind

61 Gov. agency

63 Attila was one

64 Would dad offer son a scorpion instead of this? (Luke 11:12)

21 ELISABETH'S JOY

by Patricia Mitchell

• • • • • •

ACROSS

1 "Are heavy ___" (Matt. 11:28)
6 Flows partner
10 Two cups make one
14 Greek marketplace in Paul's day
15 The sluggard might do this (Prov. 6:9)
16 Galilee, Samaria, or Judea
17 Breastplate stone (Ex. 28:17)
18 Mary "entered ___ the house of Zacharias, and saluted Elisabeth" (Luke 1:40)
19 The Ten Commandments
20 Caesarea to Nazareth (dir.)
21 Educational inst.
23 Polish port
25 Experts, for short
26 Fido's org.
27 Zacharias felt this way to see Gabriel (Luke 1:12)
30 Judgment, council, and hell fire (Matt. 5:22)
34 Hairdo no-no (1 Peter 3:3)
35 Coastal hazes
36 Climate and natural resources org.
38 Yuck!
39 Bard's before
40 What you want to be when 59 Across
42 Elisabeth and Zacharias, e.g.
43 "Till thou hast ___ the very last mite" (Luke 12:59)
44 Spirits
45 Warriors of 1 Chron. 12:2, perhaps
48 Twain's Tom
49 Elisabeth "brought forth a ___" (Luke 1:57)
50 Je ne ___ quoi (Fr.)
51 "No child, because that Elisabeth was ___" (Luke 1:7)
54 Bethsaida native, familiarily (John 1:44)

55 Large tree
58 Samoan capital
59 Paul was this from Seleucia to Cyprus (Acts 13:4)
61 Ahasuerus reigned from here to Ethiopia (Est. 1:1)
63 Paul's destination in 59 Across (Acts. 13:4)
64 "Then drew ___ unto him all the publicans and sinners" (Luke 15:1)
65 Simeon's sobriquet (Acts 13:1)
66 No doubt Elisabeth couldn't wait to ___ Mary what happened
67 Zacharias couldn't do this for a while (Luke 1:22)
68 Dales

DOWN

1 People wondered why Zacharias was this (Luke 1:21)
2 Dramatic conflict
3 Did Zacharias feel like one to argue with Gabriel? (Luke 1:18)
4 Epoch
5 Where Gabriel went after visiting Zacharias (Luke 1:26)
6 Elisabeth's son would have "power of ___" (Luke 1:17)
7 Paul was in one (Acts 26:29)
8 Deli order
9 Mottos
10 Caiaphas had one (Matt. 26:3)
11 Modern Persia
12 What Gabriel brought (Luke 1:13)
13 Brick making, e.g. (Ex. 5:14)
22 Fish
24 10 grams (abbr.)
25 One with a haughty spirit, e.g. (Prov. 16:18)
27 Laban and Jacob had one (Gen. 31:49–50)

28 Nebuchadnezzar's nails (Dan. 4:33)
29 Elisabeth's tribe (Luke 1:5)
30 Actress Day
31 Both Elisabeth and Zacharias were this (Luke 1:7)
32 Elisabeth's baby would "make ___ a people" (Luke 1:17)
33 Jael's weapon (Judg. 4:21)
35 Gabriel to Zacharias: "___ not" (Luke 1:13)
37 Like a wing
40 Helping
41 Among those devils entered (Matt. 8:31)
43 Team flag
46 Elisabeth's child preached to this people (Luke 1:80)
47 Edgar Allen

48 Okinawan weapon
50 Day 5 creation (Gen. 1:21)
51 Judah took Tamar's (Gen. 38:15)
52 Church section
53 The Jordan River in some places today
54 Church bell might do this
55 Gabriel's appearance put Zacharias on it (Luke 1:12)
56 "One of the people might lightly have ___ with thy wife" (Gen. 26:10)
57 Hill site of Paul's sermon (Acts 17:22)
60 Where 41 Down ran (Matt. 8:32)
62 Our righteousness is this (Isa. 64:6)

22 ESAU'S ERROR
by Patricia Mitchell

• • • • • •

ACROSS

1 Jacob and Esau had one, big-time (Gen. 27:41)
5 Top story
10 Women's magazine
14 Rebekah was one to Jacob in trickery (Gen. 27:8)
15 Animals in a region
16 Genesis includes these for Esau and Jacob
17 Esau sold it (Gen. 25:33)
19 Orchestra voice
20 Cry softly
21 What Christ did for your sins (Rom. 5:11)
23 Esau's father had lost this sense (Gen. 27:22)
26 Esau's father ___ for Jacob's impersonation of Esau (Gen. 27:27)
28 Esau "came out ___, all over like an hairy garment" (Gen. 25:25)
31 Charged particle
32 What Jesus does (Luke 1:68)
33 Jacob drew this from Esau (Gen. 27:41)
34 Jacob ___ gifts to Esau to appease him (Gen. 32:20)
37 Esau's dad (Gen. 25:26)
39 Crucifix
40 What Jacob told his father was not this
42 Asian capital
45 Incense descriptor
49 Winter river sight, at times
50 Camera stand
53 Computing phrase
54 "Thy dwelling shall be. . .of the ___ of heaven" (Gen. 27:39)
55 "I mean not that other men be ___" (2 Cor. 8:13)
56 Frothy

58 Power controlling device, for short
60 How Esau and Jacob may have addressed their father
61 "___ before men" (Matt. 6:1)
63 Frogs, toads, e.g.
69 What a 63 Across might do
70 Jacob wanted to ___ ___ Esau's inheritance (Gen. 25:31) (2 wds.)
71 Scat!
72 Ezekiel's vision (Ezek. 37:1)
73 Psalmist asks God to do this to his transgressions (Ps. 51:1)
74 Esau does this when Jacob gives him stew (Gen. 25:34)

DOWN

1 Charge
2 Roman count
3 Presidential initials
4 Fido's activity
5 Hairdo
6 Chinese ethnic group
7 Tower
8 Breathe in
9 "Lead on softly, according as the ___" (Gen. 33:14)
10 Black
11 West African country
12 London WC
13 Joppa to Jerusalem (dir.)
18 The meat Jacob served his father, perhaps
22 Element
23 Esau's niece Dinah to his nephew Zebulun, for short (Gen. 30:20–21)
24 Jacob's debt to Esau, e.g.
25 Economic measure
26 Esau to Jacob: "___ me, I pray thee" (Gen. 25:30)

27 "The LORD shall ____ to me another son" (Gen. 30:24)
29 When the patriarchs lived, e.g.
30 Noel month (abbr.)
32 2016 Games city, for short
35 At trickery, Jacob was this
36 Mill about
38 ____ of Galilee
40 Feet did this, KJV style
41 Aaron's budded (Num. 17:8)
42 Jacob ____ from Esau (Gen. 27:43)
43 Whiz
44 Walter Cronkite, e.g.
45 Jacob would ____ Esau (Gen. 27:15–16)
46 Sticky black substance
47 Computer corp.
48 Esau emitted an "exceeding bitter ____" (Gen. 27:34)

51 Esau might ____ Jacob's family in revenge (Gen. 32:6)
52 Chemical compound
56 Nursery item
57 Esau: "Let my father ____, and eat" (Gen. 27:31)
59 Rebekah would ____ her husband's plans to bless Esau (Gen. 27:5)
60 Mount Sinai, e.g.
61 Mass garment
62 MGM's Lion
64 School org.
65 KJV hast
66 What Esau might have said when he realized what Jacob did (Gen. 27:34)
67 Commandment word
68 Distress call

ESTHER:
23 THE BLESSED QUEEN
by Patricia Mitchell

• • • • • • •

ACROSS

1 Concorde, e.g.
4 British W.C.
7 Shushan to 22 Across (dir.)
10 Jews may have used one in defense (Est. 8:11)
12 Tool of trade, perhaps, for Andrew and Peter (Matt. 4:18)
13 Esther's appearance (Est. 2:7)
14 Leah to Joseph and Rachel to Reuben (Gen. 35:23–24)
16 Ahasuerus's exclamation to find Haman at Esther's couch (Est. 7:8)
17 Ahasuerus to Esther: "___ ye also for the Jews" (Est. 8:8)
18 Description of Esther (Est. 2:7) (2 wds.)
21 Ahasuerus's calls for young virgins, for short
22 Abraham's native place (Gen. 11:27–28)
23 Esther may have felt this when urged to intercede (Est. 4:16)
26 Chemical symbol
27 Esther was one (Est. 2:7)
31 Scooby-___
32 Skunklike African animal
35 Haman would ___ the king's decree to destroy Jews (Est. 3:8–9)
36 Mordecai to Esther: "Who knoweth whether thou art come to the kingdom for ___ ___ ___ ___ ___" (Est. 4:14) (5 wds.)
41 Esther's pronoun
42 Fern seed
43 Haman had a lot of it (Est. 6:6)
44 Esther was given Haman's (Est. 8:7)
47 Spielberg's alien
48 Esther must not be this (Est. 4:8)

49 Mordecai acted as this to Esther (Est. 2:7)
50 "Go to the ___, thou sluggard" (Prov. 6:6)
51 Where Haman ended up (Est. 7:10) (4 wds.)
61 Mordecai sent letters to the Jews "with words of ___ and truth" (Est. 9:30)
62 Hospital patients do this
63 Haman's plans could be called this (Est. 3:8–9)
64 63 Across homonym
65 Jerusalem to Damascus (dir.)
66 "Singin' in the Rain" Kelly
67 "They shall not hunger ___ thirst" (Isa. 49:10)
68 Esther asked the Jews not to do this for three days (Est. 4:16)
69 Comprehensive dictionary

DOWN

1 Wound cap
2 Skid
3 Charlie's sort
4 What a sluggard does
5 Honolulu's island
6 The king's command to his servants was this (Est. 1:10)
7 "Cause Haman to make haste, that he may do as Esther hath ___" (Est. 5:5)
8 Shushan is one
9 One might be among those singing (Song 2:12)
11 Energy measurement
13 TGI day (abbr.)
15 A psalm often has one
17 Haman's mind did this, perhaps
19 Haman was one, in the foolish sense
20 Austrian river (var.)

23 Passports are these
24 Particle of dust turned to one under Aaron's rod (Ex. 8:16)
25 Ness and Lomond
27 Bread spread
28 Sukkot shelter
29 Sackcloth partner
30 Mr. Ed's negative, perhaps
33 Jesus would do this on the third day
34 Elf
37 Excited (with up)
38 Christians were martyred in one, at times
39 Ahasuerus would not ___ for Vashti's refusal
40 Chinese sauce
45 Church part
46 Chinese philosophical concept

50 Ornamental stud
51 "I stand. . .and knock: if any man. . .___ the door, I will come in" (Rev. 3:20)
52 Christians' nemesis in Rome
53 Esau had a lot of this (Gen. 27:11)
54 Often in cubes
55 Wax mate
56 One of Columbus's ships
57 In the king's dream, one of these was iron (Dan. 2:33)
58 Black and white treat
59 Ahasuerus enjoyed too much of this (Est. 1:10)
60 "If Mordecai be of the ___ of the Jews" (Est. 6:13)

EVE:
THE FIRST WOMAN
by Patricia Mitchell

• • • • • •

ACROSS

1 Cave dwellers

5 John the Baptizer's food, according to tradition

10 Eve to Serpent: "God hath said, Ye shall ___ eat of it" (Gen. 3:3)

13 God would ___ the sin of Adam and Eve (Gen. 3:14)

15 Eden was this before the Fall

16 Easter mo., often

17 Eve placed this on the serpent (Gen. 3:13)

18 Eve's was a biggie (Gen. 3:6)

19 Serpent to Eve: "Ye shall not surely ___" (Gen. 3:4)

20 Eve had one for the fruit of the tree (Gen. 3:6)

21 Chowder mollusk

23 God clothed Adam and Eve in "coats of ___" (Gen. 3:21)

25 Satan called God this, in effect (Gen. 3:4)

26 Satan preyed on those of Eve (Gen. 3:6)

28 "I will put ___ between thee and the woman" (Gen. 3:15)

31 Satan's temptations are often double ___

32 Adam to God: "I heard thy ___ in the garden, and I was afraid" (Gen. 3:10)

33 Tea choice

34 ___ Squad, classic TV show

37 Eve may have been this, as she had time to speak to a serpent

38 Salome or Delilah, e.g.

40 Pedal-powered transport

41 Eve told God she was ___ astray by the serpent (Gen. 3:13)

42 Mob activity

43 "Shall be called ___" (Gen. 2:23)

44 God's punishment for disobedience (Gen. 2:17)

45 Adam and Eve were these before the Fall (Gen. 2:23)

46 Mexican spirit

49 Colorado's Zebulon M.

50 Music genre

51 "Time and ___ wait for no man"

52 Noah's vessel

55 Grand ___ Opry, radio program

56 Church steeple

59 Downtown

61 Formerly (Fr.)

62 Despite Eve's sin, God would ___ a promise (Gen. 3:15)

63 For a covering, Adam and Eve would ___ fig leaves (Gen. 3:7)

64 Climate channel

65 God's promise of a Savior ___ sin's sting (1 Cor. 15:54–57)

66 Eve ___ off God's warning, so to speak (Gen. 3:6)

DOWN

1 God's promise of a Savior would take this form (Luke 2:11–12)

2 52 Down's homonym

3 "The serpent was more subtil ___ any beast" (Gen. 3:1)

4 Ruble replacement in the Kyrgyz Republic

5 Humidor item

6 Eve's hubby

7 Team sports figure, for short

8 Nabal, for one (1 Sam. 25:3)

9 "Male and female created he them; and ___ them" (Gen. 5:2)

10 Lowest point

11 Eve would do this in response to God's question (Gen. 3:13)

12 Eve might have had one

14 Those who memorize Bible verses can do this

22 "Little Lord Jesus ___ down His sweet head" (song)

24 Eve's boy Cain, e.g.

25 Plague pests (Ex. 8:17)

26 Chop

27 Eve's paradise

28 "Tree of knowledge of good and ___" (Gen. 2:9)
29 Stem point
30 Like earth inheritors (Matt. 5:5)
31 God created Adam and Eve on the ___ day (Gen. 1:27, 31)
34 Silent performer
35 Eve's word to the serpent's suggestion, maybe (Gen. 3:6)
36 "in ___ and caves of the earth" (Heb. 11:38)
38 Tube
39 Not one of the law shall remain unfulfilled (Matt. 5:18)
40 "Adam said, This is now ___ of my bones" (Gen. 2:23)
42 Many times in the Bible, God would ___ His promise of a Savior
43 After they sinned, Adam and Eve did this, in a way (Gen. 3:7) (2 wds.)

44 After Adam and Eve sinned, punishment was ___
45 "Adam and his wife ___ themselves from" God (Gen. 3:8)
46 Cut of beef
47 Girl's name
48 Title of Solomon's visitor (1 Kings 10:1)
49 Docks
51 Eve "saw that the ___ was good for food" (Gen. 3:6)
52 Eve's murdered son
53 Eve is the mother of the human ___ (Gen. 3:20)
54 "Adam ___ Eve his wife; and she conceived" (Gen. 4:1)
57 School org.
58 After creation, vegetation produced after ___ kind (Gen. 1:11–12)
60 God made Eve from Adam's ___ (Gen. 2:22)

25 EZRA: THE SCRIBE

by Patricia Mitchell

• • • • • •

ACROSS

1 Dance
4 "Who is there ___ you of all his people?" (Ezra 1:3)
9 Damage
12 "Un bel di vedremo," e.g.
14 Ezekiel may have seen one (Ezek. 37:4)
15 "At ___ in the body. . .absent from the Lord" (2 Cor. 5:6)
16 A good man will do this (Ps. 112:5)
17 Matador's passes at bull
18 Arabian Sea gulf
19 Ezra going to Jerusalem did not rest at one of these (2 wds.)
21 Patron
23 Tool likely used in Temple project (Ezra 5:8) (var.)
24 Ezra "did ___ no bread" in mourning (Ezra 10:6)
25 Cyrus or Artaxerxes
28 Really cool
31 Thin strand
34 Third largest island in the world
36 When Temple construction ceased, the builders could do this (Ezra 4:24)
38 Luau dish
40 Whoremonger (Eph. 5:5)
41 God's gift to the faithful remnant (Ezra 9:8)
43 Hiker's nemesis
44 Brew
45 Building wing
46 Islands off of Portugal
48 "Finished on the third day of the month ___" (Ezra 6:15)
51 Throw
53 On the holy day, everyone does this (Neh. 8:10)
54 Subsidiary (abbr.)
56 Flow mate
58 Ezra was a ready one (Ezra 7:6)

61 "___ the house of the LORD" (Ezra 7:27)
66 Location of 30 Down
67 What an angry mob does
69 Human rights org.
70 Baby pooches
71 Temple vessels were in Babylon because Sheshbazzar did this (Ezra 1:11)
72 All the people enjoyed one (Neh. 8:12)
73 Jerusalem to Dead Sea (dir.)
74 "Then ___ we those elders" (Ezra 5:9)
75 It colored the rich man's garment (Luke 16:19)

DOWN

1 Is there any in Gilead? (Jer. 8:22)
2 Black and white treat
3 Gourmet ice-cream container, often
4 Temple builders would ___ stones and timber (Ezra 6:4)
5 Nebuchadnezzar, an oppressor, was ___ than Cyrus, a benevolent ruler
6 Jews' marriages with heathens was a bad one to Ezra (Ezra 9:1–3)
7 Mother Teresa, e.g.
8 "___ hath been shewed from the LORD" (Ezra 9:8)
9 Style
10 The people's response to Ezra's blessing (Neh. 8:6)
11 Ezra did this to his clothing (Ezra 9:1–3)
13 Festive activities of Neh. 8:10, e.g.
15 Port-au-Prince location
20 Reaction of natives when not permitted to work on the Temple (Ezra 4:4–5)

22 Ezra's expertise (Ezra 7:6)
25 Eucalyptus-loving marsupial
26 Natives were this (see 20 Down)
27 Jerusalem to Babylon (dir.)
29 __-Saxon
30 Doo ___ Parade, 66 Across event
32 The rock in Horeb did this
   (Ex. 17:6)
33 Skin features
34 Lingerie item
35 17 Across arena cheer
37 School org.
39 Taxing org.
42 How Ezra felt (see 11 Down)
43 Relative of Eve's tempter
47 Asian humped ox
49 "See ya later!" (Sp.)
50 God took one from Adam
   (Gen. 2:22)

52 Scarab
55 Vice __
57 Cyrus knew God's Temple was
   ___ in Jerusalem (Ezra 1:2)
58 Several of the items Judas
   received from Jesus (John 13:26)
59 Small freshwater fish
60 "Offer the first of thy ___ fruits"
   (Ex. 22:29)
61 "Ezra opened the ___ in the sight
   of all the people" (Neh. 8:5)
62 Scottish cap, for short
63 The face of the deep is this
   (Job 38:30)
64 "He shall ___ the burnt offering"
   (Lev. 1:6)
65 December log
68 "__ a Small World," Disney ditty

GABRIEL: THE ARCHANGEL

26

by Patricia Mitchell

• • • • • •

ACROSS

1 Never say this to Gabriel!
6 Investment choices
9 It's for lovers (abbr.)
11 Rights org.
12 Downwind
13 Tramps
16 Temptation, often
17 Gabriel to Mary: "Elisabeth, she hath also conceived a son in her old ___" (Luke 1:36)
18 How Gabriel might respond if you said 1 Across
19 Gabriel's message, Part 1 (Luke 1:28) (3 wds.)
23 It came to ___: KJV for "when"
24 "Fear not" are words Gabriel would use and ___
25 Pasty glue
29 13th letter of the Greek alphabet
30 Gabriel's promise: "The Lord ___ ___ ___" (Luke 1:28) (3 wds.)
33 ___ voyage (Fr.)
36 Mary and Joseph would ___ Jesus (Luke 1:80)
37 Sports org.
38 Press
40 After His resurrection, Jesus did this with His disciples (Luke 24:43)
41 Design process (2 wds.)
44 Fashionable
45 Post-jail sentence
46 Gabriel's message, Part 2 (Luke 1:28)
50 Car rental agency
52 Joseph might have been doing this during Jesus' birth if Nikon had been around (2 wds.)
58 Cuisine choice
59 Parents should not be this (Prov. 23:13)

60 Connection
61 Wildebeest location
62 Kind of messenger Gabriel was
63 Herodias' daughter needed one (Matt. 14:6)
64 Grizzly bear state (abbr.)
65 Daniel and lions met here (Dan. 6:16)
66 Gabriel's message, Part 3 (Luke 1:28)

DOWN

1 Never do this to Gabriel!
2 Astronomer Sagan
3 "Jealousy is the ___ of a man" (Prov. 6:34)
4 Card series
5 U.K. politician (abbr.)
6 Puts on, KJV style
7 Impressionist painter
8 Huldah was one (2 Kings 22:14)
9 Popularity
10 Sackcloth mate
13 "We should be saved. . .from the hand of all that ___ us" (Luke 1:71)
14 Pacific tourist destination
15 Reuben, Judah, and Simon (abbr.)
20 "They ___ upon him" (Matt. 27:30)
21 "The charity of every one of you all toward ___ other aboundeth" (2 Thess. 1:3)
22 God's Word is this
25 Space station
26 Paul and shipmates where this in a storm (Acts 27:15)
27 Pakistani valley in the news
28 A good soldier of Christ does not do this (2 Tim. 2:3)
29 Rebekah put goat skins on Jacob's (Gen. 27:16)

31 Jacob to Esau
32 Movie 2001's talking computer
33 100 cents in Ethiopia
34 You can fiddle with its middle
35 Gabriel's time in France
39 Bethlehem to Jerusalem (dir.)
41 Angel to shepherds: "This shall be a ___ unto you" (Luke 2:12)
42 ___ and span
43 Mary "___ in her mind what manner of salutation this should be" (Luke 1:29)
46 "The king had ___ ___ a navy of Tharshish" (1 Kings 10:22) (2 wds.)
47 What place God needs to have in your life (Matt. 6:33)

48 Mary was this with Gabriel's message (Luke 1:38)
49 Little girl in Cancun
50 "Kings of armies did flee ___" (Ps. 68:12)
51 Harpy
53 Gabriel's tidings (Luke 1:19)
54 Gabriel was "sent to speak ___" Zacharias (Luke 1:19)
55 Range
56 "They shall fall by the ___ of the sword" (Luke 21:24)
57 "We have ___ his star in the east" (Matt. 2:2)
58 Fido's org.
63 Jericho to Jerusalem (dir.)

GIDEON:
27 GOD'S MAN OF VALOR
by Laura Lisle

• • • • •

ACROSS

1 Recedes
5 Inflexible
10 Mountain Time (abbr.)
13 Japanese dress
14 Mockery
15 Soft white cheese
16 "Upon the ___ of the rock" (Job 39:28)
17 "___ be unto thee; fear not" (Judg. 6:23)
18 Consumer
19 Sixth tribe of Israel (abbr.)
21 Gideon's job (Judg. 6:11)
23 Teaspoon (abbr.)
26 "He shall be cast into the ___ of lions" (Dan. 6:7)
28 "The ___ shall not always be forgotten" (Ps. 9:18)
29 It might fall on your head
32 These should be redeemed (Num. 3:48) (pl.)
33 Hyundai is one
34 Author of Acts (Gr., Philem. 1:24)
36 "Cast him into the ___ of ground" (2 Kings 9:26)
37 Deborah's right-hand man
38 Syllables in songs (2 wds.)
42 Drop
43 "The children of Israel did ___" (Judg. 2:11)
44 Midianite prince who lost his head
46 Network
49 Trims
51 "Let all thy wants ___ upon me." (Judg. 19:20)
52 "Gideon went up by the ___ of them" (Judg. 8:11)
53 "I ___ not my heart from any joy" (Eccl. 2:10)
57 ___ Lanka
59 Reverberate
60 Bullwinkle is one
62 She follows Judges
66 "There was no such ___ done" (Judg. 19:30)
67 Lawn tool
68 Paul's mission field ___ Minor
69 "A people that do ___ in their heart" (Ps. 95:10)
70 Sleep disorder
71 Dozes

DOWN

1 Keyboard component
2 It reaches from end to end (Ex. 26:28)
3 Lingerie
4 "Shew me a ___ that thou talkest with me" (Judg. 6:17)
5 Jack the ___
6 Wrath
7 "And one ___ for a sin offering" (Num. 29:38)
8 Give 'em an ___, they want a mile
9 Lydia's profession (Acts 16:14)
10 Joins together
11 Trusty horse
12 "I will ___ until thou come again" (Judg. 6:18)
15 Stuck together
20 "___ to your faith virtue" (2 Peter 1:5)
22 "All the ___ of the world shall remember" (Ps. 22:27)
23 "Let it become a ___" (Ps. 69:22)
24 First king of Israel

25 Falafel holder
27 Mr. Ryan
30 "Israel remembered ___ the
   LORD their God" (Judg. 8:34)
31 Jewish holiday (Est. 9:26)
32 Tree where Gideon met the angel
   of the Lord (Judg. 6:11)
35 Biblical ground transportation
37 Baby essential
38 "Many are called, but ___ are
   chosen" (Matt. 22:14)
39 Assert
40 Italian money
41 Alcoholic (slang)
42 Interlock
44 Psalmist's instrument
45 Gideon's was made of gold

47 Canaanite killed by Deborah
48 Samson to his father: "Get ___
   for me" (Judg. 14:3)
49 Swedish citizen
50 Kinder
54 Mrs. Peel
55 Ice-skating maneuver
56 "I will break ___ this tower"
   (Judg. 8:9)
58 Cyrus' kingdom today (Ezra 1:1)
61 "___ there come people down
   by the middle of the land"
   (Judg. 9:37)
63 America (abbr.)
64 Part of ear to be anointed
   (Lev. 14:17)
65 Owns

HAGAR:
THE OTHER WIFE
by Laura Lisle

• • • • •

ACROSS

1 Nebraska city
6 "___ the right, O LORD" (Ps. 17:1)
10 What to do with swaddling (Luke 2:7)
14 Ishmael dwelt here (Gen. 21:21)
15 Loops' location (Ex. 26:5)
16 Drag (Luke 12:58)
17 Concerning
18 Mystery "hid from ___" (Col. 1:26)
19 Woodwind
20 "I will ___ on softly" (Gen. 33:14)
21 Interfere
22 "___ shall be thy name" (Gen. 35:10)
24 Hagar's job (Gen. 16:2)
26 Grown-ups
27 "Enter ye in at the ___ gate" (Matt. 7:13)
30 Blunder
31 Possessive pronoun
32 Constellation near Taurus
33 ___ Lanka
36 Root beer brand (3 wds.)
37 "Fools ___ for want of wisdom" (Prov. 10:21)
38 Ishmael's brother (Gen. 25:9)
40 "___ me come unto thee" (Matt. 14:28)
41 Relating to birds
43 "Is he a homeborn ___?" (Jer. 2:14)
44 Change direction
45 Stowed
46 Capital of Lesotho
49 "Son of man ___ suffer" (Mark 8:31)
50 Ladies' bow

51 Number of years Abram dwelt in Canaan (Gen. 16:3)
52 Slaps
56 Opera solo
57 Entice
59 In advance, as in Rom. 9:23
60 "I am the first and the ___" (Rev. 1:17)
61 Widows might be (1 Tim. 5:13)
62 Private teacher
63 "I ___ from the face of my mistress" (Gen. 16:8)
64 Heavenly pavement (Rev. 21:21)
65 Thrill

DOWN

1 Australian export
2 Lion's hair
3 Region
4 Hagar, "Sarah's ___" (Gen. 25:12)
5 Sluggard's example (Prov. 6:6)
6 "God hath ___ the voice of the lad" (Gen. 21:17)
7 Innovative
8 "The eyes of Israel were dim for ___" (Gen. 48:10)
9 Remnant (Neh. 11:20)
10 Spiral
11 Capital of Morocco
12 "Garments smell of myrrh, and ___" (Ps. 45:8)
13 Orange exterior
21 Joseph was cast into this for his first trial (Gen. 37:22)
23 Scrapes by
25 Radio signals travel on these
26 "I am an ___ in their sight" (Job 19:15)
27 Thrust
28 Siamese

29 "___ your heart" (Joel 2:13)
30 Monk
32 Good-bye (Fr.)
33 German region
34 Rant
35 Frosted
39 "Desire of the ___ killeth him" (Prov. 21:25)
42 Jumbo (2 wds.)
45 "___, stand thou" (Josh. 10:12)
46 Wall picture
47 "___, shine; for thy light is come" (Isa. 60:1)

48 Last worse than first (Luke 11:26)
49 The Lord "___ out heaven" (Isa. 40:12)
50 Abraham's meal (Gen. 18:8)
51 Plow the earth (Gen. 2:5)
53 Small particle
54 Ride horseback
55 Wizened
58 "Why make ye this ___, and weep?" (Mark 5:39)
59 John "___ the little book" (Rev. 10:10)

HAMAN TRADES PLACES
by Laura Lisle

● ● ● ● ●

ACROSS
1 Wicked fall into (Ps. 141:10)
5 Country facing judgment (Ezek. 30:5)
9 Clang
13 Give off
14 Persona non ___
15 ___ mater
16 Banquet beverage (Est. 5:6)
17 Mordecai's garment material (Est. 8:15)
18 Ball of thread
19 Nut (2 wds.)
21 Vashti and Esther
23 Pod vegetables
24 Pitch
25 Sway
28 Role play
31 Hebrew 12th month (Est. 3:7)
32 "My life is ___ with grief" (Ps. 31:10)
34 A woman should "___ her nails" (Deut. 21:12)
36 Roman days of fasting (Est. 4:16)
37 "David ___, and stood upon the Philistine" (1 Sam. 17:51)
38 "They shall ___, and not be weary" (Isa. 40:31)
39 Hook site (Job 41:2)
41 Wanderer
43 "At thy rebuke they ___" (Ps. 104:7)
44 "He appointed the moon for ___" (Ps. 104:19)
46 "Who can understand his ___?" (Ps. 19:12)
48 Mordecai's seat (Est. 2:19)
49 Removed as confirmation (Ruth 4:7)
50 Hebrew 10th month (Est. 2:16)

53 Wired for Internet
57 "Thy ___ is as a flock of goats" (Song 4:1)
58 Lazy person
60 Extinct bird
61 Defunct football league
62 Month Pur was cast (Est. 3:7)
63 Leave out
64 Goliath's plan regarding Israel (1 Sam. 17:25)
65 Nerd
66 Give out a measure, as in Mark 4:24

DOWN
1 Mr. Gingrich
2 Ruler
3 Prong
4 More abrupt
5 What the Lord hears (James 5:4)
6 "He laid his ___ upon the Jews" (Est. 8:7)
7 Colorado tribe
8 Haman attended (Est. 5:5)
9 Warm-up lap (2 wds.)
10 French pronoun
11 Bible's last word
12 Kept in the heart (Heb. 10:16)
14 Ruth does this (Ruth 2:2)
20 "I ___ Mordecai the Jew" (Est. 5:13)
22 Large vase
24 Tattoo type
25 Adam's eldest son
26 Bye! (Sp.)
27 "I will ___ up a shepherd" (Zech. 11:16)
28 Cleans a hole
29 Monte ___
30 More accurate

33 Flat

35 "Salvation unto the ___ of the earth" (Acts 13:47)

40 Anxiously

41 What Esther required (Est. 2:15)

42 Take away the antlers

43 What Paul obtained (Acts 22:28)

45 Mordecai ___ at the king's gate (Est. 2:19)

47 Beryl on 4th (Ex. 28:20)

49 "___ thou unto the king" (Est. 5:14)

50 Thump

51 "At ___ and quiet" (Job 21:23)

52 Hit

53 Otherwise, as in Ex. 10:4

54 Where Jews departed from (Acts 18:2)

55 Redact

56 Be fond of

59 "Curse God, and ___" (Job 2:9)

HANNAH'S CHILD
OF PROMISE
by Laura Lisle

• • • • •

ACROSS

1 Trades
6 It may be gray
10 Carmel to Joppa (dir.)
14 Assistants
15 The ___ should bury their dead (Matt. 8:22)
16 "___ and female created he them" (Gen. 1:27)
17 Stupid
18 "There be now an ___ betwixt us" (Gen. 26:28)
19 Modern-day Persia
20 Actress Moore
21 Large computer co.
22 "Why ___ thou not?" (1 Sam. 1:8)
24 Defensive alliance
26 "Eli the ___ sat" (1 Sam. 1:9)
27 CSI data
30 "From thence they went to ___" (Num. 21:16)
31 Not urban
32 "We are thy bone and thy ___" (2 Sam. 5:1)
33 "___ with the dew of heaven" (Dan. 4:33)
36 Island greeting
37 "He that hath an ___" (Rev. 2:7)
38 Dry measure (1 Sam. 1:24)
40 Crave
41 "Christ must ___ have suffered" (Acts 17:3)
43 "Samuel ___ and went to Eli" (1 Sam. 3:6)
44 "As a ___ that is told" (Ps. 90:9)
45 To think
46 Is appropriate
49 "Hannah ___ up after they had eaten" (1 Sam. 1:9)
50 Roman stoic
51 Yang's partner
52 Rocket builders
56 Alabama's Crimson
57 "Their ___ shall be broken" (Ps. 37:15)
59 Aka buffalo
60 "Barzillai was a very ___ man" (2 Sam. 19:32)
61 "He that gathered little had no ___" (Ex. 16:18)
62 The pride of Vidalia, GA
63 Made of gold and silver (Est. 1:6)
64 Epochs
65 Stone on Aaron's ephod (Ex. 28:19)

DOWN

1 "He is risen, as he ___" (Matt. 28:6)
2 Hannah abstained from this (1 Sam. 1:15)
3 The first man
4 Elkanah's other wife (1 Sam. 1:2)
5 Nazareth to Jerusalem (dir.)
6 Seasoning (Sp.)
7 Enlarge
8 "She wept, and did not ___" (1 Sam. 1:7)
9 Cleaves
10 "Saul sought to ___ David" (1 Sam. 19:10)
11 "Gather up thy ___" (Jer. 10:17)
12 "By the ___ of God they perish" (Job 4:9)
13 "But Hannah ___ not up" (1 Sam. 1:22)
21 "That which groweth of ___ own accord" (Lev. 25:5)
23 Frivolous, silly people
25 Second-largest ocean
26 Equals
27 What Hannah does at Shiloh (1 Sam. 1:9–10)

28 "The greater light to ___ the day" (Gen. 1:16)
29 Canaanite chariot material (Josh. 17:16)
30 First sign of growth (Mark 4:28)
32 Senses
33 Stop!
34 This wind brought the locusts (Ex. 10:13)
35 Formal "you" in KJV
39 Cleaning feathers
42 Edible
45 Charged particle
46 Neutral color
47 "The days of thy mourning shall be ___" (Isa. 60:20)

48 The raven ___ Elijah (1 Kings 17:6)
49 Chances
50 Wound that killed Eglon (Judg. 3:21)
51 YMCA counterpart
53 Paul forbidden to preach here (Acts 16:6)
54 Chimney dirt
55 Green Gables dweller
58 Bashan's were made of oak (Ezek. 27:6)
59 It may be feathery or scaly

HEROD THE TETRARCH

31

by Laura Lisle

• • • • •

ACROSS

1 Kingdom or state treasury (abbr.)
5 Child protection agency
8 "He maketh ___ to cease" (Ps. 46:9)
12 Against
13 Lures
15 Weapons of iron (2 Sam. 12:31)
16 Type of jazz vocals
17 Buick model
18 What Herod did to children in Bethlehem (Matt. 2:16)
19 Fortification
21 She wept for the children (Matt. 2:18)
23 How God spoke to Joseph (Matt. 2:12)
25 Con's opposite
26 Flare
29 Took Isaac's place (Gen. 22:13)
31 Desert plant
35 Designer Laura
37 Scientist playground
39 "And ___ shall be a sign unto you" (Luke 2:12)
40 "If any man will ___ thee" (Matt. 5:40)
41 Fiendish
44 "___, and it shall be given you" (Matt. 7:7)
45 Streetcar
47 Average work performance
48 Dress top
50 It's cut with a pruning hook (Isa. 18:5)
52 Roman number of Herods in the Bible
54 Tetrarch of Galilee (Luke 3:1)
55 Hind's mate (Song 2:9)
57 Heavenly messenger
59 Neckwear (17th cent.)

62 Waterways
65 Newsman Sevareid
66 Animals that heard the Good News first
68 Ivy League school
70 Given to Jesus to drink (Matt. 27:34)
71 It may be past or present
72 Send forth
73 Leer
74 "My time is not ___ come" (John 7:6)
75 "In ___ was there a voice heard" (Matt. 2:18)

DOWN

1 Musical syllables
2 Andes inhabitant
3 Wound in Jesus' side
4 Strong tower of Ps. 61:3
5 He ordered a census (Luke 2:1)
6 One who is slovenly, greedy, or gluttonous
7 Herod tracked it (Matt. 2:7)
8 Failure
9 Shaft
10 The earth will do this one day (Isa. 24:20)
11 Jerusalem to Bethlehem (dir.)
13 French province
14 Smack
20 In Isaiah they clap their hands (Isa. 55:12)
22 What stones might do (Luke 19:40)
24 Infectious disease
26 Times of denial
27 Women should not "___ authority" (1 Tim. 2:12)
28 "Nabal did ___ his sheep" (1 Sam. 25:4)

30 Jesus, the Son of ___
32 Seat
33 IT leader
34 "Saul ___ counsel of God" (1 Sam. 14:37)
36 Yelp
38 Apron top
42 ___ chi
43 Singer Leonard
46 "This is again the second ___" (John 4:54)
49 Impediment
51 Joseph's role in Egypt (Gen. 42:6) (abbr.)
53 Herod Antipas' sin (Matt. 14:4)

56 Magi's origin
58 Open-mouthed stare
59 Where the eagle dwells (Job 39:28)
60 Rivulet
61 "___ rejoiced with exceeding great joy" (Matt. 2:10)
63 "Eli, Eli, ___ sabachthani?" (Matt. 27:46)
64 Western actor Pickens
65 Id's companion
67 Bethlehem to Jerusalem (dir.)
69 Seventh Greek letter

HEZEKIAH: JEHOVAH FOLLOWER

32

by Laura Lisle

• • • • •

ACROSS

1 "Is there no ___ in Gilead?" (Jer. 8:22)
5 Tides
9 China island: ___ Kong
13 Off-Broadway award
14 Saw logs
15 Nighttime (Gen. 19:1)
16 Samuel's role (1 Sam. 9:19)
17 Particle
18 Asian humped ox
19 Plasterwork
21 Hezekiah's water holder (2 Kings 18:31)
23 "My ___ is easy" (Matt. 11:30)
25 Egyptian delicacy (Num. 11:5) (sing.)
26 Christian org. for young athletes
29 "The LORD will ___ me" (2 Kings 20:8)
31 "Salute every ___ in Christ Jesus" (Phil. 4:21)
34 Coffee holder
35 Inches forward
37 Air (prefix)
39 "We shall also ___ with him" (2 Tim. 2:12)
41 "Lot is cast into the ___" (Prov. 16:33)
42 Turkish ruler
43 "They shall ___ as lions' whelps" (Jer. 51:38)
44 Cain's eldest son (Gen. 4:17)
46 Danish krone (abbr.)
47 Material of Heavenly gate (Rev. 21:21)
50 Remain
51 Yes, as in John 11:27
52 Gloomy
54 "A rod out of the ___ of Jesse" (Isa. 11:1)

56 Cleaner brand
59 Tombs
63 The king "___ his garments" (2 Sam. 13:31)
64 Disconcert
66 Shipshape
67 Word of sorrow (Amos. 5:16)
68 Tightly twisted
69 Attacked Hezekiah (Isa. 36:2)
70 Hiding places (Rev. 6:15)
71 Disciple nickname
72 "Rejoicing in ___" (Rom. 12:12)

DOWN

1 Springsteen nickname
2 Aid
3 Instead: "In ___ of"
4 Seat of gold (Ex. 25:17)
5 Bethel to Shiloh (dir.)
6 Pear type
7 Cooking technique from Luke 24:42
8 Senses
9 King who saw a shadow (2 Kings 20:10)
10 "I will pass ___ you" (Ex. 12:13)
11 Gaza to Joppa (dir.)
12 African antelope
14 Food cured
20 Musician Leonard
22 Four o'clock beverage
24 "Fly away as an ___" (Prov. 23:5)
26 God's anger (Isa. 42:25)
27 How beasts move (Ps. 104:20)
28 Senile
30 Rests against
32 The Lord hears them (Isa. 41:17)
33 Three-wheeler
36 What the leopard can't change (Jer. 13:23)
38 Gumbo ingredient

40 "They sang praises with ___"
(2 Chron. 29:30)
42 More timid
45 Attention-getting
48 Hind's partner (Prov. 5:19)
49 Zambia capital
53 Batman's partner
55 Asian bird
56 Appearance of death horse
(Rev. 6:8)

57 Persia today
58 "God called the dry ___ Earth"
(Gen. 1:10)
60 Coffee alternative brand
61 Tap in lightly
62 Eye infection
63 A little bit
65 "So many as the stars of the ___"
(Heb. 11:12)

33 HOSEA: THE LONG-SUFFERING SPOUSE

by Laura Lisle

• • • • •

ACROSS

1 Caribbean dance
6 Jewish calendar month
10 Chimney
14 Jacob's father (Gen. 25:26)
15 "___ not ye unto Gilgal" (Hos. 4:15)
16 Speech defect
17 Playfully romantic
18 "Not an ___ be left behind" (Ex. 10:26)
19 Beehive state
20 "Go quickly, and ___ his disciples" (Matt. 28:7)
21 Exacerbate
23 Self
24 Native ruler in Africa
26 "Moses ___ up the tabernacle" (Ex. 40:18)
28 Citizen of Libya
31 Bible teacher Moore
32 Epoch
33 They are bent to backsliding (Hos. 11:7)
36 "For as in ___ all die" (1 Cor. 15:22)
40 "God waited in the days of ___" (1 Peter 3:20)
42 Charm
43 Tubular pasta
44 "Man doth not live by bread ___" (Deut. 8:3)
45 What Esther wrote regarding Purim (Est. 9:29)
48 An age
49 "The ___ was fair and beautiful" (Est. 2:7)
51 Hosea's son (Hos. 1:9)
53 "Raw" color
56 May be a good or bad sign
57 Body sys. consisting of brain and spinal cord

58 Iraq river
61 Festive party
65 "Go, take ___ thee a wife" (Hos. 1:2)
67 Paul before Damascus Road
68 Absurd
69 "Surely he shall not ___ quietness" (Job 20:20)
70 Gape
71 Male honeybee
72 Flintstone or Astaire
73 "To abound and to suffer ___" (Phil. 4:12)
74 "He reproved kings for their ___" (Ps. 105:14)

DOWN

1 "I will ___ up mine eyes" (Ps. 121:1)
2 John's prison, ___ of Patmos
3 Goliath's coat (1 Sam. 17:5)
4 Hosea's payment for Gomer (Hos. 3:2)
5 Fall mo.
6 Where Achan was destroyed (Josh. 7:24)
7 Achor was a "___ of hope" (Hos. 2:15)
8 Old Testament prophet
9 Umpire
10 Winter malady
11 Liquid measure
12 Utilization
13 Israel didn't have one (Hos. 3:4)
21 "They shall not offer ___ offerings" (Hos. 9:4)
22 Part of the altar (Ex. 27:5)
25 Traveler's aid
27 Son of Jotham (Hos. 1:1)
28 Comedian Jay
29 Og's bedstead material (Deut. 3:11)

30 Israel served ___ (2 Kings 17:16)
31 "___ out all mine iniquities" (Ps. 51:9)
34 "The one ___ five hundred pence" (Luke 7:41)
35 "The fining ___ is for silver" (Prov. 17:3)
37 Carpe ___
38 Particle
39 Short
41 Prelude to Gethsemane (Mark 14:26)
45 Intermediary
46 Trees of sacrifice (Hos. 4:13)
47 "My beloved is like a ___" (Song 2:9)
50 "Go to the ___, thou sluggard" (Prov. 6:6)

52 Goat or rabbit hair
53 Scratch
54 "The cloud filled the ___ court" (Ezek. 10:3)
55 Perfume maven Lauder
56 Bread sacrifice type (Lev. 8:26)
59 Challenge to combat
60 "The sun to ___ by day" (Ps. 136:8)
62 Priest of Jeshua (Neh. 12:7)
63 Rahab "bound a scarlet ___" (Josh. 2:21)
64 Experts
66 "Honour the face of the ___ man" (Lev. 19:32)
68 Savings accts.

34 Isaiah: The Faithful Prophet

by Laura Lisle

• • • • •

ACROSS

1 Wilderness tree (Isa. 41:19)
6 Fashionable
10 Connect
14 "The LORD ___ shall be exalted" (Isa. 2:11)
15 Crazy (Sp.)
16 Taboo
17 "Your hands are full of ___" (Isa. 1:15)
18 Prayer ending
19 Jainism believer
20 Half
21 "My heart standeth in ___ of thy word" (Ps. 119:161)
22 Phantoms
24 G-man Eliot
26 "___ for ashes" (Isa. 61:3)
27 Hog side
30 "This people draw ___" (Isa. 29:13)
31 Painting prop
32 Jacob had 10 (Gen. 32:15)
33 Noah's building project
36 Diacritic mark
37 Shortened (abbr.)
38 Netherlands' capital
40 "Come down ___ my child die" (John 4:49)
41 "Unto us a ___ is born" (Isa. 9:6)
43 Musical composition
44 Adjust
45 "Holy One of ___" (Isa. 1:4)
46 His birth foretold in Isaiah (Isa. 9:6)
49 "___ us a son is given" (Isa. 9:6)
50 "___ good tidings unto the meek" (Isa. 61:1)
51 Licensed caregiver
52 Seraphims held (Isa. 6:6)
56 Rejoicing, "The earth ___ again" (1 Sam. 4:5)
57 Bearded or Japanese
59 Transitional state
60 "God hath spoken ___" (Ps. 62:11)
61 "Call his ___ Immanuel" (Isa. 7:14)
62 Askew
63 "He shall ___ his flock" (Isa. 40:11)
64 "Strain at a ___, and swallow a camel" (Matt. 23:24)
65 Sound or mega

DOWN

1 Taxis
2 Women's magazine
3 Gloom and ___
4 "The LORD hath ___ me" (Isa. 61:1)
5 "___ like crimson" (Isa. 1:18)
6 "Nails like birds' ___" (Dan. 4:33)
7 Groom's first-year location (Deut. 24:5)
8 "Out of whose womb came the ___?" (Job 38:29)
9 Coagulate
10 Green-skinned pear
11 "Shall the axe ___ itself?" (Isa. 10:15)
12 "Keep the ___ of the Spirit" (Eph. 4:3)
13 Thousands of pounds
21 Tree the carpenter planted (Isa. 44:14)
23 Most unpleasant
25 Diverse
26 Razor consumes this (Isa. 7:20)
27 Lavish party
28 Hideout
29 "Howl, ye inhabitants of the ___" (Isa. 23:6)

30 "Not many ___, are called"
    (1 Cor. 1:26)

32 "They shall walk, and not ___"
    (Isa. 40:31)

33 Water (Sp.)

34 Describes Paul's speech
    (2 Cor. 11:6)

35 Musical actor Howard

39 Cruelty

42 Muting

45 No room here

46 Chattering bird (Isa. 38:14)

47 Command the idol, "Get thee
    ___" (Isa. 30:22)

48 "The heathen ___" (Ps. 46:6)

49 Toppled

50 University instructor (abbr.)

51 Peru capital

53 Leave out

54 " Believe ye that I am ___?"
    (Matt. 9:28)

55 These were cast for Jesus' clothes
    (John 19:24)

58 "David ___, and stood upon the
    Philistine" (1 Sam. 17:51)

59 Canine retriever (abbr.)

ISHMAEL: THE OTHER SON

35

by Laura Lisle

• • • • •

ACROSS

1 Astronaut employer
5 "And ___ of the son of the bondwoman" (Gen. 21:13)
9 Small flute
13 Old Testament prophet
14 Groups
15 Carved image (2 Chron. 33:7)
16 Beasts' homes (Job 37:8)
17 Fastener
18 "Set me as a ___ upon thine heart" (Song 8:6)
19 Central African country
21 Ishmael's father (Gen. 17:23)
23 Salad type
25 Ninth month (abbr.)
26 Car speed measurement
29 Hagar "___ from her face" (Gen. 16:6)
31 Leaven
34 Yes, as in Ps. 23:4
35 ___-cotta (clay)
37 Object
39 Bird homes (Luke 9:58)
41 "Give ___ unto my prayer" (Ps. 17:1)
42 Incline
43 Female voice
44 Formal statements
46 Animal companion
47 "Thou God ___ me" (Gen. 16:13)
50 "The Lord hath ___ of them" (Matt. 21:3)
51 "Ye shall not ___ my face" (Gen. 43:5)
52 "Planted in a good ___" (Ezek. 17:8)
54 Restaurant
56 Haunted
59 Dryads

63 Animal out of the wood (Ps. 80:13)
64 Nineteenth U.S. president
66 Realm
67 Cleves or Aragon (var.)
68 "His hand will be against ___ man" (Gen. 16:12)
69 Far Side's Larson
70 Dye color (Ex. 25:5) (pl.)
71 Dried up
72 God opened Hagar's (Gen. 21:19)

DOWN

1 Zilch (Sp.)
2 "The people shall say, ___" (Deut. 27:16)
3 ___ of Solomon
4 Organizational group (abbr.)
5 "Go to the ___, thou sluggard" (Prov. 6:6)
6 Italian currency
7 Jabs
8 Unclean bird (Lev. 11:13) (var.)
9 Back of car swerving
10 Thought
11 What Samaria's king is like (Hos. 10:7)
12 Building extension
14 Useful
20 Eutychus fell from (Acts 20:9) (pl.)
22 Tharshish cargo (1 Kings 10:22) (sing.)
24 Where Hagar and Ishmael rested (Gen. 16:14)
26 Asian starling
27 Apple skins
28 Move quickly, as in Gen. 19:22
30 Empty
32 Red lights

33 Indian lodge
36 Bow-shaped
38 Assign, as in Ps. 108:7
40 Corns (2 wds.)
42 "Wherefore look ye so ___?" (Gen. 40:7)
45 Small
48 Distress call
49 Brought to the storehouse (Mal. 3:10)
53 "Therefore shall a man ___ his father and his mother" (Gen. 2:24)

55 "In the ___ of God made he man" (Gen. 9:6)
56 "The LORD is ___ out against me" (Ruth 1:13)
57 "His ___ will be against every man" (Gen. 16:12)
58 Colorist
60 "I ___ thee, go in unto my maid" (Gen. 16:2)
61 "Behold, ___ am I" (Gen. 27:1)
62 Declares
63 Block
65 Before, as in John 4:49

JACOB: THE USURPER
by Laura Lisle

• • • • •

ACROSS

1 Western state
5 Wise king (abbr.)
8 Musical symbol
12 "I sink in deep ___" (Ps. 69:2)
13 Brief witty speech
15 Jacob held Esau's ___ (Gen. 25:26)
16 Urgent request
17 Learner
18 "Fear not: believe ___" (Luke 8:50)
19 Baltic state
21 Brains (slang)
23 Rental car company
25 "The LORD shall ___ to me another son" (Gen. 30:24)
26 Part of the offering in Lev. 8:26
29 How the rich ruler felt (Mark 10:22)
31 Lettuce and toppings
35 Color between red and yellow
37 Ballet steps
39 Jacob's priestly son (Gen. 34:25)
40 Unrefined metal
41 Country bordering Latvia
44 Convert into leather
45 "Thou hast now ___ foolishly" (Gen. 31:28)
47 Isaac did before blessing his son (Gen. 27:4)
48 Cat food brand
50 Actress Hilary
52 Bookstore section (abbr.)
54 "I will surely give the ___ unto thee" (Gen. 28:22)
55 N.T. author, for short
57 Imitation chocolate
59 Jacob's new name (Gen. 32:28)
62 Jacob's favored son (Gen. 37:3)
65 "The truth shall make you ___" (John 8:32)
66 Legitimate
68 To maintain, as in Gen. 17:9
70 "Eli, Eli, ___ sabachthani?" (Matt. 27:46)
71 Jacob dwelt in these (Gen. 25:27)
72 Paul was forbidden to preach here (Acts 16:6)
73 Troop
74 Springsteen's "Born in the ___"
75 Shofar, as in Josh. 6:5

DOWN

1 Referee (abbr.)
2 Plow, as in Gen. 2:5
3 Region
4 "Among the ___, and I will sing praises" (2 Sam. 22:50)
5 Weightlifting exercise
6 "Get thee ___ of thy country" (Gen. 12:1)
7 "A false witness that speaketh ___" (Prov. 6:19)
8 Harmonic
9 "I have ___ him to the LORD" (1 Sam. 1:28)
10 Morays
11 "He shall ___ away as a dream" (Job 20:8)
13 "Grievous words ___ up anger" (Prov. 15:1)
14 Judgment seat (Gr.)
20 Brink
22 Spots
24 Southern Mexican Indian
26 Where God's people will sleep (Ezek. 34:25)
27 "Their tongue is as an ___" (Jer. 9:8)

28 Matador's passes at bull
30 Jacob's fifth son (Gen. 29:32 –30:6)
32 Induct (2 wds.)
33 ___ -garde
34 Jacob's daughter (Gen. 34:1)
36 Shiloh to Jericho (dir.)
38 Drink slowly
42 Sticky black substance
43 Vehicles
46 "I will cause the enemy to ___ thee" (Jer. 15:11)
49 Isaac's wife (Gen. 24:67)
51 Soldier killed while in active service
53 Tortilla rollup
56 "Our hearts did ___" (Josh. 2:11)
58 Decays
59 Cyrus' kingdom today (2 Chron. 36:22)
60 Very large truck
61 Instead: "in ___ of"
63 Mexican money
64 Jesus, "___ of all things" (Heb. 1:2)
65 Winter malady
67 Body sys. consisting of brain and spinal cord
69 "A meat offering baken in a ___" (Lev. 2:5)

37 JAMES THE DISCIPLE

by Laura Lisle

● ● ● ● ●

ACROSS

1 "___ that great city Babylon" (Rev. 18:10)
5 Ancient Greek marketplace
10 "Ye ___. . .by works a man is justified" (James 2:24)
13 "Resist the ___, and he will flee" (James 4:7)
15 Small appliance maker
16 Cable network
17 Burning, as in Ex. 3:2
18 Type of offering
19 Sackcloth partner
20 Cable music network
21 Stuck-up person
23 Offspring (Matt. 22:25)
25 "Every good ___. . .is from above" (James 1:17)
26 James to Jesus (Mark 6:3)
28 Tyrannus led one (Acts 19:9)
31 Insolent
32 Constellation (Job 9:9)
33 "Receive ___ meekness the engrafted word" (James 1:21)
34 Unruly crowd
37 Crossing place in Gen. 32:22
38 "Weeping and gnashing of ___" (Matt. 25:30)
40 Musical instrument (Isa. 5:12)
41 Peacock partner (2 Chron. 9:21)
42 Vulture gathers with (Isa. 34:15)
43 Keyed
44 ___ of Olives
45 "A time ___, and a time to heal" (Eccl. 3:3) (2 wds.)
46 Home of the Braves
49 Emaciated
50 "And if children, then ___" (Rom. 8:17)
51 Horsefly
52 Greek letter
55 Suffix meaning direction
56 Shewbread sat upon this (Ex. 25:30)
59 Turn over
61 Is (pl.)
62 Seen at transfiguration (Luke 9:30)
63 Uncanny
64 Father, familiarly
65 Tear, as in John 19:24 (sing.)
66 Unhatched insect

DOWN

1 Eve's husband
2 Goat side (Matt. 25:33)
3 Tel ___ (Israel's capital)
4 What John called the elder (Rev. 7:14)
5 Monastery superior
6 Dig
7 Mariner's tool (Ezek. 27:29)
8 "Eyes of the LORD ___ to and fro" (2 Chron. 16:9)
9 Early church site (Acts 15:35)
10 Hide away
11 Pursue, as in 1 Peter 3:11
12 Anesthetic (arch.)
14 Leprosy scab
22 Football assoc.
24 Pig's home
25 Gift from above (See 25 Across)
26 Lure
27 Wife of Boaz (Ruth 4:13)
28 Divan
29 Prune, as in Lev. 25:3
30 "Labourer is worthy of his ___" (Luke 10:7)
31 Bitter's opposite (James 3:11)
34 Short

35 Australian gemstone
36 Hangs on priest's garment
  (Ex. 28:34)
38 Tight
39 Volcano
40 Dawdling
42 Creature of Lam. 4:3 (sing.)
43 This is hard to tame (James 3:8)
44 Endanger, as in Ruth 4:6
45 Anointing spot (Lev. 14:28)
46 In the lead

47 ___ firma
48 Covered
49 "___ them which persecute you"
  (Rom. 12:14)
51 Dressed
52 South American nation
53 Trim
54 Notion
57 Lager
58 Container
60 Vigor

JEHOVAH: THE GREAT AND MIGHTY ONE

38

by Laura Lisle

• • • • •

ACROSS

1 Will come out of Jacob (Num. 24:17)
5 Try
9 Hungry
14 Coca-___
15 Scent
16 Sifter (Amos 9:9)
17 "Cast me not ___" (Ps. 51:11)
18 Judgment seat (Gr.)
19 Ms. Lauder
20 Deep sleep
21 Bahrain capital
23 "Behold, I ___ an Angel" (Ex. 23:20)
24 Romp around
26 Après ___
28 Business name ending (abbr.)
29 Pine
31 Cooking measurement (abbr.)
34 Pizza brand
37 Noah found this in the eyes of the LORD (Gen. 6:8)
39 Snack
40 "Even to your old ___ I am he" (Isa. 46:4)
41 Arab Peninsula country
42 Closes, as in 2 Sam. 13:17
44 "For their ___ is mighty" (Prov. 23:11)
47 Until, as in Job 18:2
48 Exploiter
50 Gov. agency responsible for food and drug regulations
51 Grown in a pod (sing.)
52 Best, as in Ps. 81:16
56 Ali, with 40 Thieves
59 Absolute ruler
63 Fasted's opposite
64 What the trumpets sound (Joel 2:1)
66 Raise, as in John 2:20
67 PC Security card (abbr.)
68 Types, as in Ps. 78:45
69 Ship part (Isa. 33:23)
70 Gas burner used in laboratories
71 "Thou God ___ me" (Gen. 16:13)
72 Prophet of Tekoa (Amos 1:1)
73 Not now

DOWN

1 Kerchief
2 The Lord is a strong one (Ps. 61:3)
3 Crockett battle site
4 R&B singer Charles
5 Southern crop
6 Eve's garden
7 Core
8 Trolley
9 Employ
10 Ending for Jehovah, meaning "Lord our banner" (Ex. 17:15)
11 Lavish party
12 Evening, as in Gen. 19:1
13 "A prophet mighty in __" (Luke 24:19)
21 Cooper automobile
22 Tree of Isa. 44:14
25 "I will make darkness ___" (Isa. 42:16)
27 Cask
29 "His ___ is not turned away" (Isa. 9:12)
30 Dorm dweller
31 "The tongue can no man ___" (James 3:8)
32 Former wound
33 Writing tool in Isa. 8:1
34 What Maaseiah kept (Jer. 35:4)
35 Patmos is one

36 Unusual (Dan. 2:11)
38 Cannot be scourged (Acts 22:25)
39 Jerusalem to Salim (dir.)
43 Take to court, as in Matt. 5:40
45 Exertions
46 Condense
49 Hypocrites' look (Matt. 6:16)
51 "Thou shalt see my back ___"
   (Ex. 33:23)
53 "God created the heaven and the
   ___" (Gen. 1:1)
54 "A precious corner ___"
   (Isa. 28:16)

55 Dallas dweller
56 Deep voice
57 Sweet-smelling herb from Ps.
   45:8 (sing.)
58 Gave birth, as in Gen. 4:2
60 Writer Bombeck
61 Jesus' coat was without this
   (John 19:23)
62 El __, TX
65 Montana time zone
67 Stroke an animal

JEREMIAH: THE GREAT PROPHET

39

by Laura Lisle

• • • • •

ACROSS

1 Agricultural org.
4 "Believe ye that I am ___?" (Matt. 9:28)
8 Eight ounces
14 He had loaves (John 6:9)
15 Entice
16 Discomfort
17 Israel did this (Jer. 23:13)
18 Volcano
19 Frightened
20 Terrier
22 Pouch
23 What the Ammonites did not have (Jer. 49:1)
24 "Before I formed thee. . .I ___ thee (Jer. 1:5)
27 Bird's seat
31 Shut, as in Ps. 107:42
33 "___, though I walk through the valley" (Ps. 23:4)
35 French affirmative
36 Made in the ___
38 Word receiver in Jer. 9:20
39 Pixies
40 Unsurpassed to the present (2 wds.)
44 Uncooked nature
46 "The prophets prophesy ___" (Jer. 14:14)
47 Adam's wife
49 Nocturnal flyer (Lev. 11:19)
50 Hovercraft
51 Cut
52 "He maketh the storm a ___" (Ps. 107:29)
55 Earthquake
58 The Lord gives a pleasant one (Jer. 3:19)
61 This was embroidered for a priest (Ex. 28:39)

63 Pod vegetable
65 Small chapel
67 What a woman buys in Prov. 31:16 (2 wds.)
70 What Publius' father has in Acts 28:8
71 Part to dip (Luke 16:24)
72 What Simon did at night (Luke 5:5)
73 Curse
74 Israel to Babylon (dir.)
75 What Israelites were in Babylon
76 Used to write with (Jer. 36:18) (pl.)
77 Hebrews crossed the ___ Sea

DOWN

1 "The LORD, the God of all ___" (Jer. 32:27)
2 Comedies
3 Adept
4 A wager (2 wds.)
5 Hand-dyed fabric
6 Jeremiah's girdle material (Jer. 13:1)
7 Arrival time info.
8 Curse
9 Take off the lid
10 "Thoughts of ___, and not of evil" (Jer. 29:11)
11 Where watchers come from (Jer. 4:16)
12 "___ not vain repetitions" (Matt. 6:7)
13 "Thou hast ___ captivity captive" (Ps. 68:18)
21 Rainbow fish (pl.)
25 "Lift up thine ___" (Jer. 3:2) (sing.)
26 "Waters ___ the stones" (Job 14:19)

28 Paul's destination in Acts 28:14
29 Used to drink in Jer. 52:19
30 Snake speech
32 Greek letter
34 City of Joshua in Josh. 15:52
37 A woman's affirmation (Num. 5:22)
39 Inviolate
40 "___! for that day is great" (Jer. 30:7)
41 Fourth plague (Ex. 8:16)
42 Leah's son (Gen. 29:34)
43 This comes from the north in Jer. 4:6
45 Corps of women serving in the armed forces
48 Gov. agency for environmental regulations

53 Raider
54 Military branch
56 Short period
57 Disturbance
59 Mr. Ryan
60 Princes' state (Jer. 51:57)
62 Used a keyboard
64 Totals
66 Chopping tools (Jer. 46:22)
67 Daniel "___ no pleasant bread" (Dan. 10:3)
68 Herod's nickname in Luke 13:32
69 Roman number of doorkeepers in Jer. 52:24
70 Gov. agency housed in the U.S. Dept. of Justice

JEROBOAM: MIGHTY MAN OF VALOR

40

by Laura Lisle

• • • • •

ACROSS

1 Author Bombeck
5 Zero
10 Volume
14 Complain bitterly
15 "Come, let us ___ him"
16 ___ mater
17 Where Paul wintered (Acts 28:11)
18 Model
19 "Iniquity shall ___ her mouth" (Ps. 107:42)
20 Pickup maker
22 Tan color
23 "Dogs shall ___ Jezebel" (1 Kings 21:23)
24 Female sheep (Gen. 21:28)
26 Color of pottage (Gen. 25:30)
27 Iota, as in Matt. 5:18
30 Divide, as in (Ps. 108:7)
33 Ladies' undergarment
35 Flightless birds
37 Forms in which Jeroboam's story is told (1 Kings 14:19)
42 This animal chews cud in Lev. 11:6
43 Long time
44 Plow (Gen. 2:5)
45 Not amiable
49 Flexible tube
50 Presidential initials
51 "Thou shalt see it with thine ___" (2 Kings 7:2)
53 "Sing unto him a ___ song" (Ps. 33:3)
54 Pouch
57 Before, as in Ex. 1:19
59 Alias
61 Approximate date
63 Keillor and William Lloyd
69 Twelfth Hebrew month (Est. 3:7)

70 Tower
71 "Every ___ shall bow" (Isa. 45:23)
72 TV host Jay
73 "The ___ of thine eye" (Prov. 7:2)
74 Economics (abbr.)
75 "She ___ not near to her God" (Zeph. 3:2)
76 "Jeroboam ___ by the altar" (1 Kings 13:1)
77 Remove, as in 1 Kings 11:11

DOWN

1 Actor McCormack
2 "Be not ___ with thy mouth" (Eccl. 5:2)
3 Distance in Matt. 5:41
4 Tylenol's competitor
5 Southern Mexican Indian
6 Made of wood and stone (Deut. 29:17) (sing.)
7 "A time to ___; a time to keep" (Eccl. 3:6)
8 Paul's destination in Acts 27:12
9 That girl
10 Aram offspring (Gen. 10:23)
11 Jeroboam made his offering upon this (1 Kings 12:33)
12 Ascended with the prayers in Rev. 8:4
13 Flavorful
21 Elihu kin (Job 32:2)
22 Lotion brand
25 Ephraim to Shechem (dir.)
27 Son of Jehoshaphat (2 Kings 9:14)
28 Gulf nation
29 Territory
31 "___ Jeroboam built Shechem" (1 Kings 12:25)

32 Eat away
34 Hormone
36 Vassal
38 "He ___ of Jeroboam shall come" (1 Kings 14:13)
39 It slew a prophet (1 Kings 13:24)
40 Otherwise, as in Ex 10:4
41 Killed
46 Belief
47 Stray, as in (Ps. 119:118)
48 Longed for, as in 1 Kings 3:26
52 Winter sport
54 Blanch
55 Helper

56 Bird of Jer. 8:7
58 Where Jeroboam fled in 1 Kings 11:40
60 Beggar
62 "Before the cock ___" (Luke 22:61)
64 Dog food brand
65 Rolled chocolate candy brand
66 "___ in three years came the navy" (1 Kings 10:22)
67 Glowing sign
68 "I will ___ rain upon the earth" (1 Kings 18:1)
70 Not (Fr.)

JEZEBEL: THE EVIL QUEEN
by Laura Lisle

• • • • •

ACROSS

1 Won't remove iniquity (Jer. 2:22)
5 Bobcat
9 Paul's fleshly messenger (2 Cor. 12:7)
14 Motor vehicle
15 Track
16 Cotton fabric
17 "Praise him for his mighty ___" (Ps. 150:2)
18 "World without end. ___" (Eph. 3:21)
19 "Let us lay ___ every weight" (Heb. 12:1)
20 Patterns
22 Pharisees did this to the weightier matters of the law (Matt. 23:23)
24 Pod vegetable (sing.)
25 The Lord will "___ his people" (Joel 2:18)
26 Ahab and Jezebel worshipped these
28 "___ painted her face" (2 Kings 9:30)
29 NJ neighbor (abbr.)
32 Worker bee
33 Jacob's pillow (Gen. 28:18)
35 Samaria to Jerusalem (dir.)
36 "Bread ___ in secret is pleasant" (Prov. 9:17)
37 Arrest
38 Offered with meat (Lev. 2:13) (pl.)
40 "I ___ no pleasant bread" (Dan. 10:3)
41 "___ the harvest, when the bud is perfect" (Isa. 18:5)
43 The Lord hears these (James 5:4)
44 Esau's color (Gen. 25:25)
45 All the poor man had (2 Sam. 12:3)

46 "Thou shalt not ___ the deaf" (Lev. 19:14)
47 "Immediately the cock ___" (Matt. 26:74)
49 "Why make ye this ___?" (Mark 5:39)
50 Elijah's resting place (1 Kings 17:3)
53 Choked
57 Halos
58 Manasseh put this in the house of the Lord (2 Chron. 33:7)
60 Air (prefix)
61 Tier
62 "The tongue can no man ___" (James 3:8)
63 Jael's weapon (Judg. 4:21)
64 Comforts
65 "Saul ___ David from that day" (1 Sam. 18:9)
66 Elijah rested under this in 1 Kings 19:4

DOWN

1 France and Germany river
2 That hurts!
3 Attorney (abbr.)
4 Defer
5 Alpaca cousins
6 Sweet potatoes
7 Samaria to Galilee (dir.)
8 One scared of foreigners
9 Characteristic
10 "Be not ___ in thy spirit" (Eccl. 7:9)
11 Leave out
12 "In thy majesty ___ prosperously" (Ps. 45:4)
13 "I have ___ to be baptized of thee" (Matt. 3:14)
21 Montana capital

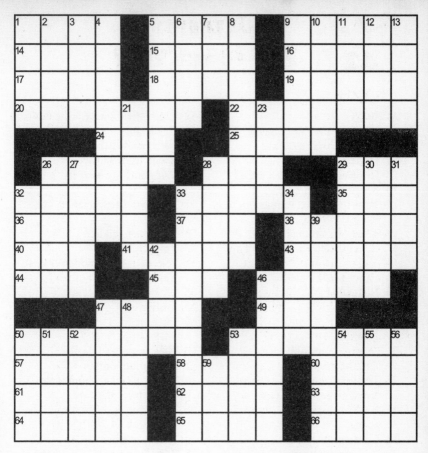

23 Appearance

26 Angry

27 "She ___ upon the Assyrians" (Ezek. 23:12)

28 "They look and ___ upon me"(Ps. 22:17)

29 Cafés

30 ___ Lauder cosmetics

31 "Some more, some ___" (Ex. 16:17)

32 "Followers of God, as ___ children" (Eph. 5:1)

33 1937 Disney classic (2 wds.)

34 Spanish gold

39 Cocky

42 "He will keep the ___ of his saints" (1 Sam. 2:9)

46 "Jesus ___ a little child" (Matt. 18:2)

47 Bird of Isaiah 38:14

48 The sun does this each day

50 Point

51 Island dance

52 Epochs

53 "Let fire ___ down from heaven" (2 Kings 1:12)

54 May be in first or park

55 Canal

56 Portion

59 "God called the light ___" (Gen. 1:5)

JOB:
PUT TO THE TEST

42

by Laura Lisle

• • • • •

ACROSS

1 "His ___ abhorreth bread" (Job 33:20)
5 One-celled creature
10 Jerusalem to Bethlehem (dir.)
13 Beautiful Japanese city
15 "Can that which is unsavory be ___?" (Job 6:6)
16 Boxer Muhammad
17 "Count me for a stranger: I am an ___" (Job 19:15)
18 Canned chili brand
19 Number of Job's children (Job 1:2)
20 First state in U.S. (abbr.)
21 "Lift up thy face without ___" (Job 11:15)
23 "Not ___ your liberty" (1 Peter 2:16)
25 Trade possessions
26 "My ___ scorn me" (Job 16:20)
28 Place of lodging
31 Soak
32 Contract
33 "He maketh peace in his ___ places" (Job 25:2)
34 T.B. vaccine
37 "American Idol" host Seacrest
38 "Upon the ___ of my feet" (Job 13:27)
40 Sore that afflicted Job (Job 2:7)
41 Extension (abbr.)
42 Brand of coffee alternative
43 Main artery
44 "Gat our bread with the ___ of our lives" (Lam. 5:9)
45 Hummed
46 Pre-Columbian civilization
49 "In his ___ remaineth strength" (Job 41:22)
50 Make joyful
51 "He shall not be ___" (Job 15:29)

52 Coloring substance
55 Pig's abode
56 "Who provideth for the ___ his food?" (Job 38:41)
59 "Let mine ___ be as the wicked" (Job 27:7)
61 Twentieth English letter
62 To be
63 "And their children ___" (Job 21:11)
64 "Times ___ not hidden" (Job 24:1)
65 "There is no darkness, nor shadow of ___" (Job 34:22)
66 Parent/teacher groups (abbr.)

DOWN

1 Put ammunition in
2 "Howl, ye inhabitants of the ___" (Isa. 23:6)
3 "But the eyes of the wicked shall ___" (Job 11:20)
4 Stretch to make do
5 Fable writer
6 First Gospel writer, familiarly
7 Airport flight arrival info.
8 "To ___ I am ashamed" (Luke 16:3)
9 "I will speak in the ___ of my spirit" (Job 7:11)
10 Soft shiny fabric
11 Starbucks' daily
12 "Gavest thou the goodly ___ unto the peacocks?" (Job 39:13)
14 "How much less shall I ___ him?" (Job 9:14)
22 VHS alternative
24 "The righteous ___ it" (Job 22:19)
25 Star Trek phaser setting
26 Small fencing sword
27 Toupees (slang)

28 "Thou shalt give him his ___" (Deut. 24:15)
29 Gold and "precious ___" (Job 28:16)
30 Type of jazz vocals
31 Hebrew term for hell
34 "Let the day perish wherein I was ___" (Job 3:3)
35 State your source
36 "The righteous see it, and are ___" (Job 22:19)
38 "Gray hairs are ___ and there" (Hosea 7:9)
39 Newsman Sevareid
40 "Oh that they were printed in a ___!" (Job 19:23)
42 Tired: ___ out
43 Curved

44 "He maketh the deep to boil like a ___" (Job 41:31)
45 Wintry month (abbr.)
46 Saltine cracker brand
47 "He shall not ___ it, nor change it" (Lev. 27:10)
48 One to whom money is due
49 From the sixth to the ___ hour there was darkness (Matt. 27:45)
51 "My sinews take no ___" (Job 30:17)
52 Make an impression
53 YWCA companion
54 "I made a covenant with mine ___" (Job 31:1)
57 "Abimelech took an ___ in his hand" (Judg. 9:48)
58 Road to the cross: ___ Dolorosa
60 Quick sleep

JOEL: THE MINOR PROPHET

43

by Laura Lisle

• • • • •

ACROSS

1 Refuse
6 "___ out the land" (Josh. 14:7)
10 Jesus used this to heal (Mark 7:33)
14 Foolish
15 Used for perfume (Prov. 7:17) (sing.)
16 Comedian Jay
17 "Who shall ___ him up?" (Gen. 49:9)
18 Lilies "___ not" (Matt. 6:28)
19 Cyrus' kingdom today (2 Chron. 36:22)
20 Women's magazine
21 "To the ___ first" (Rom. 1:16)
22 String
24 "That ye be not ___ shaken" (2 Thess. 2:2)
26 "Put ye in the ___" (Joel 3:13)
27 Dog star
30 Gasp
31 "I will ___ thee, O LORD" (Ps. 30:1)
32 Tropical fruit
33 Expression of surprise
36 They are like prophets (2 Kings 17:13)
37 "Neither shall ___ thrust another" (Joel 2:8)
38 Act of kindness
40 Cooking measurement (abbr.)
41 More loyal
43 Fairy-tale writer
44 "Inheritance may be ___" (Luke 20:14)
45 Israel's invaders look like these (Joel 2:4)
46 Astringent chemical
49 Rich man's fate (James 1:11)
50 Whalebone

51 Tree that languisheth (Joel 1:12)
52 Remnant
56 "Believe ye that I am ___?" (Matt. 9:28)
57 Where Paul wintered (Acts 28:11)
59 "They look and ___ upon me" (Ps. 22:17)
60 David made one (1 Sam. 27:10)
61 Christmas (Fr.)
62 Woolen cloth
63 Esau and Jacob (Gen. 25:27)
64 "Be ___ and rejoice" (Joel 2:21)
65 They are withered (Joel 1:12)

DOWN

1 Shrek
2 Says there is no God (Ps. 14:1)
3 "My face is ___ with weeping" (Job 16:16)
4 Tax man
5 Caustic substance
6 Locusts' past activity (Joel 1:4)
7 "Merciful, ___ to anger" (Joel 2:13)
8 Luau dish
9 Shouting
10 Slippery
11 Won't separate us from Christ (Rom. 8:35)
12 Absurd
13 Grasping tool (sing.)
21 Jesus' dad, to friends
23 Disaster due to force of nature (3 wds.)
25 Oil treated whetstone
26 Not as insane
27 For fear that, as in Amos 5:6
28 Iron tools (2 Sam. 12:31)
29 "But a ___ between me and death" (1 Sam. 20:3)

30 Window sections
32 Priests do this in Joel 1:9
33 Car rental agency
34 "Shew piety at ___" (1 Tim. 5:4)
35 God's are everlasting (Deut. 33:27)
39 Policeman
42 Corrupting
45 O.T. prophet (abbr.)
46 Banned
47 Appease
48 "Ye must ___ be subject"
   (Rom. 13:5)

49 "The ___ is wasted" (Joel 1:10)
50 Hook
51 The king of Israel seeks this in
   1 Sam. 26:20
53 "The spirit ___ him" (Mark 9:20)
54 "Pharisees began to ___ him"
   (Luke 11:53)
55 Found in a lion's carcass in Judg.
   14:8
58 Solomon, to friends
59 Fast plane

JOHN: THE BELOVED DISCIPLE

by Laura Lisle

• • • • •

ACROSS

1 In ___ (together)
5 Oregon time zone
8 He walked with God (Gen. 6:9)
12 Char
13 Partly frozen rain
15 Ms. Aragon or Cleves (var.)
16 Restrain
17 Egg's fate (Isa. 34:15)
18 Idol
19 "Let us ___ together" (Isa. 1:18)
21 Trinity's home (1 John 5:7)
23 Wave offering (Lev. 23:12)
25 Jordan River to Jerusalem (dir.)
26 Last Supper room (Luke 22:12)
29 Hunted animal (Prov. 6:5)
31 Suffix meaning material-forming
35 Shred (2 wds.)
37 Sphere
39 Family-oriented health ctr.
40 Mad at John and James (Matt. 20:24)
41 Chewy candy
44 Disciples urged Jesus to do this (John 4:31)
45 Nighttime (John 6:16)
47 The Lord delivered David from this (1 Sam. 17:37)
48 Teeter
50 Tree product
52 MGM mascot
54 A pillar of cloud ___ the way (Ex. 13:21)
55 John doesn't write with this (3 John 1:13)
57 Cooking style in Luke 24:42
59 Type of sewer system
62 Mathematical conclusions
65 Crown of glory will not (1 Peter 5:4)
66 Woodworker's tool

68 Stringed instrument (Amos 6:5)
70 "Will of God abideth for ___" (1 John 2:17)
71 He will restore all things (Matt. 17:11)
72 Gospel singer Franklin
73 Beastly homes (Job 37:8)
74 "I write unto you, young ___" (1 John 2:13)
75 "He that was ___ came forth" (John 11:44)

DOWN

1 Super speedy transport (abbr.)
2 "Proclaim the acceptable ___ of the Lᴏʀᴅ" (Isa. 61:2)
3 "How excellent is thy___" (Ps. 8:1)
4 Folder
5 Two-dimensional
6 "For the joy that was ___ before him" (Heb. 12:2)
7 Virginia ___ University
8 Innocently
9 "Appointed unto men ___ to die" (Heb. 9:27)
10 Immediately, as in Matt. 13:20
11 "As a ___ gathereth her chickens" (Matt. 23:37)
13 Removed this in holy place (Josh. 5:15)
14 "Neither do I condemn ___" (John 8:11)
20 Express indifference
22 Poisonous snake (Rom. 3:13)
24 Ecological food chain (2 wds.)
26 Speak (Lev. 5:1)
27 Annoyance
28 Enclosed sections of windows
30 Sin, as in Ps. 95:10
32 One-celled water creature

33 Hot liquid burn
34 Spouses
36 Baby dog
38 Covenant sign (Gen. 9:13)
42 Last O.T. book (abbr.)
43 Salk's vaccine
46 Pliers
49 "___, let us love one another" (1 John 4:7)
51 Fish holder (John 21:11)
53 Kin to fatherless (Lam. 5:3) (sing.)
56 Pharaoh's river

58 Mined metals
59 Jesus came "to ___ the world" (John 12:47)
60 Nod is east of (Gen. 4:16)
61 Sea after rebuke (Luke 8:24)
63 "It rained ___ and brimstone" (Luke 17:29)
64 Body
65 Nourished
67 "___ them about thy neck" (Prov. 6:21)
69 One with loaves and fishes (John 6:9)

JOHN THE BAPTIST: FORERUNNER OF THE LORD

by Laura Lisle

• • • • •

ACROSS

1 Nazareth to Jordan River (dir.)
4 "___ them upon the door posts" (Deut. 11:20)
9 Resort
12 Frilly
14 He arrested John (Matt. 14:3)
15 "___ the sick, cleanse the lepers" (Matt. 10:8)
16 Woodwind instrument
17 Impersonating
18 Leave out
19 They trust in Jesus (Matt. 12:21)
21 Pacific current (2 wds.)
23 Joseph's brother, for short (Gen. 35:24)
24 Tyre to Jerusalem (dir.)
25 Mongolian desert
28 Disciple nickname (Matt. 10:3)
31 Tinter
34 "Thou art ___ the Son of God" (Luke 4:41)
36 "Give us this ___ our daily bread" (Matt. 6:11)
38 Fair weather color (Matt. 16:2)
40 Jonah did this with the fare (Jonah 1:3)
41 ". . .shall not live by bread ___" (Matt. 4:4)
43 Lion's voice (Ps. 104:21)
44 One (Sp.)
45 Baby essential
46 Trashy
48 Photographer Geddes
51 Animal home
53 "Winds and the sea ___ him" (Matt. 8:27)
54 Snake (Isa. 11:8)
56 Gov. agency for U.S. workforce
58 Afternoon nap (Sp.)

61 Keying in again
66 Hannah made for Samuel (1 Sam. 2:19)
67 Debris
69 "Am I ___, or a whale?" (Job. 7:12) (2 wds.)
70 Askew
71 Mordecai rode (Est. 6:11)
72 Stave
73 Light brown
74 Pledge (Heb. 6:13)
75 Lest, as in John 4:49

DOWN

1 Plod
2 "The ___ leaped in her womb" (Luke 1:41)
3 Economics (abbr.)
4 Large ocean mammal in Ez. 32:2
5 John's message (Matt. 3:2)
6 Rainbow goddess
7 2,000 pounds
8 Sword has two (Rev. 2:12)
9 Prefix meaning half
10 Creation feels this (Rom. 8:22)
11 Singing voice
13 "___ in my flesh shall I see God" (Job 19:26)
15 John ate this in Mark 1:6
20 Wading bird
22 Psychedelic drug
25 African nation
26 Constellation (Job 9:9)
27 "___ me come unto thee" (Matt. 14:28)
29 Seasoning (Sp.)
30 Tribe of Israel (Gen. 49:16)
32 Wear away
33 "Be ye therefore ___ also" (Luke 12:40)

34 Computer part
35 Charges
37 Affirmative, as in Mark 7:28
39 Not wet (Gen. 8:13)
42 John's mother, to friends (Luke 1:57)
43 "Will a man ___ God?" (Mal. 3:8)
47 Jesus baptized with the ___ Ghost
49 Mean-spirited
50 NY time zone
52 West Texas city
55 "Make his ___ straight" (Mark 1:3)

57 Additional, as in Matt. 5:9
58 Scram!
59 Hawkeye State
60 Make money
61 Highly unusual, as in Dan. 2:11
62 French "not"
63 The inhabitant of this can't escape (Isa. 20:6)
64 "Draw ___ with a true heart" (Heb. 10:22)
65 "Enter in at the strait ___" (Luke 13:24)
68 Fourth contained beryl (Ex. 28:20)

46 JONAH: IN THE BELLY OF THE WHALE

by Laura Lisle

• • • • •

ACROSS

1 Times
5 Moses' brother (Ex. 4:14)
10 Farming org.
13 Exotic bird
15 ___ Arabia
16 This should be made bare (Isa. 47:2)
17 Florida metropolis
18 Clean feathers
19 "___ Father which art in heaven" (Matt. 6:9)
20 Don't do this unto the law (Deut. 4:2)
21 Jonah's ride (Jonah 1:3)
23 Music used as practice
25 Fashionable
26 Counterpart
28 Jonah was this during the storm (Jonah 1:5)
31 Visitor from Sheba (1 Kings 10:1)
32 Pass time, as in Ps. 90:9
33 Beehive State
34 Ministry org. for young athletes
37 Side where Jonah sat (Jonah 4:5)
38 Called to fast in Nineveh (Jonah 3:7)
40 Stubborn Israel's made of brass (Isa. 48:4)
41 "Go to the ___, thou sluggard" (Prov. 6:6)
42 "Light of the ___ is the eye" (Matt. 6:22)
43 Test, as in Ex. 20:20
44 Crimps
45 Appeared, as in Acts 15:25
46 In abundance
49 "The LORD sent out a great ___ into the sea" (Jonah 1:4)
50 What the gourd delivered Jonah from (Jonah 4:6)
51 This ate Jonah's gourd (Jonah 4:7)
52 Morse code "T"
55 Confederate Gen. Robert E.
56 Famous potatoes
59 "___, go to Nineveh" (Jonah 1:2)
61 Found in a nest (Isa. 10:14)
62 Unyielding
63 Lowest point
64 Anointed part (Lev. 8:23)
65 A friend of the world is one (James 4:4)
66 Shamgar's weapon (Judg. 3:31)

DOWN

1 Poetess Lazarus
2 Insect killer
3 Learning institution (abbr.)
4 O.T. prophet to his friends
5 Savory jelly
6 Senior org.
7 Herbal tithe (Luke 11:42)
8 Keats' specialty
9 Wicked city turned good (Jonah 3:5)
10 Cake ingredient (Ex. 29:2)
11 Violent quarrels
12 "___ with thine adversary quickly" (Matt. 5:25)
14 Desired, as in Jonah 4:8
22 Philistines' injury (Judg. 15:8)
24 Lepers cleansed (Luke 17:17)
25 Penny
26 Not ins
27 "Sun ___ upon" Jonah's head (Jonah 4:8)
28 Before God's throne (Rev. 15:2) (2 wds.)

29 Length of measure (Ex. 28:16)
30 For fear that, as in Mark 13:5
31 Wharfs
34 Jonah "fled ___ the presence of the LORD" (Jonah 1:10)
35 Sheltered inlet
36 Reverent
38 Lock, as in 2 Sam. 13:17
39 Baritone Nelson
40 Manna "___" worms the next day (Ex. 16:20)
42 Campsite warmer
43 Scribe
44 Fixed charge

45 Man's title, as in John 12:21
46 Metal tip on the end of a lance
47 Ragu's competition
48 Superior
49 *Toy Story* cowboy
51 Sudden fancy
52 Prank
53 Seven churches site (Rev. 1:4)
54 Fasted in Nineveh (Jonah 3:8)
57 Boom
58 Life, as in Job 11:17
60 Sin is filthy like this (Isa. 64:6) (sing.)

JONATHAN: BEST FRIEND FOREVER

by Laura Lisle

• • • • •

ACROSS

1 Loads
6 Slice
10 "There is none ___ beside him" (Deut. 4:35)
14 Moses' brother (Ex. 4:14)
15 "A thousand ___ with Jonathan" (1 Sam. 13:2)
16 Complain
17 Military groups
18 Grown in Bashan (Isa. 2:13)
19 Went with Saul to Gibeah (1 Sam. 10:26)
20 Limited (abbr.)
21 Geek
23 Practical jokes
25 Jonathan's father hath troubled this in 1 Sam. 14:29
26 To plow, as in 1 Sam. 8:12
27 Stick fast
30 Bedcover
34 Bird of Isa. 38:14
35 Bird appendage
36 Edge
38 Avian homes (Luke 9:58)
39 Burnt offering (Ex. 29:18)
40 Expected, as in Luke 12:46
42 Jonathan would not do this (1 Sam. 20:34)
43 Where jewels may be (Isa. 3:21)
44 Start over
45 "What ___ thou, O sleeper?" (Jonah 1:6)
48 Hinder progress
49 Repetition (abbr.)
50 Type of jazz
51 Affection
54 Sharpen (Ps. 7:12)
55 Vigor's partner
58 Paul visited this place (Acts 19:22)

59 Afghan ruler
61 "___ my heart to fear thy name" (Ps. 86:11)
63 Tear, as in Joel 2:13
64 Walk through water
65 Gets up, as in Ps. 119:62
66 Long narrative
67 David did this to the lion (1 Sam. 17:36)
68 Inspections

DOWN

1 Jonathan's father (1 Sam. 13:16)
2 Trample, as in Amos 2:7
3 Waterless
4 Tater snack
5 Entangles
6 Jonathan gift to David (1 Sam. 18:4)
7 "___ us not into temptation" (Luke 11:4)
8 Stolen by Philistines (1 Sam. 6:18)
9 Ask in advance
10 Begin a journey
11 Elkanah was blessed because of Hannah's (1 Sam. 2:20)
12 Egyptians "___ into the bottom" (Ex. 15:5)
13 Where cherubim stood (Ex. 25:19)
22 Gilgal to Gilead (dir.)
24 "Esau ___ to meet him" (Gen. 33:4)
25 Days before Easter
27 Pimples
28 Pilate's wife suffered many things in this (Matt. 27:19)
29 Hurry, as in 1 Sam. 20:38
30 Animal, as in Gen. 8:19
31 Jonathan's son's condition (2 Sam. 4:4)

32 Rub out
33 Jezebel beautified (2 Kings 9:30)
35 Ringling ___
37 Measure (Mark 4:24)
40 Protective covering
41 David and Jonathan did this (1 Sam. 20:41)
43 Abdon had 30 (Judg. 12:14)
46 Naval fleet
47 Fishing essential for Peter and Andrew (Matt. 4:18)
48 Cast forth like morsels (Ps. 147:17)

50 Shakespeare's was tamed
51 Will hear rumors of (Mark 13:7)
52 Of glass in Rev. 4:6 (2 wds.)
53 Pharaoh gave this to Joseph (Gen. 41:42)
54 "Open thy mouth ___, and I will fill it" (Ps. 81:10)
55 Credit card
56 Detail
57 Benjamin had 5 times more (Gen. 43:34)
60 Minor prophet (abbr.)
62 Call off

JOSEPH: GOD'S MAN IN EGYPT

48

by Laura Lisle

• • • • •

ACROSS

1 Did well
5 "We cry, '___, Father'" (Rom. 8:15)
9 Tool
13 Favorite (slang)
14 Squirrel's dinner
15 Truth-girded, as in Eph. 6:14 (sing.)
16 Against
17 Infatuate
18 Run easily
19 Savor
21 Joseph's coat had many (Gen. 37:3)
23 Bowed to Joseph (Gen. 37:9)
25 Brass was used to do this (2 Chron. 24:12)
26 The trees of the Lord are full of this (Ps. 104:16)
29 Warm-up activity (abbr.)
31 "Shalt thou indeed ___ over us?" (Gen. 37:8)
34 Kimono sash
35 In worship everyone hath one of these (1 Cor. 14:26)
37 When Joseph dined (Gen. 43:16)
39 Found in sacks (Gen. 42:35)
41 Ball holder
42 Ephod stone (Ex. 39:12)
43 Eve's garden
44 Joseph's brothers "___ him" (Gen. 37:5)
46 Gideon's sign (Judg. 6:37)
47 Organic compound
50 "Midianites ___ him into Egypt" (Gen. 37:36)
51 Concord e.g.
52 Tubalcain worked with this (Gen. 4:22)

54 Arabian Peninsula country
56 Saloon
59 Wields
63 Dream bovine (Gen. 41:2)
64 Less restricted
66 Sign of dad's favor to Joseph (Gen. 37:3)
67 Asa destroyed this (1 Kings 15:13)
68 ___ Park, CO
69 Metric weight unit
70 "Thou shalt ___ me thrice" (Matt. 26:34)
71 Stagger, as in Ps. 107:27
72 Herod "___ all the children" (Matt. 2:16)

DOWN

1 At a distance, as in Mark 5:6
2 Bird's home (Jer. 5:27)
3 "Ye thought ___ against me" (Gen. 50:20)
4 Jeans fabric
5 Low or high card
6 Pear type
7 Housekeeper's tool
8 Branched horn
9 Referring indirectly
10 "I stand at the ___, and knock" (Rev. 3:20)
11 Fastens
12 Timnah to Gilead (dir.)
14 Hates, as in Rom. 12:9 (sing.)
20 Soaked
22 "The LORD our God is ___" (Deut. 6:4)
24 Under (poet.)
26 "___ evil beast hath devoured him" (Gen. 37:20)
27 "But his bow ___ in strength" (Gen. 49:24)

28 Trees in the desert (Isa. 41:19)
30 Two in Deut. 17:8
32 "Words of the wise are as ___"
   (Eccl. 12:11)
33 Scale components
36 Ditto (2 wds.)
38 Former Speaker Gingrich
40 Completely
42 Large whitish antelope
45 Gantry and Bernstein
48 Sin, as in Ps. 95:10

49 Shingler
53 Nordic
55 These were hardened (Neh. 9:16)
56 Wait
57 At once, as in Matt. 13:20
58 Measure
60 Annoy
61 Old wife tells one, as in 1 Tim. 4:7
62 Store
63 Baby goat (Lev. 4:28)
65 Slippery as an ___

JOSEPH: FATHER OF OUR LORD

by Laura Lisle

• • • • •

ACROSS

1 Coffee (slang)
5 Turf
10 Santa's helper
13 Bad smells
15 Netherlands' capital
16 "Raven" author
17 Lloyd Webber heroine
18 May be barbed, as in Job. 41:7
19 "___ no man any thing" (Rom. 13:8)
20 Type of partnership (abbr.)
21 "Jesus was ___ in Bethlehem" (Matt. 2:1)
23 Caesar decreed that all should be ___ (Luke 2:1)
25 Mary to Joseph
26 "With the blood of the ___ of Jesus" (Rev. 17:6)
28 Broken bone treatment
31 Long, narrow boat
32 Awakened, as in Matt. 2:14
33 Pretentiously artistic
34 Not hers
37 Gripping tool
38 "___, and take the young child" (Matt. 2:13)
40 Wise men's home (Matt. 2:1)
41 Extension (abbr.)
42 Joseph, "___ not to take unto thee Mary thy wife" (Matt. 1:20)
43 Lily type
44 Chisel
45 Resurrection Day
46 Woman's sunshade (arch.)
49 Joseph told to "___ into Egypt" (Matt. 2:13)
50 Gives off
51 Fades
52 Witch

55 Drink slowly
56 Imbecile
59 Indoor football stadium
61 "Voice of ___ crying" (Matt. 3:3)
62 Stairway post
63 To be rebuilt in Amos 9:11
64 "Joseph, thou ___ of David" (Matt. 1:20)
65 "___ to God in the highest" (Luke 2:14)
66 Wicked men set one (Jer. 5:26)

DOWN

1 Old Testament prophet
2 Advertisement (abbr.)
3 Earth at creation (Gen. 1:2)
4 "Blessed ___ thou among women" (Luke 1:42)
5 British county
6 "___ them that are unruly" (1 Thess. 5:14)
7 Hence, as in Acts 10:30
8 "Their feet ___ to evil" (Prov. 1:16)
9 Herod's plan is to ___ "the young child" (Matt. 2:13)
10 Synthetic resin
11 Man to angels (Ps. 8:5)
12 Five loaves and 2 fishes ___ many in John 6:9
14 Texas river
22 Frequently, as in 2 Tim. 1:16
24 Daniel "___ no pleasant bread" (Dan. 10:3)
25 "There came ___ men" (Matt. 2:1)
26 Paul speech site (Acts 17:22)
27 Wager
28 Jesus "shall ___ his people" (Matt. 1:21)
29 Grand ___ race

30 "To save that which was ___" (Matt. 18:11)
31 Marker
34 Jesus healed them (John 5:3)
35 Patmos
36 Wise men's guide (Matt. 2:9)
38 Air (prefix)
39 Insult, as in 2 Chron. 32:17
40 "His soul shall dwell at ___" (Ps. 25:13)
42 Complaining
43 He decreed all should be taxed (Luke 2:1)
44 Flying rodent of Lev. 11:19

45 Tree of Hos. 4:13
46 Cents south of the border
47 Type of acid
48 Mature
49 "Body ___ joined together" (Eph. 4:16)
51 One who does
52 Noah, "___ of the righteousness" (Heb. 11:7)
53 New Testament prophetess
54 Pant
57 First state (abbr.)
58 Battle site ___ Jima
60 Track

JOSHUA: THE SUCCESSOR

50

by Patricia Mitchell

• • • • • •

ACROSS

1 Come to ___: KJV for "It will happen" (Gen 4:14)
5 Sign of despair on Joshua's head (Josh. 7:6)
9 Nonfunctioning smeller (Ps. 115:6)
13 Women's magazine
14 Dueling sword
15 At battle's end, Amalek was this (slang)
16 Joshua went ___ the mount of God (Ex. 24:13)
17 "The LORD said unto Joshua, ___ not, neither be thou dismayed" (Josh. 8:1)
18 One way to accomplish 19 Across
19 "The ___ of the LORD's host said unto Joshua, Loose thy shoe from off thy foot" (Josh. 5:15)
21 Joshua was one
23 Bard's before
24 Presented to the people by Moses, Joshua ___ the Israelites (Num. 27:22–23)
25 Israelites' loot from Ai (Josh. 8:26–27)
29 Joshua said, "How long are ye slack to go to possess the land, which the LORD ___ of your fathers hath given you?" (Josh. 18:3)
30 Deutsche ___, German railway
32 Sweet potato
33 Distribute
36 Southern states, popularly
37 ___ Lanka
38 Baseball glove
39 Rahab ___ ___ the spies (Josh 2:1) (2 wds.)
40 Jericho was one (Josh. 6:1)
41 Swee' ___, Popeye tot
42 Joshua was minister to him (Ex. 24:13)

43 Broadway awards
44 "Is there any taste in the white of an ___?" (Job 6:6)
45 John will not use these to write (3 John 1:13)
46 One of the watchers of Joshua's battle with Amalek (Ex. 17:10)
47 Bean
49 Joshua's dad (Ex. 33:11)
50 "Their works are works of iniquity, and the ___ of violence is in their hands" (Isa. 59:6)
53 "The people served the ___ all the days of Joshua" (Judg. 2:7)
55 Joshua's priest (Num. 27:22)
57 Israelites' dwellings (Josh. 22:6)
60 Mount of 2 Down
62 One of the Ten Commandments, e.g.
63 Ancient Greek marketplace
64 Stringed instrument
65 "I was blind, now ___ ___" (John 9:25) (2 wds.)
66 Star
67 Stravinsky's first name
68 Small amounts, as of paint

DOWN

1 The city of Gibeon "made ___ with Joshua and with the children of Israel" (Josh. 10:4)
2 What Joshua built at 60 Across (Josh. 8:30)
3 Land feature of 60 Across
4 Labor Day month
5 "How shall I defy, whom the LORD hath not ___?" (Num. 23:8)
6 Turn over
7 "The way. . .of the Red ___" (Ex. 13:18)
8 Period of time
9 Feature of a daring aerial escapade (2 wds.)
10 Horse nibble

11 Govt. benefits program
12 Vacation time in Versailles
15 Mississippi university
20 Bible fragrance source (Prov. 7:17)
22 Describes Achan as "all Israel stoned him with stones" (Josh. 7:25)
26 Poultry products producer
27 One of the Stooges
28 Burning incense ___ a fragrance (Gen. 8:20–21)
29 Fishing cord
30 Adder's threats to horse heels (Gen. 49:17)
31 Geometry word
33 A pillar of a cloud would ___ the Israelites to move (Ex. 13:21)
34 Reason "Jericho was straitly shut up" (Josh. 6:1–3)
35 Canned chili choice

36 Writing table
39 Hermit
40 Pro
42 White-flowered plant
43 Piper's product (Matt. 11:17)
46 Nutty tool
48 Extreme prefix
49 Cool!
50 Street of noted 1906 revival
51 Only he and Joshua entered the land (Num. 26:65)
52 Joshua's yuccas
54 Go-to place for a pastrami on rye
56 Sinai wilderness descriptor
57 What Simon could do (Acts 10:6)
58 Pharaoh's problem (Ex. 5:2)
59 Veteran's Day mo.
61 John the Baptizer would eat one (Matt. 3:4)

JUDAH:
SON OF PRAISE
by Patricia Mitchell

• • • • • •

ACROSS

1 Judah's older brother (Gen. 35:23)
5 Flustered responder to Peter's knock (Acts 12:13–14)
10 Slightly open
14 The brothers saw their treatment of Joseph as one (Gen. 42:21)
15 Judah's reaction when the cup was found in Benjamin's sack (Gen. 44:16)
16 Make again
17 Tamar's attitude, in a way (Gen. 38:25)
18 County in Ireland
19 Joseph made his steward do this to his brothers' sacks (Gen. 44:1)
20 Ceased
22 Benjamin was framed as one of these (Gen. 44:12)
24 Game ref.
25 Judah's sister (Gen. 30:20–21)
27 People like the praying Pharisee (Luke 18:11)
29 With 39 Down, Judah's feelings after he saw Tamar's evidence (Gen. 38:24–26)
32 "The ___ of our house are cedar" (Song 1:17)
35 Reuben was this when he returned to Joseph's pit (Gen. 37:29)
38 Lot's wife would ___ behind, become pillar of salt (Gen. 19:26)
39 Celtic language
40 Before (poet.)
41 Rifle (2 wds.)
43 Time of the patriarchs, e.g.
44 Pineapples in 70 Across
46 French vote
47 Last word in prayer
48 Disband (Brit.)
49 Synthetic fiber
51 Article of Tamar's evidence (Gen. 38:25)

54 Speaking to Eve, Satan would ___ the truth, as in Gen. 3:5
57 Topper
59 Tamar does this to Judah in Gen. 38:25 (slang)
62 RMNP destination
64 Judah's was to sell Joseph to the Ishmeelites (Gen. 37:27)
66 Whimsical
68 British nobleman
69 Popular potted plant
70 German city
71 Joseph to his brothers: Bring your youngest brother, or ___! (Gen. 42:20)
72 Institution (abbr.)
73 Jacob's cuisines (Gen. 25:34)
74 Judah thought to kill Joseph was a bad one (Gen. 37:26)

DOWN

1 What the hind's feet might do (Ps. 18:33)
2 Do not do this to God's Word (Rev. 22:19)
3 Rigoletto composer
4 Describes the brothers' feelings entering Joseph's house (Gen. 44:14)
5 Record label datum
6 "Has" in Scotland (dial.)
7 Judah's son (Gen. 38:4)
8 Bits (dial.)
9 Thieving member of Judah's tribe (Josh. 7:1)
10 Rainbow shape
11 City of Judah (Josh. 15:63)
12 First name
13 Frolic
21 La-de-___
23 Police box in Tokyo
26 Headgear for Gabriel and Michael
28 Bonnet dweller, at times
30 Judah was one

31 The brothers would ___ ___ each other in their plot against Joseph (Gen. 37:20) (2 wds.)

33 Eventually, the brothers found themselves in a ___ of remorse, as in Gen. 44:18

34 Look over

35 Judah took the ___ in entering Goshen (Gen. 46:28)

36 "Rule, Britannia!" composer

37 Truck drivers, often

39 See 29 Across

41 Judah's granddad (Gen. 29:16)

42 Gal's pal

45 Ten Commandments word

47 Flavoring mentioned by Jesus (Matt. 23:23)

50 The brothers would ___ Jacob an explanation for Joseph's absence plotted in Gen. 37:20

52 Joseph's coat does this if washed in hot water? (Gen. 37:3)

53 Er's position among Judah's sons (Gen. 38:3–5)

55 Kept over, manna turned worse than this (Ex. 16:20)

56 Describes Joseph's questions to his brothers (Gen. 44:15)

57 Record player, sometimes

58 Yemeni gulf

60 "___ his life for my sake" (Matt. 16:25)

61 "Er. . .was wicked. . .and the LORD ___ him" (Gen. 38:7)

63 Bob follower

65 Insect commended for foresight (Prov. 30:25)

67 Lancaster PA airport code

JUDAS ISCARIOT: THE BETRAYER

by Patricia Mitchell

• • • • • •

ACROSS

1 Connery of Bond fame
5 Noah's float
8 Those who "gnash the teeth" might do this, too (Lam. 2:16)
12 Tropical tubers
14 Caesar's seven
15 Clearly, Jesus was not preparing this (John 21:9)
16 Judas to Jesus (Matt. 26:25) (3 wds.)
17 Greek goddess of dawn
18 Judas' money, he thought (Matt. 27:3)
19 Hotel arrangement, for short
20 Aim of Simon Peter's sword (John 18:10)
22 Concorde was one
24 Bravo in Toledo
25 Vivien of Scarlett fame
27 Civil rights org.
29 "If thou hadst ___ here" (John 11:21)
31 "Judas then, having received a ___ of men" (John 18:3)
32 Peter could not do this (Matt. 14:30)
35 To avoid one, Judas identified Jesus (Matt. 26:48) (2 wds.)
37 Jesus identified the soldiers held ___ Him in Matt. 26:57
41 Novelist McEwan
42 Hiram's evergreen gift to Solomon (1 Kings 5:10)
43 "Saw we thee an hungred, and ___ thee?" (Matt. 25:37)
44 Asian starling
46 "O death, where is thy ___?" (1 Cor. 15:55)
48 Chief priests, to hear Judas' proposal (Mark 14:11)
49 Chief priests "sought to ___" Jesus (John 5:16)
51 StarKist fish

53 Very, in music
55 Señora's diacritic
58 Judas would ___ for death rather than repentance (Matt. 27:5)
59 Kansas City summer hour
61 Sodom and Gomorrah were reduced to this (Gen. 19:28)
62 Series ender, often
64 Judas' reaction to see Jesus condemned, maybe (Matt. 27:3)
66 "The sucking child shall play on the hole of the ___" (Isa. 11:8)
68 Jesus' answer to the soldiers (John 18:5) (3 wds.)
70 Daniel's den dwellers (Dan. 6:16)
71 Two in Acapulco
72 Architect Frank ___ Wright
73 Chances of winning
74 Sailed with the navy of Tarshish (2 Chron. 9:21) (sing.)
75 Paul and Barnabas' sailing destination, e.g. (Acts. 13:4)

DOWN

1 "That thou ___ up the gift of God" (2 Tim. 1:6)
2 Artist's item
3 "There shall ___ false Christs" (Matt. 24:24)
4 Modern response to a statement like: "Judas was a nice guy."
5 Jesus would ___, "Thou hast said" (Matt. 26:25)
6 River (Sp.)
7 Judas, betrayest thou the Son of man with a ___?" (Luke 22:48)
8 Jitney
9 Org.
10 Judah: "A lion's ___" (Gen. 49:9)
11 Some ice creams
13 "Draw thee waters for the ___" (Nah. 3:14)
15 "Then entered ___ into Judas" (Luke 22:3)
21 "___, excuse me."

23 Crackle and Pop's pal
26 Computer corp.
28 There was one in the garden when Judas arrived (John 18:4–6)
30 Cool
31 O.T. offerings, often
32 Alike, for short
33 Jesus said, "I am the ___, the truth, and the life" (John 14:6)
34 "There was no room for them in the ___" (Luke 2:7)
36 One dozen, to Felix, the Roman governor (Acts. 23:24)
38 Football assoc.
39 Beverage Pharisees could have made with mint (Luke 11:42)
40 Of the twelve disciples, Judas made himself the ___ man out
45 "An ___ tied" (Matt. 21:2)
46 Jesus to Judas: "Thou hast ___" (Matt. 26:25)

47 Judas did not have the ___ to resist temptation
48 Goes with a guy
50 The Promised Land would have none of these (Deut. 8:9)
52 Nothing
53 Rose pest
54 "Judas also, which betrayed him, ___ with them" (John 18:5)
56 How-to exhibits, for short
57 Pre-1970's gas choice
58 Norwegian capital
60 Christian author Joni Eareckson
61 Church part
63 Judas would ___ his position among the disciples
65 Body coordinator
67 What Jesus gave to Judas at the Last Supper (John 13:26)
69 Last name in boxing

LABAN THE TRICKSTER
by Patricia Mitchell

• • • • • •

ACROSS

1 "___ an alarm" (Num. 10:5)
5 "Abraham. . .saw the place ___ off" (Gen. 22:4)
9 Cabbage dish
13 Flot preceder
14 Biblical accounts of the patriarchs, e.g.
15 Sour cream addition, perhaps (sing.)
16 The kingdom of God should be the ___ thing (Matt. 6:33)
17 Paul's physician (Col. 4:14)
18 Lazarus's sores undoubtedly did this in Luke 16:20
19 Laban to Rebekah (Gen. 24:29)
21 Jesus' disciples did not do this (Matt. 9:14)
23 There was no room here for Mary and Joseph (Luke 2:7)
24 Response to Laban's trickery in Gen. 29:25, perhaps
25 After three days, Jacob was ___ by Laban (Gen. 31:22)
29 Brooks are "blackish by reason of the ___" (Job 6:16)
30 Smile
32 Pronoun for Leah or Rachel
33 God to Laban: "___ not to Jacob either good or bad" (Gen. 31:24)
36 Laban "brought [Jacob] to his ___" (Gen. 29:13)
37 "Give me my wife, for my days ___ fulfilled" (Gen. 29:21)
38 Big ships are "turned about with a very small ___" (James 3:4)
39 Taking the gates of Gaza was one of Samson's (Judg. 16:3)
40 Samoan capital
41 LAX info
42 Isaac to Esau: "I am old, I know not the day of my ___" (Gen. 27:2)
43 Basketball player Olajuwon
44 What Laban and Jacob do at the feast in Gen. 29:22
45 God to Moses: "Rehearse it in the ___ of Joshua" (Ex. 17:14)
46 Basketball assoc.

47 A modest woman's hair should not sport these (1 Peter 3:3)
49 "Lift up now thine eyes, and ___. . . I have seen all that Laban doeth unto thee" (Gen. 31:12)
50 Jacob to Isaac: "___ and eat of my venison" (Gen. 27:19)
53 Racetrack activities
55 Oval shape
57 Describes the mob outside Pilate's palace (John 19:12)
60 A sinner does this
62 "Soldiers cut off the ropes of the ___" (Acts 27:32)
63 A craftsman ___ the doors of the temple in 1 Kings 7:50
64 De ___ : anew
65 "The waters thereof ___ and be troubled" (Ps. 46:3)
66 Laban tricked Jacob more than ___
67 Leah when she married Jacob, probably
68 Indian of South America

DOWN

1 Disney deer
2 Laban would ___ (Gen. 30:27)
3 God to Job: "Canst thou. . .loose the bands of ___?" (Job 38:31)
4 Balaam's donkey after abuse: "Was I ever ___ to do so unto thee?" (Num. 22:30)
5 Laban would ___ that Jacob had kidnapped his daughters (Gen. 31:26)
6 Rural club, the long way (2 wds.)
7 Noah's vessel
8 Shallow area
9 The archers' actions (Gen. 49:23)
10 Mary's cuz (Luke 1:36)
11 ___ Maria
12 Jacob proposed to ___ Laban's daughter, Rachel (Gen. 29:18)
15 Trigonometry term
20 Twain boy
22 12 Down went badly ___ for Jacob (Gen. 29:25)

26 "Descended in a bodily ___ like a dove" (Luke 3:22)

27 Scary

28 "God came to Laban the Syrian in a ___ by night" (Gen. 31:24)

29 "___ ___ hath sent me" (Ex. 3:14) (2 wds.)

30 Jacob chose "the spotted and speckled among the ___" (Gen. 30:32)

31 Judges follower

33 Jacob watered these of Laban (Gen. 29:10)

34 A decorative flower in Ex. 25:33 would have had one

35 Rachel would ___ Jacob when he saw her (Gen. 29:10)

36 He who has 45 Across, "let him ___" (Mark 4:9)

39 Laban gathered all the men "and made a ___" (Gen. 29:22)

40 Modern ID: Esau ___ Edom (Gen. 25:30)

42 Jacob and Laban's deceit ___ trust in either one

43 First murder victim (Gen. 4:8)

46 Mandella

48 Laban's invitation to Jacob: "___ with me" (Gen. 29:19)

49 Jacob to Laban: "Did not I ___ with thee?" (Gen. 29:25)

50 Shekel measure (Num. 7:14)

51 Laban's brother-in-law (Gen. 28:5)

52 Tank dweller

54 "Jacob ___ and called Rachel and Leah to the field" (Gen. 31:4)

56 Son of Merari (1 Chron. 24:27)

57 Laban lived long ___

58 Jacob to Laban: "What is my ___, that thou hast so hotly pursued after me?" (Gen. 31:36)

59 Laban and Jacob did not treat each other with this

61 "Asahel was as light of foot as a wild ___" (2 Sam. 2:18)

54

LAZARUS: A NEW LEASE ON LIFE
by Patricia Mitchell

• • • • • •

ACROSS

1 Paul's interrogator (Acts 22:27) (abbr.)
5 Shelter for the prodigal son, perhaps (Luke 15:15)
8 Mussolini title
12 Island greeting
14 ___ Jima
15 With 29 Across, shortest verse of the Bible (John 11:35)
16 Not a consonant
17 Wheel tooth
18 Martha hoped for ___ ___ for Lazarus (John 11:21–22) (2 wds.)
19 Bethany to Jericho (dir.)
20 Jesus' sayings would ___ the Pharisees, as in Matt. 15:12
22 "The hole of the ___" (Isa. 11:8)
24 Lazarus does this in John 11:1
25 Jesus went to Lazarus's (John 11:38)
27 Place at which Lazarus sat with Jesus (John 12:2)
29 See 15 Across
31 Mustard seed (Mark 4:31)
32 "Love the Lord thy God. . .with all thy ___" (Matt. 22:37)
35 Sweetener, like the honey Jesus ate in Luke 24:42
37 Psalm valley (Ps. 84:6)
41 Samson's were strong (Judg. 16:29–30) (abbr.)
42 The Lord is not ___ with those He loves, Prov. 3:12, e.g.
43 Business ending, often (abbr.)
44 Roman bye-bye
46 Winds from the north (Job 37:9)
48 Graduate of 39 Down (abbr.)
49 With 68 Across, Jesus' words to Lazarus (John 11:43)
51 Martha served one (John 12:2)
53 Subway
55 Having wings

58 Disciples wanted to ___ Jesus' plan to go to Bethany (John 11:8)
59 Jerusalem to Bethany (dir.)
61 At the sisters' house, there would have been much (John 11:19)
62 Equine nibble
64 Sun Valley resort locale
66 "God shall ___ unto him the plagues" (Rev. 22:18)
68 See 49 Across
70 "Rejoice, because your ___ are written in heaven" (Luke 10:20)
71 Spy guys and gals org.
72 Apollos was one (Acts 18:24–26)
73 Group (abbr.)
74 Pronoun referring to Mary or Martha
75 Condition

DOWN

1 Lazarus lay in one (John 11:38)
2 Mary "rose up hastily" and others went ___ (John 11:31)
3 Jesus displayed this in John 11:43
4 Martha to Jesus: "Thou art ___ Christ" (John 11:27)
5 "A certain man was ___, named Lazarus" (John 11:1)
6 Number of Lazarus's sisters (John 11:1)
7 Exercise
8 Christmas mo.
9 Business as ___
10 Marie ___, chemist
11 JavaScript word
13 Jesus made it clear Lazarus wasn't this (John 11:14)
15 Osaka site
21 We're these for Christ (2 Cor. 5:20) (abbr.)
23 Maybe Martha wanted Mary to do this in the kitchen (Luke 10:40)

26 Tanner's tool, perhaps (Acts 9:43)
28 Baby Jesus' need, perhaps
30 Sheer fabric
31 Proverbs 10:23, e.g.
32 Joey sits in mama's
33 You may see one in 15 Down
34 Red, white, and blue
36 A fool might pull one (Prov. 10:23)
38 Jesus came so "___ men through him might believe" (John 1:7)
39 Chicago seminary
40 Naval figure (abbr.)
45 Halloween mo.
46 Book after Joel
47 People came to "see Lazarus also, whom he had raised from the ___" (John 12:9)
48 ___ ___ carte, menu choice (2 wds.)
50 You can fiddle with their middles

52 Moses held the brass serpent this way (Num. 21:9)
53 He who is "greedy of gain" (Prov. 1:19) might be called one
54 Tests
56 Light cake
57 Drunkard's companion (Prov. 23:21)
58 Girl (Sp.)
60 Jesus loves ___ of us
61 Twelfth month (Est. 3:7)
63 "Jesus saith unto ___, Loose him" (John 11:44)
65 "As a ___ gathereth her chickens" (Matt. 23:37)
67 Jesus knew "what death he should ___" (John 18:32)
69 Jesus "called Lazarus ___" of the tomb (John 12:17)

LEAH:
THE UNLOVED WIFE

55

by Patricia Mitchell

• • • • • •

ACROSS

1 Likely in Leah's heart because Jacob did not love her (Gen. 29:30)
5 Rachel would ___ with Jacob over her barrenness (Gen. 30:1)
9 Transport for Leah and the family (Gen. 31:17) (sing.)
14 White fruit
15 ___ Major, Big Dipper locale
16 Leah thought she would ___ herself to Jacob (Gen. 29:32)
17 Laban and Jacob agreed not to cross a boundary "for ___" (Gen. 31:52)
18 Andrew's tools (Matt. 4:18)
19 Feelings Jacob believed Esau had (Gen. 33:1) (abbr./slang)
20 Leah's father-in-law (Gen. 25:26)
22 Leah did not ___ around Rachel's feelings (Gen. 30:15)
24 "Ye have made it a ___ of thieves" (Matt. 21:13)
25 Martha certainly put one on the table (John 12:2)
27 Strap for 9 Across
31 Mongolian desert
32 Bilhah's son (Gen. 35:25)
34 African antelope
35 "Who is a ___ man?" (James 3:13)
38 Transparent sheet (abbr.)
40 Jacob, when he discovered Laban's trick (Gen. 29:25)
42 Awry (Scot.)
44 Rhoda answered Peter's (Acts 12:13)
46 "Noses have they," but they won't smell these (Ps. 115:6)
47 Their covenant was meant to ___ the bitterness between them (Gen. 31:44)
48 "Scatter thou the people that delight in ___" (Ps. 68:30)
50 Stake
51 Luau dish
52 Leah's feelings to know she was not loved (Gen. 29:31)
55 Where Paul would have debarked in Perga (Acts 13:13)

57 They made Leah's heart glad (Gen. 30:20)
59 Of Laban's daughters, Jacob would ___ Rachel (Gen. 29:18)
61 Government dept.
64 Perhaps Leah's was pale (Gen. 29:17)
66 Chocolate substitute
68 Leah's dad (Gen. 29:16)
71 Leah's were weak (Gen. 29:17)
73 Pilate's 13
74 Buckinghamshire village
75 It was sown among the wheat (Matt. 13:25)
76 "If ye ___ to them of whom ye hope to receive" (Luke 6:34)
77 Describes Pharaoh when he refused to let Israel go (Ex. 5:2)
78 "Give me children, or ___ I die" (Gen. 30:1)
79 Jacob was on ___ to see Esau coming (Gen. 33:1)

DOWN

1 Rose bug
2 "We. . .do not ___ to pray for you" (Col. 1:9)
3 "Of ___ are we" (Gen. 29:4)
4 Writer Bombeck
5 In Joseph's dream, it bowed before him (Gen. 37:9)
6 Jacob thought Rachel ___ than Leah (Gen. 29:17–18)
7 Active
8 Perhaps Job did this as he groaned (Job 23:2)
9 "See ya!" in Assisi
10 Leah responded with this when Rachel requested the mandrakes (Gen. 30:15)
11 Pharaoh's cup, maybe (Gen. 40:11)
12 "To ___ from the words of knowledge" (Prov. 19:27)
13 Name for one of Daniel's denizens, maybe? (Dan. 6:16)
21 Head honcho

23 Oolong
26 TV network
28 Laban would ___ ___ Jacob with the promise of Rachel (Gen. 29:26–27) (2 wds.)
29 Jesus was this in the storm (Mark 4:37–38)
30 "Rebekah their sister, and her ___" (Gen. 24:59)
31 Computer expert (slang)
33 Intelligence agency
35 Summer stingers
36 Ice house
37 "The sons of Jacob came upon the ___, and spoiled the city" (Gen. 34:27)
39 The Ten Commandments
41 Twelfth month (Est. 3:7)
43 KJV yea
45 Some home decorators
49 ___-rac, zigzag trim

53 Communication method
54 Do not do this to one word of Scripture! (Rev. 22:19)
56 Series ender, often (abbr.)
58 Spies on (arch.)
60 Crown of life receivers must be this (Rev. 2:10)
61 Cooking method for fish
62 "Thou hast now done foolishly in so ___" (Gen. 31:28)
63 Laban to Jacob: "___ with me" (Gen. 29:19)
65 Green Gables girl
67 Shaft
68 Acid
69 One of the ship's hairy passengers (1 Kings 10:22)
70 Rachel's last, for short (Gen. 35:24)
72 Philip to Nathanael: "Come and ___" (John 1:46)

56 LOT: THE NEPHEW
by Patricia Mitchell
• • • • • •

ACROSS

1 Lot's wife's lesson (Matt. 6:33) (Part 1)
4 Describes Lot's choice of Sodom
7 TV initials
10 St. Catherine's city
12 "These ___ the generations of Terah" (Gen. 11:27)
13 Milk mates, often
15 Scarf
16 Hollywood talent org.
17 Artist Andrew
18 Heat unit
19 Abraham did not ___ the Lord by pleading (Gen. 18:32)
21 To rescue Lot, Abram "pursued them unto ___" (Gen. 14:14)
23 Under brimstone, Sodom and Gomorrah would do this (Gen. 19:24–28)
24 Rachel ___ her father's idols (Gen. 31:19)
26 Holy Roman Empire's western border river
28 Salt Lake City site
30 Lot's wife's lesson (Matt. 6:33) (Part 2)
31 One of Lot's choices (Gen. 13:9)
34 The men of Sodom were not interested in these (Gen. 19:5)
36 Ally of Abram (Gen. 14:13)
40 Lot lived a long time ___
41 ___ Jose
42 Borrower's note, as in Ex. 22:14
43 Lot's wife's lesson (Matt. 6:33) (Part 3)
45 Men probably did this as they walked Sodom's streets
47 Lot to his sons-in-law: Go, or ___! (Gen. 19:14)
48 Paul was shipwrecked on one (Acts 28:1)
50 Cell body
52 "Samuel sent. . .every ___ ___ his house" (1 Sam. 10:25) (2 wds.)
54 Lot's wife's lesson (Matt. 6:33) (Part 4)
57 Moving mooer with Abram and Lot (Gen. 13:5)
58 Delivery co.
60 "The ___ was risen. . .when Lot entered" (Gen. 19:23)
61 "___ thee two tables" (Ex. 34:1)
63 Goliath wasn't one (1 Sam. 17:4)
65 Remains of Sodom, Gomorrah
67 The Lord would ___ Sodom for ten's sake (Gen. 18:32)
69 Letter stem
70 Abram didn't ___ with Lot over land (Gen. 13:9)
71 Weight unit for gems as in Ex. 28:18
72 Sea crossed by Israel (Ex. 15:22)
73 ___-time: Revelation's subject
74 Jehu's was notable (2 Kings 9:20)

DOWN

1 Like the flies of Exodus 8:21
2 A Nazarite's hair remained this way (Num. 6:5)
3 Besides Lot, Abram rescued his goods, ___ (Gen. 14:16)
4 How Lot's wife looked (Gen. 19:26)
5 Son of Jether (1 Chron. 7:38)
6 The men of Sodom were ___ in their sins (Gen. 13:13)
7 Lot's hesitation would ___ the angel's patience (Gen. 19:22)
8 Makes bigger, with "up"
9 Our (Fr.)
10 One who is "slow to speak" doesn't do this (James 1:19)
11 Before wrecking, Paul's ship was this (Acts 27:14)
13 Lot ___ "flocks, and herds, and tents" (Gen. 13:5)
14 The men of Sodom were not this (Gen. 13:13)
20 "Worthy to open and to ___ the book" (Rev. 5:4)
22 It comes before Obadiah
25 "God. . .sent Lot ___" (Gen. 19:29)
27 It has 50 states

29 Angel to Lot: "___ thee, escape thither" (Gen. 19:22)
30 Classification in biology
31 Lot "seemed as one that mocked unto his sons in ___" (Gen. 19:14)
32 To beg the angel, Lot had plenty of this (Gen. 19:20)
33 Abram to Lot: "___ we be brethren" (Gen. 13:8)
35 Lot's behavior in many instances would ___ his reputation
37 What was left of Sodom and Gomorrah
38 Aurora
39 Parsed by the Pharisees (Luke 11:42)
44 Surely the fire and brimstone created a big one!
45 What the prodigal son wasn't offered for food (Luke 15:16)
46 Meat alternative
47 Malchus's temporary loss (John 18:10)
49 What Lot's wife may have been concerned about (Gen. 19:26)

51 Capital of Belarus
52 "Wherewith the ___ filleth not his hand" (Ps. 129:7)
53 "Come. . .when he is not ___" (Luke 12:46)
55 "He spreadeth ___ pointed things" (Job 41:30)
56 Lot's granddad (Gen. 11:27)
57 Music choices
59 The Lord would ___ Lot, but he needed to leave Sodom (Gen. 19:20–22)
60 "Reuben said unto them, ___ no blood, but cast him into this pit" (Gen. 37:22)
62 Moses parted the waters so the Israelites didn't get this (Ex. 14:22)
64 "I will ___ evil beasts out of the land" (Lev. 26:6)
66 Men of Sodom's problem (Gen. 13:13)
68 Cooking spray brand

LUKE: THE
BELOVED PHYSICIAN
by Patricia Mitchell

• • • • • •

ACROSS

1 Sinai desert climate
5 "Let us go forth therefore unto him without the ___" (Heb. 13:13)
9 "God. . .raised up Jesus, whom ye ___" (Acts 5:30)
13 Way you can memorize Bible verses
14 Philip's preaching, e.g. (Acts 8:35)
15 *Aida* is one
16 First gardener
17 Bloody river (Ex. 7:17)
18 "___ stood up in the midst of the disciples" (Acts 1:15)
19 Luke wrote so readers would do this (Luke 1:1)
21 "All they which dwelt in ___ heard the word" (Acts 19:10)
23 Legume
24 Greek goddess
25 Matthew collected this (Matt. 9:9)
29 Simon tried to ___ the apostles with money (Acts 8:18)
30 Paul's sermons were more than just one of these
32 Paul warned the voyage would ___ the ship not just a little (Acts 27:10)
33 Painter Richard
36 Explore thoroughly
37 Dessert choice
38 He follows Luke
39 "Through the wrath of the LORD of hosts," people are these (Isa. 9:19)
40 Luke was one, for short
41 Perga to Derbe (dir.)
42 Lucre descriptor (1 Tim. 3:3)
43 To some, the first Christians belonged to these
44 Today, Paul and Luke might use this for their journeys
45 Giant of folklore
46 "Thou shalt. . .bring forth a ___" (Luke 1:31)
47 Elijah "made a ___ about the altar" (1 Kings 18:32)
49 Health org.
50 Joseph would pay one in Bethlehem (Luke 2:5)

53 One of these asked Jesus, "What shall I do to inherit eternal life?" (Luke 10:25) (abbr.)
55 47 Across was not this, but around the altar (1 Kings 18:35)
57 Texas tourist site
60 Shopping area
62 Jesus to His followers
63 Seed sower (Luke 8:5)
64 What 63 Across wanted from his labor
65 Craftsman would do this to the four wooden pillars (Ex. 36:36)
66 Tools for 63 Across
67 Luke's second treatise
68 Laodicea, known for its eye salve, may have had a cure for one (Rev. 3:18)

DOWN

1 Some were present at Pentecost (Acts 2:11)
2 Event near 57 Across, perhaps
3 Where Julius planned to take Paul (Acts 27:1)
4 Not quite: prefix
5 Joseph and Mary would have traveled in one for protection on the road in Luke 2:4
6 Ram in the sky
7 Not good: prefix
8 Paul demanded to take his to Caesar (Acts 25:11)
9 Jesus was pierced with one (John 19:34)
10 Agrippa would have ___ Paul go had he not demanded to see Caesar (Acts 26:32)
11 Poet's "before"
12 "What king, going to make ___ against another king, sitteth not down first?" (Luke 14:31)
15 Vinegar given to Jesus on the cross may have acted slightly like this (John 19:29)
20 Snaky fish (pl.)
22 What a sword does (Luke 2:35)
26 The wind would ___ the ship toward Clauda (Acts 27:15–16)
27 "Men ought always to pray, and not to ___" (Luke 18:1)

28 Some people are choked with these and "bring no fruit to perfection" (Luke 8:14)
29 Writing tool
30 "Ye should. . .not have loosed from ___" (Acts 27:21)
31 Mary said, "He that is mighty hath done. . .great things; and ___ is his name" (Luke 1:49)
33 It took 10 plagues before Pharaoh would ___ the Israelites (Ex. 12:31)
34 Threat to whales, often
35 "___ was in the days of Herod" (Luke 1:5)
36 What Daniel heard, maybe (Dan. 6:22)
39 Pharisees: "Let us not ___ against God" (Acts 23:9)
40 What Simon Peter might have drawn today (John 18:10)
42 Luke (Col. 4:14)
43 The young man found the ___ of discipleship too steep (Matt. 19:20–22)

46 The hairy ___ of willful sinners will be wounded (Ps. 68:21)
48 Listings in Matt. 10:2
49 Joshua would ___ land to tribes (Josh. 18:10)
50 "Every tree is known by his own ___" (Luke 6:44)
51 When the women went to Jesus' tomb (Luke 24:1)
52 Jesus would ___ those that would "take him by force, to make him a king" (John 6:15)
54 Christian community org.
56 Prophecy: "As one gathereth ___ that are left, have I gathered all the earth" (Isa. 10:14)
57 Burnt offerings residue
58 W.C. in London
59 Luke's feeling toward Jesus' ministry (Acts 1:1–4)
61 Shape of God's promise to Noah (Gen. 9:16)

MARK: THE EVANGELIST

58

by Patricia Mitchell

• • • • • •

ACROSS

1 Elisabeth and Mary's needs (Luke 1:41–42)

6 Jesus: "This cup is the new testament in my blood, which is ___ for you" (Luke 22:20)

10 Judas carried one (John 12:6)

13 There was one between Paul and Barnabas about Mark (Acts 15:39–40)

15 East Indian dress

16 Forbidden fruit eater

17 Paul felt this about Mark (Acts 15:37–38)

18 "We know that thou art ___" (Mark 12:14)

19 Pssst!

20 Jesus fed many with two (Mark 6:38)

22 Mark highlights these in his gospel

24 Butcher's hook

26 Eject

28 Swerve

29 Offspring of the beast "like to a bear" (Dan. 7:5)

30 What might have been in Mark's mother's home

31 Tooth-leaved tree

32 Spherical body

33 Pinch

34 "If I should ___ with thee, I will not deny thee" (Mark 14:31)

35 Jesus made great calm on this (Mark 4:39)

37 Mark wanted to show that Jesus was this (Mark 1:1) (2 wds.)

41 Ananias told one (Acts 5:3)

42 Abode

43 Santa's helper

44 Goliath does this to the army of Saul (1 Sam. 17:8)

47 Former Italian magistrate

48 Crucifixion need (John 20:25) (sing.)

49 Fencing sword

50 One may have been thrown over the colt Jesus rode (Mark 11:7)

51 El ___, Texas

52 Mark wrote of Jesus' resurrection to prove His ___ over death

54 Jesus would ___ His disciples "what things should happen unto him" (Mark 10:32)

56 Describes the morsels in Psalm 147:17

57 Paul's vote on taking Mark on a second journey (Acts 15:39)

59 "___ were gathered" (Acts 4:26)

63 The disciples ___ the colt to Jesus (Mark 11:7)

64 God came ___ the mount Sinai (Ex. 19:20)

65 Pilot Earhart

66 Direction Mark traveled from Perga to Jerusalem

67 Pre-Easter season

68 Taken by Samson from Gaza (Judg. 16:3)

DOWN

1 One might be at your desk

2 Perhaps Mark: what the naked young man did (Mark 14:52)

3 Modern job opportunity for Matthew (Matt. 9:9)

4 Features of many coastlines

5 Stems of letters

6 Boomer

7 Scribes and Pharisees did this to Jesus frequently

8 Sound of two who "shall come to poverty," perhaps (Prov. 23:21)

9 Both those mentioned in Prov. 23:21 had a bad one

10 KJV: look!

11 Route

12 One of the "fountains of the great deep," perhaps (Gen. 7:11)

14 KJV yea

21 What cannot stand if divided (Mark 3:25)

23 "Multitude of ___" (Ps. 97:1)
24 Jesus, to some followers
25 Shorten
27 Response to manna kept overnight, as in Ex. 16:20
29 Paul's port on the way to Tyre (Acts 21:1) (var.)
30 Mark might have run one, naked (Mark 14:51–52)
31 Assistant
33 Paul may have stood on one to preach
34 Feature of many cathedrals
36 King Solomon had one in 1 Kings 9:26
37 Paul to Barnabas: I'll ___ ___ someone more reliable than Mark! (Acts 15:37–39) (2 wds.)
38 Sailed by Mark to reach Perga
39 Hodgepodge
40 Sports assoc.

42 What one of "them ye may eat" might do (Lev. 11:22)
44 Mark relates how Jesus "cast out many ___" (Mark 1:34)
45 Tops of Sinai and Ararat, e.g.
46 After Barnabas takes Mark, they ___ from the narrative
47 Ohio city
48 Chili brand
50 Some hearers at Pentecost were from here (Acts 2:11)
51 Seven cows looking like this emerged from the river (Gen. 41:2)
53 Speedway shape
55 Time of the early church was one
58 Paul would ___ for Silas in place of Mark (Acts 15:39–40)
60 Building addition
61 Tigris, e.g. (Sp.)
62 ___ Leandro, Calif.

59

MARTHA THE SERVER
by Patricia Mitchell

• • • • • •

ACROSS

1 Wise men saw one (Matt. 2:1–2)
5 Martha did this to meet Jesus (John 11:20)
9 Martha to Jesus: "Bid her . . .___ me" (Luke 10:40)
13 Clearly, an attribute of Martha
14 Beautiful Helen's city
15 Crippling disease
16 Martha's sister's choice (Luke 10:42)
17 Martha to Jesus: "I know that he shall ___ again" (John 11:24)
18 In 9 Across, Martha was this. . .
19 . . .and this
21 Martha to Jesus: ". . .my brother had not ___" (John 11:21)
23 Couldn't Martha's sister ___ the problem?
24 Martha's sister wouldn't lift one ___ finger!
25 Potato brand
29 Martha's motto: Don't just think about it, ___!
30 Bluish-white metal
32 Calais negative
33 Gear for the Bahamas
36 Physicist Marie
37 Pull
38 Jesus was not telling Martha's sister one of these
39 ___ boom
40 Was Martha's kitchen this?
41 Like Martha, it's busy (Prov. 30:25)
42 Actress Day
43 Head covering
44 Blemish
45 Ski destination
46 Temperature in Martha's kitchen, perhaps
47 Blood part
49 Sower's medium (Luke 8:8)
50 San Diego winter hour
53 Martha to Jesus: "Dost thou not ___?" (Luke 10:40)

55 Outspoken Martha didn't do this with words (2 wds.)
57 Ran wild in the desert (Job 24:5)
60 The transfiguration took place ___ a high mountain (Mark 9:2)
62 Martha's sister wiped Jesus' feet with this (John 11:2)
63 Martha said Lazarus' body would do this (John 11:39)
64 Aaron used one to fashion an idol (Ex. 32:4)
65 "They cried out all at ___" (Luke 23:18)
66 Belly (Scot.)
67 Pop
68 Martha wanted to ___ her sister into action

DOWN

1 Long stories
2 Cut of beef
3 How Martha felt in the kitchen (Luke 10:40)
4 Martha needed to ___ her to-do list (Luke 10:42)
5 Wall ___
6 Martha probably took this in her housekeeping
7 Goddess known to 14 Across
8 Describes the rich man's garments (Luke 16:19)
9 Crowd
10 Antlered animal
11 Devil is its father (John 8:44)
12 Spacecraft detachment
15 "A sword shall ___ through thy own soul also" (Luke 2:35)
20 Christian community org.
22 Paul would have seen these kinds of columns in Athens
26 The Jews would ___ Lazarus in a cave (John 11:38)
27 Elijah would ___ God's altar with water (1 Kings 18:33–34)

28 What Martha probably suffered concerning what she would serve Jesus
29 Bible patriarch, for short
30 American Indian tribe
31 Rhizome riser
33 One of what a philatelist collects
34 Dug around God's altar, as in 1 Kings 18:35
35 Extreme: prefix
36 Org.
39 Describes "the greater light to rule the day" (Gen. 1:16)
40 "Martha. . .went and ___ him" (John 11:20)
42 Fabric used in interior decorating
43 Soma
46 Sounds like a lot of this when Lazarus died (John 11:19)
48 Martha's sister caused one anointing Jesus' feet (John 12:3)

49 "Chief priests and scribes ___ and vehemently accused him" (Luke 23:10)
50 Organ substitute in some churches
51 Adhere
52 Martha, her sister and brother
54 Martha, perhaps: Everyone ___ well at my place!
56 Thump
57 Though Martha came out, Jesus needed to ___ for Mary (John 11:28)
58 Prodigal son's workplace (Luke 15:15)
59 Martha's sister chose to do this and listen to Jesus (Luke 10:39)
61 Martha's lesson for us: It's possible to be ___ busy (Luke 10:41)

60 MARY: THE VIRGIN MOTHER

by Patricia Mitchell

• • • • • •

ACROSS

1 Most women's response to the plague of frogs, as in Ex. 8:3
4 Mary's pregnancy came ___ of a relationship with a man (Luke 1:34)
9 Jesus said, "Thou shalt not ___ the Lord thy God" (Matt 4:7)
14 ___ chi, martial arts
15 What Jacob could have served Esau's pottage with (Gen. 25:30)
16 Single
17 "Mary kept ___ these things, and pondered them" (Luke 2:19)
18 One was sent to Mary (Luke 1:26–27)
19 What Mary's song of praise was, in a way (Luke 1:46–55)
20 Ships are shifted with a very small one (James 3:4)
22 Mary may have had plans, but accepted God's ___ (Luke 1:38)
24 "The mote that is in thy brother's ___?" (Luke 6:41)
25 "___ ___ Gabriel" (Luke 1:19) (2 wds.)
27 Shape of each ruling light God created (Gen. 1:16)
29 French brandy
32 Pharisees had high, though misplaced, ones (Luke 11:42)
35 Dance
36 Certain roofs
38 The angel appeared to Joseph in one (Matt. 1:20)
40 Mary and Joseph's child is theirs ___, too (Luke 2:23)
42 Comforter
44 The Gospel of Matthew opens with this
45 Usually followed by ruin
47 Ointment ran down Aaron's ___ (Ps. 133:2)
49 Without children, Elisabeth certainly was this (Luke 1:7)

50 Element of Mary's song (Luke 1:46–55)
52 John: unworthy to ___ Jesus' shoes (Luke 3:16)
54 What Lazarus of Jesus' parable did (Luke 16:20)
55 Card game
56 One-sixtieth of a minute (abbr.)
59 It must have been hard for Mary to fully ___ Gabriel's message
63 Apprehends
67 Hosea ___ Israel with sweet words (Hos. 2:14)
69 Likely shape of some of the gems in Ex. 28:18–19
71 There was one in the garden (Song 6:11)
72 Joseph "___, and took the young child" (Matt. 2:21)
73 David's harp playing soothed Saul's (1 Sam. 16:23)
74 Bethlehem to Jerusalem (dir.)
75 "The ___ of the Highest shall overshadow thee" (Luke 1:35)
76 The flight to Egypt was to ___ Herod (Matt. 2:13)
77 Member of a disbelieving generation (Matt. 23:33)

DOWN

1 Beehive State
2 One wouldn't disturb the house built on rock (Matt. 7:25)
3 "Mary. . .went into the ___ country" (Luke 1:39)
4 ___ ___ carte (2 wds.)
5 Mary's description of herself (Luke 1:38)
6 Joseph was on the ___ of leaving Mary (Matt. 1:19)
7 Beverages at Belshazzar's feast (Dan. 5:2–3)
8 Corned beef on rye source
9 The angel's message might have made Mary's face do this (Luke 1:34) (2 wds.)
10 Egypt to Nazareth (dir.)

11 Spice

12 What 64 Down did in the Temple (Luke 2:37)

13 Mary had the ___ of trust we should desire (Luke 1:38)

21 Soviet-era fighter plane

23 "With ___ nothing shall be impossible" (Luke 1:37)

26 "Go to the ___" (Prov. 6:6)

28 Psalmist, in a way

29 Mary would have entered the Temple's (Luke 2:22)

30 Big name in daytime TV

31 Associations

32 Card player's statement (2 wds.)

33 Borrower's option (Prov. 22:7)

34 Jesus' tempter (Matt. 4:10)

35 What the wise men would do (Matt. 2:11)

37 Adam's helpmeet

39 Describes 60 Down's son

41 Wound covering

43 Mary felt this way at Gabriel's greeting (Luke 1:29)

46 One who works with dough

48 Baptized into Christ, do this with Christ (Gal. 3:27)

51 Soviet-era police

53 Mary's baby (Luke 1:31)

56 Servants would ___ Jesus with their hands (Mark 14:65)

57 Continental coin

58 "Before the cock ___, thou shalt deny me thrice" (Matt. 26:34)

60 Father to Jesus: my son "___ vexed" (Matt. 17:15)

61 Track shape

62 Prego's competition

64 She praised Mary's baby (Luke 2:36–38)

65 Hamburger rolls

66 The Lord directs this (Prov. 16:9) (sing.)

68 Emmaus to Jerusalem (dir.)

70 Nazareth to Jerusalem (dir.)

MARY WHO SAT AT JESUS' FEET
by Vicki J. Kuyper

• • • • • •

ACROSS

1 There was one between Abraham and the rich man (Luke 16:26)
6 "Paul and Silas prayed, and ___ praises" (Acts 16:25)
10 Organization (abbr.)
14 Main artery
15 Black and white snack
16 Mary's sister said, "The Master . . . calleth for ___" (John 11:28)
17 Pierced Jesus' side
18 "Mary. . .which anointed the ___ with ointment" (John 11:2)
19 Moray and conger
20 Jesus, Mary, and Martha's broke when Lazarus died
22 "Why was not this ointment ___?" (John 12:5)
24 Deli request
25 Church tower song
27 Tiny amounts
29 Martha's hometown (John 11:1)
32 "The ___ of the house of David" (Isa. 22:22)
33 Easter mo., usually
34 Friends assumed Mary went to Lazarus's ____ (John 11:31)
37 Judas made one with the Pharisees (Matt. 26:15)
41 "Fade as a ___" (Isa. 64:6)
43 Traditional bread for a patty melt
44 "Filled with the ___ of the ointment" (John 12:3) (var.)
45 Display
46 "To comfort them concerning ___ brother" (John 11:19)
48 Flightless bird
49 Possible exclamation by crowd when Lazarus' tomb was opened
51 Candidate
54 Pharisees were in one over Jesus
56 Birchlike tree
57 Point

58 Definition resource (abbr.)
60 Travel with
64 Malchus lost one during Jesus' arrest (John 18:10)
66 Mary may have kept her ointment in this
68 Peculiarity
69 Jesus: be born ___ (John 3:3)
70 "Be ye therefore perfect, ___ as your Father" (Matt. 5:48)
71 Monastery superior
72 "It is a ___ thing that the king requireth" (Dan. 2:11)
73 When Jesus arrived, Mary's brother was ___ (John 11:14)
74 Tilts to one side

DOWN

1 What Judas received for his betrayal of Jesus (Matt. 26:15)
2 "Faith, ___, charity, these three" (1 Cor. 13:13)
3 Samaria, e.g.
4 Gravy thickener
5 Mary's sister
6 Sun in Barcelona
7 When Jesus called for Mary "she ___ quickly" (John 11:29)
8 Roman emperor
9 What Baal was not
10 What one did at a feast
11 Queen from this region visited Solomon (1 Kings 10:1–2)
12 In Gen. 37, Judah ___ his brother to traveling merchants
13 Without children, Mary's home was an empty ___
21 "Is any merry? let him ___ psalms" (James 5:13)
23 Roe in KJV
26 Present at Jesus' birth and burial
28 Typed error
29 Describes Elisha (2 Kings 2:23)

30 Fencing sword
31 Trolley car
35 Popeye's yes
36 Surely there are these for silver and gold (Job. 28:1)
38 Room where Mary sat at Jesus' feet, perhaps (2 wds.)
39 Mary told Martha, "The Master is ___" (John 11:28)
40 "I am the ___ vine" (John 15:1)
42 Days Lazarus was dead before Jesus arrived (John 11:17)
46 Boomed
47 Perhaps used by Judas to end his life (Matt. 27:5)
50 "Blessed are the pure in heart: for they shall see ___" (Matt. 5:8)
52 Type of Mexican liquor
53 Cast from Mary Magdalene (Mark 16:9)

54 Female singer ___ Apple
55 Brown
56 What Paul was before he became shipwrecked (2 wds.)
57 Like a wing
59 Where Mary's brother was buried (John 11:38)
61 God's heavenly creations are shaped like these
62 "Faithful children not accused of ___ or unruly" (Titus 1:6)
63 Tater ___
65 "One little ___ lamb" (2 Sam. 12:3)
67 "He loved them unto the ___" (John 13:1)

MARY MAGDALENE: THE FIRST AT THE TOMB

by Vicki J. Kuyper

• • • • • •

ACROSS

1 "[Jesus] appeared ___ to Mary Magdalene" (Mark 16:9)
6 Illegal drug
9 Droops
13 Nice farewell
14 What's easy to see in another's eye (Matt. 7:3)
15 Fake butter
16 What someone was when soldiers bet for Jesus' clothes
17 ___ "the first day of the week" Mary came to the tomb (John 20:1)
18 Pale sherry
19 Brew
20 "He is ___" (Matt 28:6)
22 Could have been used to start fire for breakfast (John 21:9)
23 Synonym for Aramaic *Raca*, as in Matt. 5:22
24 The Israelites burned offerings under this tree (Hos. 4:13)
26 KJV no
27 Skateboard with a handle
30 How some may have responded to Mary before Jesus cast out her demons (Mark 16:9)
32 Created on fourth day (Gen. 1:16)
33 Connect
36 "Many women were there beholding ___ off" (Matt 27:55)
40 The curtain being torn in two was a good one (Luke 23:45)
41 Jesus came to ___ for our sins (Heb. 2:17)
42 Jerusalem to Jericho (dir.)
43 "I write not these things to shame you, but as my beloved sons I ___ you" (1 Cor. 4:14)
44 Despot
45 Cabbage cousin
46 "Why make ye this ___, and weep?" (Mark 5:39)
48 Saul never ___ to be king of Israel (1 Sam. 9:21)
51 Executive director

54 Km/h
56 "The ___ person will speak villany" (Isa. 32:6)
57 What Mary saw at tomb (Matt. 28:2)
59 La Scala is famous for it
61 "Absalom spake . . .neither good nor ___" (2 Sam 13:22)
64 Others thought Mary's words were "___ tales" (Luke 24:11)
65 The women Mary was with had had "___ spirits" (Luke 8:2)
66 A headdress of the ancient Persians, like Queen Esther
68 "Earth shall ___" (Isa. 24:20)
69 Allows
70 One touched Isaiah's lips (Isa. 6:6–7)
71 Chances of winning
72 Seraphim do this (Isa. 6:6)
73 "Therefore ___ I to them in parables" (Matt. 13:13)

DOWN

1 Syllables used in songs (2 wds.)
2 Baal was one (Judg. 2:13)
3 Jesus told his followers he'd ___
4 Angel to Mary: "Come, ___ the place" (Matt. 28:6)
5 Little tower
6 Elisha did this to pull ahead of Ahab (1 Kings 18:46)
7 Mary saw the angel roll this from the tomb (Matt 28:2)
8 Jesus accused merchants of turning the temple into a "___ of thieves" (Mark 11:17)
9 A divan is one kind
10 The Magi chose to ___ their journey with a star (Matt. 2:9)
11 Birthplace of Columbus
12 Describes those who mourned in sackcloth and ashes
14 Aquatic rodents
21 Cain felt this Abel (Gen. 4:5)
22 Madagascar franc (abbr.)

23 Another woman with Mary at Jesus' tomb (Luke 24:10)
25 Pear-shaped instrument
27 The angel Mary saw wore clothes as "white as ___" (Matt 28:3)
28 Cause of unconsciousness
29 "Sitting ___ against the sepulchre" (Matt. 27:61)
31 Handkerchief, for short
34 Type of serpent
35 Jesus' appearance to Mary ___ the mystery of the empty tomb (Mark 16:9)
37 The angel told Mary, "___ not ye" (Matt 28:5)
38 Jesus was ___ to cast seven devils from Mary (Mark 16:9)
39 Put in Jesus' hand instead of a scepter (Matt 27:29)
41 Gideon built an altar ___ the place of Baal's (Judg. 6:28)
47 Measure of volume (abbr.)

49 Mary addressed risen Jesus, "___" (John 20:15)
50 Silver ones were brought from Tarshish (Jer. 10:9)
51 Egyptian capital
52 Mary thought Jesus' life ___ on the cross (Matt. 27:55–61)
53 David did this to Bathsheba (2 Sam. 11:2)
55 Where widow lived, perhaps (1 Kings 17:12)
58 Snaky fish (pl.)
60 Jonah felt this for a gourd (Jonah 4:10)
61 "Ye shall find the ___ wrapped in swaddling clothes" (Luke 2:12)
62 Palestine, e.g.
63 "Cometh Mary Magdalene early, when it was yet ___" (John 20:1)
65 Fairy
67 Mythical demon, whereas the ones that tormented Mary were real

MATTHEW:
THE TAX COLLECTOR
by Vicki J. Kuyper

63

● ● ● ● ● ● ●

ACROSS

1 "By ___ are ye saved" (Eph. 2:8)
6 Elijah was making one for the benefit of Baal's prophets (1 Kings 18:27)
10 Part of a doorway
14 What some Jews felt a taxman, like Matthew, was
15 Matthew learned "the Son of man is Lord ___ of the sabbath day" (Matt. 12:8)
16 Mary's ointment filled the house with this (John 12:3) (var.)
17 "___ in me" (John 15:4)
18 Matthew was one of the "twelve Jesus ___ forth" (Matt. 10:5)
19 Pharaoh was a royal ___ to Moses and God's people
20 "As ___ children" (Eph. 5:1)
21 Dawn
23 School group
24 Chances of winning
26 Matthew did this in Jesus' name (Matt. 10:7)
28 Protrusion of an organ
31 God would ___ out Laodicea (Rev. 3:16) (var.)
32 Passenger on ships from Tarshish (2 Chron. 9:21)
33 Like a leaky faucet
36 Fifth book of the N.T.
40 "Ye have ___ of all these things" (Matt. 6:32)
42 Government spy org.
43 Past times
44 Restaurant
45 "Brother of low ___" (James 1:9)
48 Eve's beginning (Gen. 2:21)
49 Glided
51 Sins
53 In 1 Sam. 17:49, David ___ Goliath with a slingshot
56 "___ the sick" (Matt. 10:8)
57 Number of Bible books by Matthew

58 Tradition says Matthew was one
61 Jesus healed the ___ (Matt. 11:5)
65 "Throughout all ___" (Eph. 3:21)
67 Most Bible scholars believe the wife of Alphaeus ___ Matthew, aka Levi (Luke 5:27)
68 Matthew was in this because of Jesus (Matt. 26:56)
69 Kate ___, model
70 Lazarus "had ___ in the grave" (John 11:17)
71 Joseph "turned ___ into the parts of Galilee" (Matt. 2:22)
72 Esau sold his birthright for this (Gen. 25:30–33)
73 Writer Bombeck
74 Riding a white ___ (Rev. 19:11)

DOWN

1 How Matthew felt after Jesus rose from the dead (John 20:20)
2 The one Jesus was given was scarlet (Matt. 27:28)
3 The Holy Spirit stopped Paul from preaching here (Acts 16:6)
4 Brook Matthew crossed toward Gethsemane (John 18:1)
5 "Come down ___ my child die" (John 4:49)
6 Matthew and the disciples did "as ___ commanded" (Matt. 21:6)
7 "Ye shall not have gone ___ the cities of Israel, till the Son of man be come" (Matt. 10:23)
8 Beano
9 This did not happen to Jesus in the tomb (Ps. 16:10)
10 Regarded as Bible's oldest book
11 Matthew would ___ life of an itinerate preacher (Matt. 10:14)
12 ___ Carlo
13 Disciples forgot this (Matt. 16:5)
21 Twelfth Jewish month (Est. 3:7)
22 "Blessed ___ the poor in spirit" (Matt. 5:3)

25 "The disciples _____ as Jesus had appointed them" (Matt. 26:19)

27 "Will ye also go _____?" (John 6:67)

28 "Dippeth his _____ with me in the dish" (Matt. 26:23)

29 Fencing sword

30 To draw in

31 Box

34 Type of tea

35 Host for demons (Matt. 8:32)

37 Matthew ate this on the Sabbath (Matt. 12:1)

38 Mathematical study of triangles (abbr.)

39 Emmaus to Bethlehem (dir.)

41 God said via the prophets, "I will wipe Jerusalem as a man wipeth a _____" (2 Kings 21:13)

45 Break

46 Perhaps used to fill jars with water at a wedding (John 2:7)

47 Epoch

50 Memory of things long past

52 Ishmael was Abraham's _____ son (Gen. 17:18–19)

53 Fizzes

54 Metal bar

55 Long-necked fowl (pl.)

56 African scavenger

59 "The young lions _____ after their prey, and seek their meat from God" (Ps. 104:21)

60 In Jesus' parable, the virgins awake and _____ their lamps (Matt. 25:7)

62 Canal

63 A disciple, like Matthew, could be regarded as one to Jesus

64 After Jesus' arrest, "all the disciples forsook him, and _____" (Matt. 26:56)

66 Jericho to Bethlehem (dir.)

68 Abraham, Isaac, and Jacob, e.g.

MICAH: THE YOUNGER PROPHET

by Vicki J. Kuyper

• • • • • •

ACROSS

1 Samaria was one Micah prophesized against

5 "___ye, O mountains" (Mic. 6:2)

9 "I ___, I shall arise" (Mic. 7:8)

13 Commentators note Micah uses these throughout his prophecies

14 Harvard's rival

15 Organized crime

16 Alcoholic brews

17 Epochs

18 How rainbows are shaped

19 "The ___ of Jacob" (Mic. 5:8)

21 Time in office

23 "___ the spirits" (1 John 4:1)

24 Morse code dash

25 Abraham's was Sarah

29 Butane

30 Joseph's brothers were ___ to him (Gen. 37:23–24)

32 Before (prefix)

33 Saul's was too big for David (1 Sam. 17:38–39) (var.)

36 Ezekiel's valley of bones must have been this (Ezek. 37:7)

37 Jesus' was thirty when he began his public ministry (Luke 3:23)

38 "What is ___" (Mic. 6:8)

39 A righteous person's prayer will ___ much (James 5:16)

40 Possible vessel Samaritan woman left at the well (John 4:28)

41 Samson had strong ones (Judg. 16:29–30) (abbr.)

42 Prophets like Micah did not deliver this kind of message

43 "Thou shalt no more worship the work of thine ___" (Mic. 5:13)

44 Ball holder

45 Aaron, after application of Ps. 133:2's ointment

46 "They hunt every man his brother with a ___" (Mic. 7:2)

47 English class assignments

49 "Ten thousands of rivers of ___?" (Mic. 6:7)

50 School group

53 Pushed with the foot

55 Naaman's ailment (2 Kings 5:1)

57 A Spartan slave

60 Little Mermaid's love

62 Micah compared his mourning to sound of these birds (Mic. 1:8)

63 The Roman Coliseum is one

64 "The LORD require of thee. . .___ mercy" (Mic. 6:8)

65 Plateau

66 "Unto the ___ of Jerusalem" (Mic. 1:12)

67 The wicked will drink this from the Lord's cup of wine (Ps. 75:8)

68 "Hear, I ___ you" (Mic. 3:1)

DOWN

1 "The LORD hath set ___ him that is godly for himself" (Ps. 4:3)

2 Micah prophesied a ___ from Bethlehem (Mic. 5:2)

3 "People is risen up as an ___" (Mic. 2:8)

4 Organization (abbr.)

5 Laughing dogs

6 "Now shall he be great unto the ends of the ___" (Mic. 5:4)

7 Pie ___ ___ mode (2 wds.)

8 "Not your ___" (Mic. 2:10)

9 Boaz ___ wheat and barley (Ruth 2:23)

10 Football assn.

11 Micah said even people who do this are hailed as prophets (Mic. 2:11)

12 Samuel was one when God called him (1 Sam. 3:8)

15 Leatherneck

20 Twelfth Jewish month (Est. 9:1)

22 Electronic messages

26 Produce eggs

27 Micah ___ God's people to return to Him (Mic. 6:9)

28 "Then shall the ___ be ashamed" (Mic. 3:7)

29 "Walk humbly with thy ___?" (Mic. 6:8)

30 Isaac and Esau liked ___ food (Gen. 25:28)

31 Canal

33 Syria traded this in the markets of Tyre (Ezek. 27:16)

34 "Scribes, which desire to walk in long ___" (Luke 20:46)

35 Micah reminded God's people, "I sent before thee ___, Aaron, and Miriam" (Mic. 6:4)

36 "Woe to them that devise iniquity, and work ___ upon their beds!" (Mic. 2:1)

39 "___ and thresh, O daughter of Zion" (Mic. 4:13)

40 Micah to God's people: "Thou shalt ___, but not be satisfied" (Mic. 6:14)

42 Japanese auto maker

43 God called Micah to ___, not hurt, His people (Mic. 6:9)

46 Sister's daughters

48 God's desire is for people to ___ for their sins (Mic. 6:8)

49 Psalm 128 likens children to "___ plants round about thy table" (Ps. 128:3)

50 Micah was "full of ___ by the spirit of the LORD" (Mic. 3:8)

51 Oklahoma city

52 Analyze properties

54 Small wooded valley

56 Sport

57 Old woman in fairy tales

58 Epoch

59 "___ the Lord GOD be witness against you" (Mic. 1:2)

61 Ashael was as light-footed as one (2 Sam. 2:18)

MIRIAM: THE WATCHFUL SISTER

by Vicki J. Kuyper

• • • • • •

ACROSS

1 Charges
4 "Then ___ Moses and the children of Israel" (Ex. 15:1)
8 Beetle
14 Conservationist group
15 Symptom of malaria
16 "The tongue of the just is as ___ silver" (Prov. 10:20)
17 Record measure
18 "It is a ___ thing that the king requireth" (Dan. 2:11)
19 Flyers
20 Carrot eaters
22 Deli order
23 Used to preserve Jesus' body (John 19:39) (sing.)
24 Snaky fish (pl.)
27 Russian country cottage
31 "Miriam answered them, Sing ye to the___" (Ex. 15:21)
33 Volkswagen model
35 ___ Sea, site of Miriam's song
36 Possible nickname for Paul's "son in the faith" (1 Tim. 1:2)
38 "God created man in his ___ image" (Gen. 1:27)
39 KJV term for Korah (Jude 1:11)
40 Father, Son, and Holy Spirit
44 When Jesus arrived, Lazarus' tomb was ___ ___ (John 11:38) (2 wds.)
46 "Learn to maintain good works for necessary ___" (Titus 3:14)
47 Cool, in slang
49 "I count all things but loss.. .that I may ___ Christ" (Phil. 3:8)
50 Chicken ___ ___king (2 wds.)
51 Yang's sidekick
52 Common among soldiers who fight in battle
55 Computer phone

58 Adventure story
61 Land measurement
63 Nickname for doubting disciple
65 Warned troy of equine gift
67 Nathan would ___ David of murder (2 Sam. 12:7)
70 Fix the socks
71 Number of books of the Bible Miriam is mentioned in
72 Card suit
73 What Moses found the Israelites worshipping
74 Business name ending
75 Where Miriam died (Num. 20:1)
76 "___ me thrice" (Matt. 26:34)
77 Type of tree planted in Isa. 44:14

DOWN

1 ___ firma
2 Dismay
3 Tropical grass
4 Mombai dress
5 Stone on ephod (Ex. 28:19)
6 Deborah was Rebekah's (Gen. 35:8)
7 "To the right!"
8 Perhaps Miriam had this as her leprosy healed
9 When we first meet Miriam in the Bible, she's one (Ex. 2:8)
10 Main artery
11 Edge
12 Genius
13 Joseph's baby brother, for short (Gen. 35:24)
21 Beds
25 MGM's Lion
26 "Light is ___ for the righteous" (Ps. 97:11)
28 Farm yield
29 Moses to God: "___ am I" (Ex. 3:4)
30 City in Yemen

32 "All the firstborn in the land of Egypt shall ___" (Ex. 11:5)

34 "Miriam became leprous, white as ___" (Num. 12:10)

37 Miriam is the Hebrew form of this name

39 Brand of cold remedy

40 Small Pacific island

41 Capital of Norway

42 Prayer for Miriam: "Let her not be as one ___" (Num. 12:12)

43 Podium

45 "The ___ of his finger in water" (Luke 16:24)

48 Genetic code

53 Nova ___

54 Israelites pass through the sea; Pharaoh's army ___ (Deut. 11:4)

56 Musical composition

57 Miriam's brother (Ex. 2:7)

59 Forest clearing

60 Miriam's other brother (Ex. 15:20)

62 Cain's eldest son (Gen. 4:17)

64 Tulle

66 Miriam asked, "Hath the LORD indeed spoken ___ by Moses?" (Num. 12:2)

67 "___ for the old paths, where is the good way, and walk therein" (Jer. 6:16)

68 Professional numbers person

69 Villain

70 What God threatened Pharaoh through Moses, He ___

MORDECAI: TRUSTED GUARDIAN
by Vicki J. Kuyper

• • • • • •

ACROSS

1 How Esther felt when she saw Mordecai in mourning (Est. 4:4)
4 "Then ___ one of the seraphims unto me" (Isa. 6:6)
8 In John 11:43, Jesus ___ Lazarus from the dead
14 A bonobo is one kind
15 Put on ___; an artificial manner
16 Storm-causing current (2 wds.)
17 Sandwich nickname
18 "Whiter than ___" (Ps. 51:7)
19 Spanish priests
20 "They ___ the passover with fire" (2 Chron. 35:13)
22 ___ Lanka
23 Discharge
24 "Mordecai the Jew was ___ unto king Ahasuerus" (Est. 10:3)
27 Horses' neck hair
31 One color of Mordecai's royal apparel (Est. 8:15)
33 Annoy
35 ___ Maria
36 Weight measurement
38 Roman three
39 Eastern ruler
40 Blotch
44 A person's self
46 "Behold ___ God!" (Isa. 40:9)
47 Conger
49 Haman ___ what he deserved (Est. 8:7)
50 "Mordecai bowed ___" (Est. 3:2)
51 First day of Purim is traditionally known as Mordecai's ___
52 "This is my blood of the new testament, which is ___ for many" (Mark 14:24)
55 Thin paper
58 "When Mordecai perceived all that was done, Mordecai ___ his clothes" (Est. 4:1)

61 Vashti's actions might make wives "despise their husbands in their ___" (Est. 1:17)
63 Hallucinogen
65 Chair support
67 Form ideas
70 Part of Ahasuerus' kingdom (see Est. 1:1)
71 "He maketh me to ___ down in green pastures" (Ps. 23:2)
72 Decorative element on Jews' garments (Num. 15:38)
73 Mordecai did this daily past the women's house (Est. 2:11)
74 "Do not ___" (James 1:16)
75 Mordecai's grandfather (Est. 2:5)
76 Women's magazine
77 Number of chapters in the book of Esther

DOWN

1 Sword
2 Poise
3 Specify
4 Mordecai joined the Jews in a three-day ___ (Est. 4:16)
5 Mordecai's royal garment material (Est. 8:15)
6 Wear away
7 Persia to Sinai (dir.)
8 Spokespersons (abbr.)
9 What Mordecai likely felt hearing of Haman's decree (see Est. 3:6)
10 Part of Ahasuerus' realm (Est. 1:1)
11 "___, give me this water, that I thirst not" (John 4:15)
12 Ethiopia to Shushan (dir.)
13 What Mordecai sent to Esther via Hathach (Est. 4:8)
21 King's probable state after a seven-day feast (Est. 1:5)
25 Caesar's twelve

26 The Kingston ___
28 "Esther certified the king thereof in Mordecai's ___" (Est. 2:22)
29 Describes Mordecai's nemesis, Haman
30 Vassal
32 Savannah time, during winter
34 "The ___ took off his ring. . . and gave it unto Mordecai" (Est. 8:2)
37 Chilled
39 Mordecai's cousin (Est. 2:7)
40 In ___ (together)
41 Part of the Jews' celebration was giving gifts to the ___ (Est. 9:22)
42 Pear-shaped instrument
43 "My voice shalt thou ___ in the morning" (Ps. 5:3)

45 Volkswagen sports car
48 Caustic substance
53 Frilly fabric
54 "LORD, thou has heard the ___ of the humble" (Ps. 10:17)
56 Fluid part of blood (var.)
57 ___ Lauder cosmetics
59 Whining voice
60 Warble
62 Ship section (Acts 27:29)
64 Source for 17 Across
66 Mordecai asked Esther "to ___ supplication" (Est. 4:8)
67 "___ a Small World"
68 Dit's partner
69 Technology that supports Web page components
70 "My heart standeth in ___ of thy word" (Ps. 119:161)

67. NAAMAN, THE LEPROUS COMMANDER
by Vicki J. Kuyper

• • • • • •

ACROSS

1 Elisha's farewell to Naaman: "Go in ___" (2 Kings 5:19)
6 "Of them he ___ twelve" (Luke 6:13)
11 U.K. time zone
14 Book of maps
15 "___ among you all, the same shall be great" (Luke 9:48)
16 A small deer in KJV
17 Bird akin to a sandpiper
18 What Naaman took home as a souvenir (2 Kings 5:17)
19 There wasn't room here for Jesus
20 U.S. President William Howard ___
21 "God: incline thine ___" (Ps. 17:6)
22 Metal tip on the end of a lance
24 One billion years
26 Men living among tombs acted this way after meeting Jesus (Matt. 8:28–34)
28 The Ten Commandments, e.g.
31 Naaman was "mighty. . . , but he was a ___" (2 Kings 5:1)
32 Damascus river (2 Kings 5:12)
33 Naaman's chapter in 2 Kings
34 King Saul's was always changing (1 Sam. 16:23)
38 Caesar's seven
39 Stretchy gloves
40 Card game
41 Rev. 22:18 warns one who ___ to God's Word (Rev. 22:18)
43 The king of Babylon looked for one (Ezek. 21:21)
44 '70's music
46 Accompanied the prophets in 1 Sam. 10:5
48 The king of Syria sent this on Naaman's behalf (2 Kings 5:5)
49 "Naaman came with his ___ and with his chariot" (2 Kings 5:9)
51 Branches used to make booths in Neh. 8:15

52 Mythical creature
53 Herb the Pharisees tithed (Luke 11:42)
54 Naaman's response to Elisha's instructions: He "went away in a ___" (2 Kings 5:12)
58 Passerby's possible reaction to Naaman's leprous affliction
59 Confess
62 Long, narrow boat
63 Judas' kiss was one for the Roman soldiers (Mark 14:44)
64 To establish as law
65 Coral island
66 "Made he a woman, and brought ___ unto the man" (Gen. 2:22)
67 Gangly
68 Simon ___ Jesus a hand in Matt. 27:32

DOWN

1 "As yesterday when it is ___" (Ps. 90:4)
2 Volcanic mountain
3 First letter of the Arabic alphabet
4 Namaan's position in the Syrian army (2 Kings 5:1)
5 Damascus to Babylon (dir.)
6 "Wash in Jordan. . .and thou shalt be ___" (2 Kings 5:10)
7 "Wise man will ___" (Prov. 1:5)
8 "All that handle the ___. . .shall come down from their ships" (Ezek. 27:29)
9 Fast plane
10 Hydrocarbon
11 What Elisha would do to Gehazi upon his return (2 Kings 5:25–26) (slang)
12 What Gehazi accepted from Naaman (2 Kings 5:23)
13 Structure of the first tabernacle (Exod. 26:12)
21 Volkswagen model
23 Cootie

25 Airport information
26 Times Naaman dipped in the Jordan (2 Kings 5:14)
27 Part of Mount Ararat where the ark docked
28 2 Down element
29 Same cite as previous
30 Told Naaman's wife about Elisha (2 Kings 5:2)
31 Cubic decimeter
33 Reputations
35 After 11 Down, what Elisha would do to Gehazi (2 Kings 5:25–27)
36 "___ to die" (Heb. 9:27)
37 Naaman "stood at the ___ of the house of Elisha" (2 Kings 5:9)
39 Run easily
42 Abraham remained this way after a century (Gen. 17:17)
44 Home to Daniel's lions
45 Retell

47 Where Naaman's wife's maid was from (2 Kings 5:2)
48 What Gehazi told to Naaman (2 Kings 5:22)
49 Netherlands' capital
50 After being healed, Naaman promised he'd no longer "sacrifice unto ___ gods" (2 Kings 5:17)
51 Binder
52 "Thou thoughtest that I was altogether ___ an one as thyself" (Ps. 50:21)
53 Alternate nickname for Fred
55 After a while
56 Naaman left Syria with 6,000 pieces of this (2 Kings 5:5)
57 Snaky fish (pl.)
60 God's genetic blueprint
61 According to 2 Kings 5:1, Naaman was a great one
62 Energy measure (abbr.)

NATHAN: TEACHER OF THE LORD'S WILL

68

by Vicki J. Kuyper

• • • • • •

ACROSS

1 David does this to Goliath with a single stone (1 Sam. 17:50)
6 In Nathan's story, Bathsheba was a ___ lamb (2 Sam. 12:1–3)
9 Jesus was upset because people went to ___ in the temple (Mark 11:15)
13 Disloyal
15 To Moses, God's walkway looked like a blue one (Ex. 24:10)
16 "The lilies. . .___ not" (Luke 12:27)
17 Nathan "bowed himself . . .___" (1 Kings 1:23)
18 Economic measure
19 David to Nathan: "Cause Solomon my son to ride upon mine own ___" (1 Kings 1:33)
20 David's exploits are part of Jewish ___
21 David ___ sorrow before his child died (2 Sam. 12:21)
24 God directed Moses to turn "the ___ into dry land" (Ps. 66:6)
25 Incense to false gods was burned beneath this tree (Hos. 4:13)
26 Middle East sultanate
27 Steak tartare is ___ than steak au poivre
29 Custard dessert
30 Past
31 Bathsheba's died (2 Sam. 12:18)
34 Nocturnal South African dog
38 David to Nathan: "He shall restore . . .because he had no ___" (2 Sam 12:6)
39 David told Nathan he wanted to build a house for the ___ (2 Sam 7:2)
40 Cab
41 What people did at the tabernacle (Exod. 38:8)
44 Job was clothed in this (Job 7:5)
45 Nathan knew the ___ story behind Uriah's death (2 Sam. 12:9)
46 University (abbr.)
48 A prophet like Nathan would be a valuable one for a king

50 David's got him in trouble (2 Sam. 11:2)
51 Two of the books Nathan is in are attributed to this prophet (abbr.)
54 Computer co.
55 Nathan to David: "Thou hast ___ Uriah" (2 Sam 12:9)
57 What Peter would do from his boat upon recognizing Jesus (John 21:7)
58 Lake bird
60 How Bathsheba felt after her baby died (2 Sam. 12:24)
61 Utterances meant to be inaudible
63 Pear-shaped instrument
64 ___ God's rules figuratively around your neck (Prov. 6:21)
65 Abana and Pharpar (2 Kings 5:12)
66 KJV pottage
67 Make a mistake
68 Disgusting

DOWN

1 Similar to instrument announcing Solomon as king (1 Kings 1:39)
2 Register (var.)
3 Jesus calmed one (Luke 8:24)
4 Nathan's job was to say what was ___, as in 2 Sam. 12:9
5 Nathan to David: God's judgment would be visible "before all Israel, and before the ___" (2 Sam 12:12)
6 Nathan would ___ ___ Bathsheba to have Solomon become king (1 Kings 1:11–12) (2 wds.)
7 "Uriah. . .___ not down unto his house" (2 Sam. 11:9)
8 Nero, e.g.
9 Remembers what just happened
10 "Let the ___ of thy servant David be established" (2 Sam 7:26)
11 Cargo ship
12 David's ___ to God was "forgive me" (Ps. 51:2)
14 Swelling
22 Nathan to David: "Thou art the ___" (2 Sam 12:7)

23 Shina language

26 David "was very ___" (1 Kings 1:15)

28 Children are one (Ps. 127:3)

29 Advertisements

30 Talk

31 Numbers worker

32 "Thou shalt call ___ name JESUS" (Matt. 1:21)

33 "___ a Small World"

34 Nathan, Elisha, and Ezekiel ___ biblical prophets

35 Affirmative in Arles

36 Better than short term memory (abbr.)

37 Nathan saw Adonijah as one (1 Kings 1:9–10)

39 "Solomon in ___ his glory" (Matt. 6:29)

42 Earth inheritors (Matt. 5:5)

43 Thin cloth

44 Vapor

46 Popeye's yes

47 Wood David's home was built from (2 Sam. 7:2)

48 "The angel . . .encampeth round ___ them" (Ps. 34:7)

49 To divert David's attention from "who ___ Abimelech" the messenger mentioned Uriah was dead, as well (2 Sam 11:21)

50 Though Adonijah was the ___ brother, Nathan helped Solomon become king (1 Kings 1:13)

51 God concerning Kedar and Hazor: "I will bring their calamity from all ___" (Jer. 49:32)

52 David's repentance could not ___ his son's death (2 Sam. 12:13–18)

53 Sloppy

54 Evils

56 For a time, David's was the cave of Adullam (1 Sam. 22:1)

57 Prima donna

59 "He hath put a ___ song in my mouth" (Ps. 40:3)

62 Nathan helped David own up to his ___ (2 Sam 12:13)

NATHANAEL CAME AND SAW
By Vicki J. Kuyper

• • • • • •

ACROSS

1 David's dad, for short (Ruth 4:17)
5 "The ___ priests answered" (John 19:15)
10 "___ to teach" (1 Tim. 3:2)
13 Dunkable sandwich cookies
15 Island nation
16 Sticky black substance
17 Eastern religion
18 Some believe "Bartholomew" may be Nathanael's ___
19 Jesus stirred this up in many of the Pharisees
20 Even filled with 153 fish, Nathanael's didn't break (John 21:11)
21 Nathanael's friend's ___ was Philip (John 1:45–46)
23 Shampoo brand
25 Peter swam to shore, but Nathanael came "in a little ___" (John 21:8)
26 Eluded
28 Billy ___, evangelist
31 Moses brought water forth from this kind of rock (Deut. 8:15)
32 Nathanael's net was pushed to this in John 21:11
33 Breathing need
34 Metric capacity measure (abbr.)
37 Jesus told Nathanael, "Ye shall see heaven ___" (John 1:51)
38 Canned chili brand
40 Disobeying God would be one
41 What Jacob called his youngest son, for short? (Gen. 35:18)
42 Jesus told Nathanael he'd see angels going up and ___ (John 1:51)
43 More pallid
44 David's sling stones come from one (1 Sam. 17:40)
45 Squirted
46 Stays
49 Nathanael saw one when he came ashore (John 21:9)
50 Women should "___ themselves in modest apparel" (1 Tim. 2:9)
51 "God took one of his ___" (Gen. 2:21)

52 Jetted tub
55 Guileless Nathanael wouldn't do this to anyone (slang)
56 Capital of Afghanistan
59 "Many ___ signs truly did Jesus" (John 20:30)
61 "Out of whose womb came the ___?" (Job 38:29)
62 Socially superior
63 Judas resorted to using one (Matt. 27:5)
64 "That which groweth of ___ own accord" (Lev. 25:5)
65 Side of the ship Jesus told Nathanael and his friends to throw the net over (John 21:6)
66 Dogs, cats, birds, e.g.

DOWN

1 Only gospel Nathanael is mentioned in
2 Canal
3 "Father hath ___ me" (John 20:21)
4 "Jacob ___ pottage" (Gen. 25:29)
5 Rocky Balboa
6 Sound physical condition
7 Caesar's trio
8 Airport info
9 "I go a ___" (John 21:3)
10 Tipped
11 Analyze
12 "Behold, I give unto you power to ___ on serpents and scorpions" (Luke 10:19)
14 Nathanael could have used this while fishing (2 wds)
22 What David did before letting the stone from his slingshot fly
24 None of the disciples asked Jesus, "Who ___ thou?" (John 21:12)
25 Lower leg
26 Counterfeit coin
27 Nathanael told Jesus, "Thou art the ___ of Israel" (John 1:49)
28 Lump
29 "The harvest of the earth is ___" (Rev. 14:15)

30 Last word in the Bible
31 Side
34 Foolish person
35 "At the name of Jesus every ___ should bow" (Phil. 2:10)
36 When Nathanael came ashore, he knew the stranger "was the ___" (John 21:12)
38 "How ___ is the fig tree withered away!" (Matt. 21:20)
39 How animals were grouped for the ark
40 How Philip referred to his friend, perhaps
42 KJV's drunkard
43 "He that deviseth to do evil shall be called a mischievous ___" (Prov. 24:8)
44 "I will break also the ___ of Damascus" (Amos 1:5)
45 Fore-and-aft sail

46 More than one radius
47 One went out from Caesar Augustus (Luke 2:1)
48 "We have found him, of whom ___ in the law. . .did write" (John 1:45)
49 ___ mignon
51 Naomi's daughter-in-law (Ruth 2:22)
52 "The kinsman said unto Boaz, Buy it for thee. So he drew off his ___" (Ruth 4:8)
53 Unwanted insect
54 Greek god of war
57 Boxer Muhammad
58 Jesus' resurrection was this kind of news to Nathanael
60 "The veil of the temple was rent in twain from the ___ to the bottom" (Mark 15:38)

NEHEMIAH: BUILDER OF THE WALL

by Vicki J. Kuyper

• • • • • •

ACROSS

1 The ___ of the Apostles
5 Nehemiah didn't take one out to build the wall (Neh. 2:8)
9 Russian country house
14 African tree
15 Writer Bombeck
16 The king agreed to ___ Nehemiah's leave (Neh. 2:6)
17 The descendants of Asaph did this (Neh. 7:44)
18 Swarm
19 "Why is the ___ of God forsaken?" (Neh. 13:11)
20 A plain near one of the towns of Benjamin (Neh. 6:2)
21 Jesus ___ for our sins
23 "My God shall supply all your ___" (Phil 4:19)
24 Glass jar
26 Bethlehem to Bethany (dir.)
28 "Let them shut the doors, and ___ them" (Neh. 7:3)
29 Nehemiah: "Did not I, because of the ___ of God" (Neh. 5:15)
31 Shusan (Susa) to Sinai (dir.)
34 Nehemiah reminded the Jews that when the Israelites ___, God provided (Neh. 9:15)
37 Keeper of king's forest (Neh. 2:8)
39 Nehemiah: "Remember me, O my God, for ___" (Neh. 13:31)
40 After listening to God's law, Nehemiah and all God's people ___ (Neh. 8:10)
41 "We are the ___, and thou our potter" (Isa. 64:8)
42 Nehemiah's list of exiles included their ___ (Neh. 7:68)
44 Railroad car connector
47 "___ the spirits" (1 John 4:1)
48 Philemon author refers to himself as "Paul the ___" (Philem. 1:9)
50 King to Nehemiah: "___ long shall thy journey be?" (Neh. 2:6)
51 There was much of this when the wall was complete (Neh. 12:27)
52 Chinese tea
56 Shorten, for short
59 Heavy cloth
63 Same genus as Eve's tempter (Gen. 3:1)
64 Architect Frank ___ Wright
66 Season leading up to Easter
67 Jerusalem's Jews were deep in this (Neh. 5:3)
68 ___ eel
69 Window glass
70 Patmos is this (Rev. 1:9)
71 Vista
72 Builders didn't ___ their weapons while working (Neh. 4:17)
73 Artaxerxes ___ Nehemiah is upset (Neh. 2:2)

DOWN

1 Organization (abbr.)
2 Porcelain
3 Choir section
4 Droop
5 ___ allowed Nehemiah to travel freely (Neh. 2:7)
6 Dunking cookie
7 The Jews' response to Ezra's blessing (Neh. 8:6)
8 "Blessed be thy glorious ___" (Neh. 9:5)
9 Telegraphic signal
10 The Israelites' declaration: "Thou, art LORD ___" (Neh. 9:6)
11 Hint
12 Elijah could have used one on the trench (1 Kings 18:35)
13 Jesus' miracles left onlookers feeling this (John 2:23)
21 "Joy of Jerusalem was heard even ___ off" (Neh. 12:43)
22 Genetic building block
25 "___ in me, and I in you" (John 15:4)

27 Lingerie item
29 Day-old manna (Ex. 16:20)
30 Eve's garden
31 Nehemiah's plea: "Build up the ___ of Jerusalem" (Neh. 2:17)
32 Sanballat tried to start one (Neh. 4:1)
33 "___ is the house of God forsaken?" (Neh. 13:11)
34 Nehemiah took one of the Jerusalem's walls (Neh. 2:13)
35 The day the wall was finished was declared ___ unto the Lord (Neh. 8:10)
36 Nehemiah to Sanballat: "Let us ___ counsel" (Neh. 6:7)
38 Sanballat probably over did this (Neh. 4:1)
39 London time zone (abbr.)
43 Before Nehemiah "had not been beforetime ___" in the king's presence (Neh. 2:1)

45 Haunted
46 Ezra read the ___ of the law aloud upon the wall's completion (Neh. 8:1)
49 "___ shall fight" (Neh. 4:20)
51 Indo-European
53 Describes Eglon, king of Moab (Judg. 3:17)
54 Describes Felix (Acts 24:3)
55 "The ___ thereof are burned with fire" (Neh. 1:3)
56 "When thou doest thine ___" (Matt. 6:2)
57 Coalition
58 "His ear through with an aul" (Ex. 21:6)
60 Swiss mountains
61 Tower of Jerusalem's wall (Neh. 3:1)
62 Green Gables dweller
65 Lydia needed this (Acts 16:14)
67 Roman god

NICODEMUS: SEEKER OF SALVATION

71

by Vicki J. Kuyper

• • • • • •

ACROSS

1 Soldier's risk
5 Paul felt one when bit by a viper (Acts 28:3)
9 Plateau
13 Basmati
14 Tub spread
15 Church governing board
16 Homophone for Esau's other name (Gen. 36:1)
17 "___ of jewels" (Song 1:10)
18 Children of Israel feared they would become these in the wilderness (Num. 14:3)
19 Pharisees asked Nicodemus, "Art thou also of ___?" (John 7:52)
21 "Noah. . .became ___ of the righteousness" (Heb. 11:7)
23 Nicodemus: "How can a man be born when he is ___?" (John 3:4)
24 Ship initials
25 There was a theological one between Samaritans and Jews (John 4:9)
29 Jesus asked Nicodemus, "___ thou a master" (John 3:10)
30 God's answer to prayer is never this
32 Resort hotel
33 Slip
36 Soldiers directed these at Jesus during the crucifixion
37 "The LORD thy God ___ thee" (Deut. 8:2)
38 Homer's "Odyssey"
39 Beer
40 Royal (Sp.)
41 "Ye do ___" (Matt. 22:29)
42 Time of day when Nicodemus came to Jesus the first time (John 3:2)
43 Hazardous
44 Prayer can be a form of this, at times

45 Establishment (abbr.)
46 "Thou art a teacher come from ___" (John 3:2)
47 "If sinners ___ thee" (Prov. 1:10)
49 Expression of surprise
50 Cool (slang)
53 "God ___ not his Son into the world to condemn" (John 3:17)
55 Metal cap on tip of cane
57 Accumulate
60 We're not to do this with one word of scripture (Rev. 22:19)
62 Zealous Christians have it
63 Destroyed
64 Describes the drink Jesus was offered on the cross (John 19:29)
65 The disciples left these when they followed Jesus (Matt. 4:20)
66 Wager
67 Brand of sandwich cookie
68 "Every ___ is known by his own fruit" (Luke 6:44)

DOWN

1 Ragu's competition
2 Large wave
3 Hot liquid burn
4 ___ Moore
5 "Every beast of the ___" (Ps. 50:10)
6 Nicodemus brought these for Jesus' burial (John 19:39)
7 Nicodemus laid Jesus in a ___ sepulcher (John 19:41)
8 Mild slang expression for surprise
9 Present at Jesus' birth and burial (Matt. 2:11, John 19:39)
10 Bethlehem to Bethany (dir.)
11 Chinese sauce
12 Spots
15 Wound with cloth around Jesus (John 19:40)
20 Potiphar's wife tried to ___ Joseph (Gen. 39:7)
22 Seventeenth Bible book (var.)

26 Hawaii, e.g.
27 "We ___ that we do know" (John 3:11)
28 How Nebuchadnezzar behaved in Dan. 4:33: ___
29 Football org.
30 "I am the ___" (John 8:12)
31 Soldiers placed on Jesus' clothes, (John 19:24) (2 wds.) (sing.)
33 Birds with webbed feet
34 Eve's first clothing (Gen. 3:7)
35 "___ and the last" (Rev. 1:17)
36 Jokes
39 "Then took they the body of Jesus, and wound it in ___ clothes" (John 19:40)
40 "Deliver the poor and needy; ___ them out of the hand of the wicked" (Ps. 82:4)
42 Friendliest
43 "The LORD will ___ from Zion" (Amos 1:2)

46 Slum
48 "Waters ___ out" (Ezek. 47:8)
49 Moses' bush was in this condition (Ex. 3:2)
50 Nicodemus was a "___ of the Jews" (John 3:1)
51 Having wings
52 Thick
54 Dorothy's dog
56 "Veil was ___ . . ." (Mark 15:38)
57 Precedes an alias
58 "No ___ can do these miracles" (John 3:2)
59 "The servant of the Lord must not strive; but be gentle unto all men, ___ to teach" (2 Tim. 2:24)
61 "I cannot redeem it for myself, lest I ___ mine own inheritance" (Ruth 4:6)

NOAH: THE GREAT BUILDER
72

by Vicki J. Kuyper

• • • • • •

ACROSS

1 Publicist, slang
6 "The Pharisees began to ___ him vehemently" (Luke 11:53)
10 Trick
14 Northern Egyptian city
15 Person, place, or thing
16 California univ.
17 Noah built one (Gen. 8:20)
18 "As the ___ of Noah were" (Matt 24:37)
19 "Sun and ___" (Ps. 148:3)
20 KJV's roe
21 "They shall ___ thee until thou perish" (Deut. 28:22)
23 What manna would do if kept overnight (Ex. 16:20)
24 "God is ___" (2 Cor. 9:8)
26 African country
28 Walk quietly
31 Noah remained in the ark this long after the dove's return (Gen. 8:12)
32 Ninevah to 4 Down (dir.)
33 "That the ___ of Noah" (Isa. 54:9)
36 Evils
40 Passed (slang)
42 Precedes alias
43 Orderly
44 Rice wine
45 Pancakes in Paris
48 By means of
49 "Noah found grace in the ___ of the LORD" (Gen. 6:8)
51 Leif Erikson, e.g.
53 Merchant, as in Gen. 37:28
56 Quote
57 Movie 2001's talking computer
58 Nap raiser
61 European mountains
65 Shine
67 Sinai or Goshen, e.g.
68 Ermine
69 "Noah was ___ hundred" when he became a dad (Gen. 5:32)
70 "Ye are forgers of ___" (Job 13:4)
71 Bulgarian capital
72 Mary is believed to have been one when she gave birth to Jesus
73 Nebuchadnezzar was not this when he ate grass (Dan. 4:33)
74 Palm Sunday celebrates Jesus' ___ into Jerusalem

DOWN

1 University (abbr.)
2 The valley of Shaveh was the king of Sodom's (Gen. 14:17)
3 One of the generous widow's (Luke 21:2)
4 Ark's stopping place (Gen. 8:4)
5 "Ye do err, not knowing the scriptures, ___ the power of God" (Matt. 22:29)
6 Soldiers came with ___ force to arrest Jesus (Luke 22:52)
7 "Let the sea ___ (1 Chron. 16:32)
8 Gals' partner
9 Christ's sacrifice ___ our forgiveness
10 Sticky stuff
11 Nut
12 "A ___ of waters" (Gen 6:17)
13 Soft drink brand
21 "Just As I Am, Without One ___"
22 Baaaad critter on the ark
25 "I do set my ___ in the cloud" (Gen. 9:13)
27 Similar
28 What Celestial Seasonings makes
29 South American Indian
30 The ark's window in Gen. 6:16 afforded Noah one
31 Noah's robe: AKA

34 Noah does this to the ark (Gen. 6:14)

35 Stretch to make do

37 Jacob's son (Gen. 34:25)

38 "Had ___ in the grave four days already" (John 11:17)

39 Deer

41 "All flesh ___" (Gen. 7:21)

45 Grains

46 "___ from his youth" (Gen 8:21)

47 "It is vain for you to rise up early, to ___ up late" (Ps. 127:2)

50 "He stayed ___ other seven days; and sent forth the dove" (Gen. 8:12)

52 Batman actor

53 Joseph accused his brothers of this (Gen. 44:11–15)

54 Synthetic fabric

55 "Noah only remained ___" (Gen. 7:23)

56 "Day and night shall not ___" (Gen 8:22)

59 Opera solo

60 "For thee have I ___ righteous before me" (Gen. 7:1)

62 Eutychus fell from the third one (Acts. 20:9)

63 There was a ___ of each animal on the ark

64 "___ upon his God" (Isa. 50:10)

66 Number of God's commandments

68 Jerusalem to Bethany (dir.)

OBADIAH: WORSHIPPER OF JEHOVAH

73

by Tonya Vilhauer

• • • • • •

ACROSS

1 "___, she is broken" (Ezek. 26:2)
4 Southwestern American tribe
8 "___ in me a clean heart" (Ps. 51:10)
14 Make bare the ___ (Isa. 47:2)
15 Obtain
16 "I cried by ___" (Jonah 2:2)
17 Time period
18 Similar
19 Fished
20 Dwelled
22 Hair product
23 "___ thee like a ball" (Isa. 22:18)
24 "Set thy ___ among the stars" (Obad. 1:4)
27 "Three full ___" (Dan. 10:2)
31 "The house of Jacob shall be a ___" (Obad. 1:18)
33 Doctors for car safety
35 "Thou shalt ___," (Mic. 6:15)
36 "Neither shall be ___ more" (Joel 2:2)
38 Option (abbr.)
39 Painter of melting clocks
40 "Thou that savest by thy right hand," as in Ps. 17:7, does this
44 Best pitcher award (2 wds.)
46 Military leave without permission
47 "Esau may be ___ off" (Obad. 1:9)
49 Tracking electrical impulses of the brain
50 "All the ___ of thy confederacy" (Obad. 1:7)
51 "Behold the fowls of the ___" (Matt. 6:26)
52 Mount Sinai in Arabia (Gal. 4:25)
55 "The ___ is full" (Joel 3:13)
58 Classification
61 Experts
63 Stretch to make do

65 Interpreter
67 A worshipper of God, as in John 9:31
70 France and Germany river
71 Day of the week (abbr.)
72 Skinnier
73 California univ.
74 Make angry
75 "The ___ of the rock" (Obad. 1:3)
76 "The spreading of ___ in the midst of the sea" (Ezek. 26:5)
77 Nervous sys.

DOWN

1 Notify
2 "The fame ___ went abroad" (Matt. 9:26)
3 Tennis player Andre
4 "Thy reward shall return upon thine own ___." (Obad. 1:15)
5 Made of oak
6 "The ___ of thine heart hath deceived thee" (Obad. 1:3)
7 "There was no room for them in the ___" (Luke 2:7)
8 "Upon the ___ of the rock" (Job 39:28)
9 "___ a right spirit within me." (Ps. 51:10)
10 "Exalt thyself as the ___" (Obad. 1:4)
11 Communication method
12 "The great ___ of his right foot" (Lev. 14:28)
13 "An utter ___ of the place" (Nah. 1:8)
21 Captivity of the children of ___ (Obad. 1:20)
25 Resort hotel
26 Baby powder
28 "The house of ___ for stubble" (Obad. 1:18)
29 Cologne (Gr.)

30 Quick drink
32 Bethlehem to Bethany (dir.)
34 Eye infection
37 Song by the Village People
39 Muzzle (2 wds.)
40 Freeway entrance
41 Earthen vessel, perhaps, as in Lev. 6:28
42 "As thou hast ___, it shall be done unto thee" (Obad. 1:15)
43 "Many shall make ___ unto thee" (Job 11:19)
45 "___, they shall drink" (Obad. 1:16)
48 "Will ___ them as gold is tried" (Zech. 13:9)
53 Vinegar is this
54 "For dust thou art, and unto dust shalt thou ___" (Gen. 3:19)
56 Stems of letters
57 Trapshooting
59 "The men that were at ___ with thee" (Obad. 1:7)
60 To glorify, as in Obad. 1:4
62 Searches
64 Goofs
66 Time periods
67 TV station
68 Pain measurement
69 "Even thou wast as ___ of them" (Obad. 1:11)
70 God will cause the ___ to go down at noon (Amos 8:9)

PAUL THE PERSECUTOR

74

by Tonya Vilhauer

• • • • • •

ACROSS

1 Path cut through grass
6 Nails
10 Period
13 Composer Roy
15 Band instrument
16 "Sir, come down ___ my child die" (John 4:49)
17 End of performance cheer
18 Part of speech
19 Large vessel
20 "He was accused of the ___" (Acts 22:30)
22 Paul was sent to ___ (Acts 15:22)
24 African country
26 Paul "preached the ___ of the LORD" (Acts 15:36)
28 "Let the peace of God ___ in your hearts" (Col. 3:15)
29 Blintz
30 "The ___ also calved" (Jer. 14:5)
31 Bishop's headdress
32 Paul was taken ___ of the temple (Acts 21:30)
33 Citizen of Denmark
34 "There ___ a great earthquake." (Acts 16:26)
35 Disgusting
37 Bomb tip
41 The one with 5 loaves and 2 fishes (John 6:9)
42 "And we know that all things ___ together" (Rom. 8:28)
43 "For a ___ and for a snare" (Isa. 8:14)
44 Legal
47 Paul did not spend ___ in Asia in Acts 20:16
48 Cola
49 "The first man ___ was made a living soul" (1 Cor. 15:45)

50 "Who is ___ into heaven" (1 Peter 3:22)
51 Arch
52 Cattle house (2 wds.)
54 "Baptized in the ___ of the Lord" (Acts 10:48)
56 With an high ___ he brought them out of Egypt (Acts 13:17)
57 Soap opera
59 "Neither have I desired the ___ day" (Jer. 17:16)
63 Ball holder
64 Depart quickly
65 Enclose
66 White-tailed sea eagle
67 The head cannot say to the feet "I have no ___ of you" (1 Cor. 12:21)
68 Paul was filled with the Holy ___ (Acts 13:9)

DOWN

1 "And this did ___ many days" (Acts 16:18)
2 Weak and sickly
3 Curve
4 Like the wooden horse
5 Paul stayed in his own ___ house (Acts 28:30)
6 "___ his son" (1 Chron. 7:27)
7 "We went ___, and set forth" (Acts 21:2)
8 "Felix. . .left Paul ___" (Acts 24:27)
9 Paul was ___ away (Acts 17:14)
10 Pious soldier in Acts 10:7
11 "Lift up my hands toward thy holy ___ (Ps. 28:2)
12 Horse's leash
14 Jacob used stones for these (Gen. 28:11)
21 "Husks that the ___ did eat" (Luke 15:16)

23 UK members
24 Guild
25 Beats
27 "___, who is called Christ" (Matt. 1:16)
29 Ghost's greeting
30 Paul beckoned with this (Acts 13:16)
31 "Press toward the ___" (Phil. 3:14)
33 Jesus pronounced Lazarus ___ in John 11:14
34 Article of merchandise
36 Hike a mountain
37 "Honorable ___ which were Greeks" (Acts 17:12)
38 Id's counterparts
39 Military officer
40 Genetic code

42 "That I may ___ Christ" (Phil. 3:8)
44 Abandon
45 Admirer
46 Peacekeepers
47 "Hear we every man in our own ___" (Acts 2:8)
48 Moses: "Slow of ___" (Ex. 4:10)
50 "___ of God" (Acts 15:40)
51 Paul tarried ___ them (Acts 25:6)
53 Group
55 "Stand in ___" (Ps. 4:4)
58 Rachel: "The LORD shall add to me another son" (Gen. 30:24)
60 ___ Schwarz, toy store
61 Ship initials
62 "___ my people go" (Ex. 5:1)

75 PETER: THE ROCK
by Tonya Vilhauer

• • • • • •

ACROSS

1 Large department store
6 First letter of the Arabic alphabet
10 Animal covering
13 Jesus went into the ___ of the high priest (John 18:15)
15 Do it again
16 Jerusalem to Jericho (dir.)
17 Mount Sinai is in ___ (Gal. 4:25)
18 "For they ___ that he was Christ" (Luke 4:41)
19 Sixth sense
20 Wine bottle
22 The "disciples went away into ___" (Matt. 28:16)
24 Penny
26 Welcome rugs
28 "Ye have ___ him go into heaven" (Acts 1:11)
29 Governing authority (abbr.)
30 Waistband
31 "Noah offered ___ offerings on the altar" (Gen. 8:20)
32 Alias (abbr.)
33 Jesus gave them ___ and bread (John 21:9)
34 Twelve (abbr.)
35 Dogmas
37 Injuries
41 Laden with fish, Simon's ___ broke in Luke 5:6
42 The vine's "blossoms ___ forth in Gen. 40:10
43 Moose relative
44 "His ___ is not changed" (Jer. 48:11)
47 Peter gets into this to go fishing in John 21:3
48 "The ___ Ghost" (Matt. 1:20)
49 Egyptian river
50 "The fallow ___" (Deut. 14:4–5)
51 Damp
52 Bitter tasting
54 Dreadful
56 Pastor (abbr.)
57 Wager
59 "Thou waterest the ___ thereof abundantly (Ps. 65:10)
63 Before (poet.)
64 Competition at the Greek games
65 Happenings
66 "God. . .hath glorified his ___ Jesus" (Acts 3:13)
67 "___, thou art God" (Acts 4:24)
68 Elicit

DOWN

1 Resort hotel
2 Peter cut off Malchus' right ___ (John 18:10)
3 Wing
4 Jack or bunny follower
5 Descendant
6 "The ___ of the covenant" (Heb. 9:4)
7 "___ of days is in her right hand" (Prov. 3:16)
8 Thoughts
9 "Winged ___ after his kind" (Gen. 1:21)
10 Toucher
11 Undetected
12 "Peter said unto them, ___, and be baptized" (Acts 2:38)
14 "Rise, Peter. . .___" (Acts 10:13)
21 Accumulate
23 Car manufacturer
24 Pepsi rival
25 Elliptic
27 "Planteth an ___" (Isa. 44:14)
29 Idle talk
30 Satan wants to ___ as wheat (Luke 22:31)
31 Fishing trade necessity

33 Peter to Jesus: Wash not only my ___ but also my hands and head (John 13:9)
34 "The mountains shall ___ down new wine" (Joel 3:18)
36 Outer's opposite
37 "Go to Caesarea. . .at the ___ hour of the night" (Acts 23:23)
38 Cry like a cat
39 Associate
40 "The ___ is red" (Matt. 16:2)
42 "___ knew Peter's voice, she opened not the gate for gladness, but ran in" (Acts 12:14)
44 "Depart from the ___ of death" (Prov. 13:14)
45 Roman statesman

46 Jesus had ___ disciples (Matt. 28:16)
47 Land plot
48 Listened to
50 Wild dog
51 "When the ship was caught. . .we let her ___" (Acts 27:15)
53 There were 450 prophets of this (1 Kings 18:19)
55 Fierce wrath, as in Ps. 88:16
58 God to Noah: "The ___ of all flesh is come before me" (Gen.6:13)
60 African antelope
61 And so forth (abbr.)
62 Directional points

PHARAOH: THE HARD-HEARTED RULER

76

by Tonya Vilhauer

● ● ● ● ● ●

ACROSS

1 Couches
6 Time period
9 "Shalt ___ a son" (Gen. 16:11)
13 Lower
14 "___ shall give Pharaoh an answer of peace" (Gen. 41:16)
15 ___ ___ of Two Cities (2 wds.)
16 "Whose soever sins ye ___" (John 20:23)
17 Root vegetable
18 "Shall I go and call to thee a ___?" (Ex. 2:7)
19 Opera solo
20 "Fountains. . .that ___ out of valleys and hills" (Deut. 8:7)
22 "Jacob ___ pottage" (Gen. 25:29)
23 Charged particle
24 Winged mammal
25 Shallow area in the sea
27 Birthmark
29 Sarah's husband (Gen. 20:2)
33 Government tax agency
34 Brew
35 Ripped up
36 "___ of ten shekels" (Num. 7:14)
39 Cancer research org.
40 Shininess
41 Duke
42 Jesus took the ___, and gave thanks (Matt. 26–27)
43 Tint
44 People without color
46 "Ten ___ of vineyard shall yield one bath" (Isa. 5:10)
49 Cool
50 "I wrote them with ___ in the book" (Jer. 36:18)
51 One-sixtieth of a minute (abbr.)
53 And so on (abbr.)
56 The Lord to Moses: "With a ___ hand shall he let them go" (Ex. 6:1)
58 Blemish
59 After God smote Pharaoh, "a ___ cry in Egypt" (Ex. 12:30)
61 "There was no room for them in the ___" (Luke 2:7)
62 Jonathon felt bad for David because "his father had done him ___" (1 Sam. 20:34)
63 Covers with gold
64 "I ___ no pleasant bread" (Dan. 10:3)
65 Golden oil empties from "two golden ___" (Zech. 4:12)
66 Joseph's brothers ___ him to the Ismeelites (Gen. 37:28)
67 Neither's partner
68 Concerning

DOWN

1 Abram's wife (Gen. 12:5)
2 Titania's husband
3 Egypt's lack of food will be this (Gen. 41:36)
4 Continent
5 Joseph ___ his father before Pharaoh (Gen. 47:7)
6 Famine shall consume this land in Gen. 41:30
7 Young lions ___ after their prey (Ps. 104:21)
8 Naval leaders
9 Heat unit
10 He that has these, let him hear (Matt. 11:15)
11 "I will ___ draw for thy camels" (Gen. 24:44)
12 "This bruised ___" (2 Kings 18:21)
15 "Let not thy ___ burn (Gen. 44:18)
20 Back talk
21 Nazareth to Tiberias (dir.)
24 "Let us make brick, and ___ them thoroughly" (Gen. 11:3)

26 "Leave his ___ and his mother" (Gen. 2:24)
28 Orchestra instrument
30 Garden tool
31 Pharaoh to Moses: "Who ___ they that shall go?" (Ex. 10:8)
32 "Pharaoh commanded his ___" (Gen. 12:20)
34 Police officer talk
36 The Israelites crossed the ___ on dry ground (Ex. 14:22)
37 Chum
38 Ball
39 People from Vienna
40 "He made him to ___ honey out of the rock (Deut. 32:13)
42 Joseph's father made him a ___ of many colors (Gen. 37:3)

43 "Pharaoh. . .shall ___ thee on a tree" (Gen. 40:19)
45 Foxes have holes, and birds have these (Matt. 8:20)
47 They smote them and let none ___ (Josh. 8:22)
48 Mariners
50 Solomon "built the ___ court" with stone (1 Kings 6:36)
52 Crown
53 Partridge sits on these (Jer. 17:11)
54 Triad
55 Jail room
57 Upon
58 Lower leg
60 "___ to your faith" (2 Peter 1:5)
62 Whirlpool

77

PHILEMON: THE AFFECTIONATE ONE
by Tonya Vilhauer

• • • • • •

ACROSS

1 Thespian's job (abbr.)
5 Tap in lightly
9 The Holy ___ is a witness to us (Heb. 10:15)
14 The shepherds "were ___ afraid" (Luke 2:9)
15 Thought
16 The tree of life yielded fruit every ___ (Rev. 22:2)
17 "I ___ have written it with mine own hand" (Philem. 1:19)
18 Liturgy of the Eucharist
19 Scholar
20 The brooks are blackish "by reason of the ___" (Job 6:16)
21 Vegetable
23 "___ to honour" (2 Tim. 2:20)
24 Jesus (Philem. 1:3)
26 "___ hospitality" (1 Peter 4:9)
28 Dit's partner
29 Stoles
31 Tint
34 Male dairy worker
37 "I ___ my God" (Philem. 1:4)
39 Abraham, "when he was called ___ ___ out. . .obeyed" (Heb. 11:8) (2 wds)
40 "___ affliction to my bonds" (Phil. 1:16)
41 Parlay
42 "If he. . .___thee ought" (Philem. 1:18)
44 ___ da Vinci
47 "The beginning and the ___" (Rev. 22:13)
48 Breastplate
50 Game presider (abbr.)
51 Not against
52 Misters
56 "___ from idolatry" (1 Cor. 10:14)
59 Suppress

63 Listen in
64 Reliable
66 "Every man a ___" (Rom. 3:4)
67 Peter, for short
68 Put up
69 Ancient Indian
70 "We launched, meaning to ___ by the coasts of Asia" (Acts 27:2)
71 "The Lord ___ to the church daily" (Acts 2:47)
72 "They might ___ after him, and find him" (Acts 17:27)
73 "Offered unto an ___" (1 Cor. 8:7)

DOWN

1 Molded salad
2 Trainer
3 Not as false
4 Solidify
5 "___ our brother" (Philem. 1:1)
6 First man (1 Cor. 15:45)
7 Plateau
8 Present's opposite
9 U.K. time zone
10 Abraham's servant to Rebekah: "Is there room in thy father's ___ ?" (Gen. 24:23)
11 Upon
12 "The ___ of Jesse" (Isa. 11:1)
13 "I do not say to ___ how thou owest unto me" (Philem. 1:19)
21 An emperor
22 "God ___ Father" (Philem. 1:3)
25 Imbecile
27 Concord, e.g.
29 Dims
30 "___ the heavy burdens" (Isa. 58:6)
31 Noah "put forth his ___" (Gen. 8:9)
32 "I wrote ___ thee" (Philem. 1:21)
33 To supplement: ___ out

34 "He laid ___ his life" (1 John 3:16)
35 "The ___ women likewise" (Titus 2:3)
36 African nation
38 "With singing, and with ___" (1 Chron. 13:8)
39 "The great ___ of his right foot" (Lev. 14:28)
43 Pronoun
45 Number representer
46 "The grace of. . .Christ be with your spirit. ___" (Philem. 1:25)
49 "I thank my ___" (Philem. 1:4)
51 Grace and ___ (Philem. 1:3)
53 "In thy ___he might have ministered" (Philem. 1:13)
54 Relationship
55 Short period of time

56 "The king of Israel is come out to seek a ___" (1 Sam. 26:20)
57 "The ___ be with you all" (2 Thess. 3:16)
58 "Saul ___ David from that day and forward" (1 Sam. 18:9)
60 First letter of the Arabic alphabet
61 "I have lift up ___ hand unto the LORD" (Gen. 14:22)
62 Walk back and forth
65 Ford vehicle
67 23rd letter of the Greek alphabet

78

PHILIP: THE HORSE LOVER
by Tonya Vilhauer

• • • • • •

ACROSS

1 Snow gliders
5 The disciples were ___ ___ in John 21:1 (2 wds.)
10 Make lace
13 Capital of France
15 "A ___ in the flesh" (2 Cor. 12:7)
16 Lyric poem
17 Having wings
18 "Sin which doth so easily ___ us" (Heb. 12:1)
19 "David hastened, and ___ toward the army to meet Goliath" (1 Sam. 17:48)
20 Both ___ and women were baptized in Acts 8:12
21 "For ___ was first formed, then Eve" (1 Tim. 2:13)
23 "God created man in his own image___" (Gen. 1:27)
25 After being baptized, Philip was "caught ___" by the Spirit of the Lord (Acts 8:39)
26 Isaiah, e.g.
28 "Thou shalt not let him_____ empty" (Deut. 15:13) (2 wds.)
31 "___ not the unclean thing; and I will receive you" (2 Cor. 6:17)
32 Backstreet
33 Abraham. . .spake unto the sons of ___ (Gen. 23:3)
34 Seize
37 He ___ the book of the covenant (Acts 8:32)
38 Philip opened his ___, and preached unto him Jesus" (Acts 8:35)
40 Idiot
41 "I believe that Jesus Christ is the ___ of God" (Acts 8:37)
42 "The angel of the ___ spake unto Philip" (Acts 8:26)
43 The Lord to Noah: "Come thou and all thy ___ into the ark" (Acts 8:3)
44 Baits
45 Young swan
46 "There shall be ___, and pestilences" (Matt. 24:7)
49 Identical
50 Open mouthed
51 "Philip went ___. . .to Samaria" to preach (Acts 8:5)
52 Before (prefix)
55 Physician, for short
56 "___ is among the mountains" (Jer. 46:18)
59 Leading
61 Epoch
62 "The thought of ___ heart may be forgiven" (Acts 8:22)
63 Metric measurement (Brit.)
64 The eunuch ___ Philip no more (Acts 8:39)
65 Nosher
66 Viewed

DOWN

1 Canned meat brand
2 Cabbage cousin
3 Iraq's neighbor
4 "Come up and ___" (Acts 8:31)
5 Treed (2 wds.)
6 "Simon offered ___ money" so he could have the power of the Holy Spirit, too (Acts 8:18)
7 Distress call
8 Before (poet.)
9 Barnabas should go as far as ___ (Acts 11:22)
10 Jewish scripture
11 Expression
12 Belief of the truth
14 Sea route

22 God called light this (Gen. 1:5)
24 Speed measurement
25 Reverent
26 Poem creator
27 Naomi's daughter-in-law (Ruth 2:22)
28 Long fish
29 Fake butter
30 Actor Alda
31 Bumps
34 Sentence part
35 Niche
36 Purple vegetable
38 To a greater degree
39 Mined metals
40 Former magistrate of Venice
42 Crescent-shaped object
43 Book of hymns

44 "The ___ of truth shall be established for ever" (Prov. 12:19)
45 Crow's cry
46 Dims
47 One hundred of these makes a shekel in Israel
48 Parrot
49 More irritated
51 Simon was amazed at the "signs which were ___" (Acts 8:13)
52 Petroleum engineer, for short
53 "It is a ___ thing that the king requireth" (Dan. 2:11)
54 Adam and Eve's garden
57 "___ I am warm" (Isa. 44:16)
58 "With ___ and bridle" (Ps. 32:9)
60 "He went on ___ way rejoicing" (Acts 8:39)

PILATE: THE GOVERNOR OF JUDAEA

79

by Tonya Vilhauer

• • • • • •

ACROSS

1 Pantomime (abbr.)
5 Regional plant life
10 "The heavens shall give their ___" (Zech. 8:12)
13 Imitation chocolate
15 Isaac blessed ___ (Gen. 27:21–23)
16 Time period
17 Creed
18 "Even to the ___ court" (Ezek. 10:5)
19 Tiger
20 Ball holder
21 Shina
23 "Multitude. . .___" and led Jesus to Pilate (Luke 23:1)
25 Pilate: "I ___ no fault in this man" (Luke 23:4)
26 One who obeys
28 Talisman
31 Stingy
32 Pilate was "willing to release ___" in Luke 23:20
33 Wander
34 Basketball assoc.
37 Middle Eastern dweller
38 Architect Frank ___ Wright
40 Fines
41 Sport's official (abbr.)
42 The ship in Acts 27:41 was run aground "where two ___ met"
43 Writings
44 Pilate washed his ___ to show his innocence in Matt. 27:24
45 Asian country
46 Dog food brand (2 wds.)
49 Some people murmured, "He is a ___ man" in John 7:12
50 "Upon the ___ of his right hand" (Lev. 14:28)
51 Endure
52 Investigation agency
55 "___ thou the King?" (John 18:33)
56 Malicious burning
59 Synthetic fiber
61 Downwind
62 "Pilate wrote a ___" (John 19:19)
63 Predictors of the future
64 "Little ___ lamb" (2 Sam. 12:3)
65 Houses
66 Herod ___ Jesus "again to Pilate" (Luke 23:11)

DOWN

1 "Give an ___ of thy stewardship" (Luke 16:2) (abbr.)
2 Samaritan: "Take ___ of him" (Luke 10:35)
3 God raised up Jesus "whom ye. . . hanged on a ___" (Acts 5:30)
4 "The Christ, the Son of ___" (Matt. 26:63)
5 Narrow inlet between cliffs
6 "Praise the Lord. . .and ___ him" (Rom. 15:11)
7 Halloween mo.
8 KJV's deer
9 Isaac was the son of ___ (Luke 3:34)
10 Decoration
11 Take off
12 Out of Jesus' side came "blood and ___" (John 19:34)
14 The ___ should not remain upon the cross (John 19:31)
22 "Go to the ___" (Prov. 6:6)
24 Representative (abbr.)
25 Foul-up
26 Sailors' "hey"
27 "He is not a God of the ___, but of the living " (Luke 20:38)
28 Partially opened
29 Bare livelihood

30 Military branch
31 Mary stood by the ___ (John 19:25)
34 Following
35 Second letter of the Greek alphabet
36 Organization (abbr.)
38 Comedian Jay
39 Woman
40 Isaac, Rebekah, Esau, and Jacob had a family ___ (Gen 27:15)
42 "When the ___ was past" Mary went to Jesus' tomb (Mark 16:1)
43 "Crown of ___" (Mark 15:17)
44 One of Noah's sons (Gen. 5:32)
45 Snake
46 ___ ___ of Two Cities (2 wds.)

47 The poor widow "___ in two mites" (Mark 12:42)
48 Scholar
49 Units of heredity
51 Tree trunk
52 "Who hath warned you to ___ from the wrath?" (Matt. 3:7)
53 Jesus to Pilate: "To this end was I ___" (John 18:37)
54 Influential org.
57 "By a ___ side," (Acts 16:13) (Sp.)
58 Remember only recent events
60 "___, Lord" (Mark 7:28)

RACHEL, THE BEAUTIFUL WIFE
by Tonya Vilhauer

• • • • • •

ACROSS

1 Rachel's father (Gen. 29:10)
6 Last day of the work wk.
9 On top
13 Saying
14 Abraham "took the ___" (Gen. 22:13)
15 Swelling
16 "___ stones at him, and cast dust" (2 Sam. 16:13)
17 Referee (abbr.)
18 Individualist
19 "Restore all that was ___" (2 Kings 8:6)
20 Telephoned
22 Trinitrotoluene, for short
23 Before (poet.)
24 Rachel ___ upon the images in Gen 31:34
25 "Am I ___ ___" (Job 7:12) (2 wds.)
27 Legate
29 Recite
33 Spots
34 Heat measurement
35 "And left ___" (Gen. 29:35) (var.)
36 Cliff debris
39 Transport
40 Uncovered
41 Jacob put a pillar ___ Rachel's grave (Gen. 35:20)
42 "It is ___ high day" (Gen. 29:7)
43 Chassis, for short
44 Caves
46 Mid-Eastern dwellers
49 Sego lily's bulb
50 Sea eagle
51 Rachel ___ and told her father what Jacob said (Gen. 29:12)
53 School group
56 "All their ___ ones" (Gen. 34:29)
58 "Let him not ___" (Gen. 31:32)
59 Therefore
61 ___ chi
62 Fizzy drinks
63 "All the ___ of his sons" (Gen. 46:15)
64 Lengthen (abbr.)
65 ___-garde
66 "Prick," as in Acts 2:37
67 Rachel wanted children or wanted to ___ (Gen. 30:1)
68 Becomes liquid

DOWN

1 Machine tool
2 Bind
3 Rachel was ___ (Gen. 29:31)
4 Glory to Jesus "throughout all ___" (Eph. 3:21)
5 "There arose. . .a ___ king over Egypt" (Ex. 1:8)
6 God withheld from Rachel "the ___ of the womb" (Gen. 30:2)
7 "In ___ was there a voice heard" as Rachel wept (Matt. 2:18)
8 Embeds
9 "Why make ye this ___, and weep?" (Mark 5:39)
10 Laban "entered into Rachel's ___" (Gen. 31:33)
11 Bode
12 "An omer is the tenth ___ of an ephah" (Ex. 16:36)
15 Laban's ___ daughter's name was Leah (Gen. 29:16)
20 "Give me my wife, for my ___ are fulfilled" (Gen. 29:21)
21 Jacob's brother (Gen. 32:6)
24 Turfs
26 Fleet
28 Boasts

30 "Any winged fowl that flieth in the ___" (Deut. 4:17)
31 Ball holder
32 When "Isaac had made an ___ of blessing Jacob," Esau returned (Gen. 27:30)
34 Leah was tender eyed; "___ Rachel was beautiful" (Gen. 29:17)
36 Pull
37 Interest rate
38 Water closet
39 Stupefied
40 "Rachel had ___ Joseph" (Gen. 30:25)
42 Bear or Berra
43 "Rachel saw that she ___ Jacob no children" (Gen. 30:1)

45 Expresses
47 Nuptial
48 Scholar
50 Privileged
52 "Where the birds make their ___" (Ps. 104:17)
53 "It came to ___" (Gen. 29:10)
54 Gait
55 Roll the stone from the well, then "___ the sheep" (Gen. 29:8) (Sp.)
57 Cab
58 To Jacob, seven years seemed like nothing "for the ___ he had" for Rachel (Gen. 29:20)
60 Loose gown worn at mass
62 ___ Walton

RAHAB'S
SCARLET RIBBON
by Laura Lisle

• • • • •

ACROSS

1 Scent
5 Brews
9 Secondhand
13 Abba, familiarly
14 The Alps' Mont ___
15 Leaf bud
16 Adam's garden
17 Singer Ronstadt
18 Chapter piece
19 Secret meeting
21 "Ye have ___ iniquity" (Hos. 10:13)
23 Rahab's advice: "___ yourselves" (Josh. 2:16)
24 Group
25 Assuage, as in Gen. 8:1
28 Female deer pelt
31 Assert
32 Swagger
34 Between David and death (1 Sam. 20:3)
36 Passover hour (abbr.)
37 Anointing essential (Ex. 29:7)
38 Govt. environmental agency
39 Leprosy sign, as in Lev. 13:2
41 Trapshooting
43 Saudi Arabia neighbor
44 Paid for someone
46 Tease
48 Eagerness
49 Proper
50 Icy
53 People from Faero Islands
57 Describes garden walking time (Gen. 3:8)
58 Australian marsupial
60 "Though he ___ me, yet will I trust in him" (Job 13:15)
61 Colt's mom
62 "I ___ not from thy precepts" (Ps. 119:110)

63 Patmos
64 "Unto the ___ of the earth" (Acts. 13:47)
65 Meat to eat (Deut. 14:4–5)
66 Mustard is one (Matt. 13:31)

DOWN

1 Iran and Iraq are members
2 Pedestal part
3 "I will ___ my mouth in a parable" (Ps. 78:2)
4 Cowman
5 "Joshua saved Rahab the harlot ___" (Josh. 6:25)
6 Small street in Luke 14:21 (sing.)
7 "World without ___" (Eph. 3:21)
8 Rahab's thread (Josh. 2:18)
9 Does with suitcases
10 The Lord is like "fullers' __" (Mal. 3:2)
11 "___ of the sword" (Josh. 6:21)
12 Jesus, "Mighty in ___ and word" (Luke 24:19)
14 They spring up (Matt. 13:26) (pl.)
20 Priest put a hole in this (2 Kings 12:9)
22 Aurora
24 Greek government
25 Horns blown in Jericho (Josh. 6:5)
26 Expel
27 Lebanon wood
28 "God ___ up the waters of Jordan" (Josh. 4:23)
29 Objects
30 Everest home
33 Rahab required one (Josh. 2:12)
35 Glass window section
40 Edible insect (Lev. 11:22) (pl.)
41 How corn is stored, as in Ex. 22:6 (past tense)

42 Rahab window hanging
   (Josh. 2:18)
43 Diffusion of water
45 Boxer Muhammad
47 "Birds of the ___ have nests"
   (Matt. 8:20)
49 More wan
50 Peak
51 Colored horse
52 Spies' escape route in Josh. 2:15
53 Jonah paid this in Joppa
   (Jonah 1:3)

54 "I am the LORD; and there is
   none ___" (Isa. 45:18)
55 Its price according to years
   (Lev. 25:50)
56 "Leah was tender ___"
   (Gen. 29:17)
59 Miner's goal

82 REBEKAH: THE MOTHER OF TWINS
by Tonya Vilhauer

• • • • • •

ACROSS

1 "A man ___ number the dust of the earth" (Gen. 13:16)
4 "___ was a plain man" (Gen. 25:27)
9 Doughnut-shaped roll
14 "Neither do thou ___ thing unto him" (Gen. 22:12)
15 Birds "thumb"
16 Man should not be ___ (Gen. 2:18)
17 Disorderly crowd
18 Rebekah drew ___ from the well in Gen. 24:45
19 Isaac ___ Rebekah (Gen. 24:67)
20 Impress
22 Rebekah "___ upon the camels" in Gen. 24:61
24 "Grow as the ___" (Hos. 14:5)
25 Space defined by boundaries
27 "And he ___, Speak on" (Gen. 24:33)
31 Meets
32 Deluxe
33 Spanish "one"
34 Threesome
36 "The LORD hath blessed thee ___ my coming" (Gen. 30:30)
38 Dull from fatigue
40 Jacob to Rebekah: "I am a ___ man" (Gen. 27:11)
42 "All over like an ___ garment" (Gen. 25:25)
43 "Make the trumpet ___" (Lev. 25:9)
44 Clumsy person
45 "___ foolish questions" (Titus 3:9)
47 Thought
51 Delight
53 Spring of water
54 Person, place, or thing

55 Evils
57 Dinner drink
59 Utilization
62 Native American lodge
65 "A time to rend, and a time to ___" (Eccl. 3:7)
66 "For my ___ are many" (Lam. 1:22)
67 "One ___ unto all" (Eccl. 9:3)
68 Specifies an alias
69 Composer Francis ___ Key
70 "Isaac was comforted after his mother's ___" (Gen. 24:67)
71 "___ not thine hand upon the lad" (Gen. 22:12)

DOWN

1 "I will give thy ___ drink also" (Gen. 24:14)
2 Absence of values
3 Half a byte
4 "My tongue cleaveth to my ___" (Ps. 22:15)
5 "___, my lord. . .lay not the sin upon us" (Num. 12:11)
6 "Neither shall all flesh be ___ off any more" (Gen. 9:11)
7 Roberto's yes
8 Rebekah was ___ (Gen. 29:31)
9 A man whose hair has fallen out is ___ (Lev. 13:40)
10 "The trees of lign ___" (Num. 24:6)
11 Executive head of a state
12 Vane direction
13 "Which had ___ me in the right way" (Gen. 24:48)
21 Pearl maker
23 "Jacob hid them under the ___" (Gen. 35:4)
25 "They sent ___ Rebekah" (Gen. 24:59)

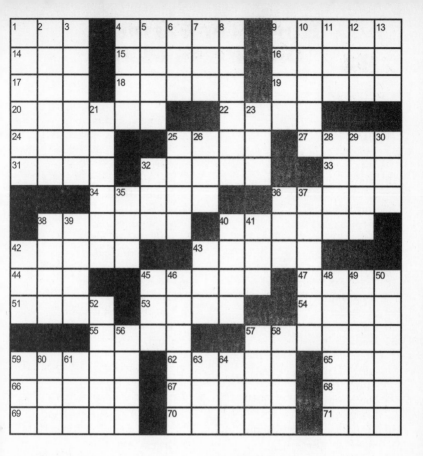

26 Cool (slang)
28 "She is thine ___" (Lev. 18:14)
29 Type of worm
30 Buck's mate
32 "O ___, we came indeed down" (Gen. 43:20)
35 Manta
36 "Take a wife unto my ___ Isaac" (Gen. 24:4)
37 Salt addition
38 "High places of ___" (Num. 22:41)
39 Rebekah was weary of her ___ (Gen. 27:46)
40 "A good ___ by great water" (Ezek. 17:8)
41 Soil
42 Pig
43 Sun's name

45 Punching tool
46 Empowered
48 Type of fin
49 Gold finder's exclamation
50 Anyhow
52 "These ___ Milcah did bear to Nahor" (Gen. 22:23)
56 Isaac to Abimelech: "___ I die for her" (Gen. 26:9)
57 "Have ___ thee away in peace" (Gen. 26:29)
58 "From the children of ___" (Gen. 49:32)
59 Ship initials
60 Attack
61 "Many years ___" (Ezra 5:11)
63 "The serpent beguiled ___" (2 Cor. 11:3)
64 Green pod vegetable

83 RUTH: THE FAITHFUL DAUGHTER-IN-LAW

by Tonya Vilhauer

• • • • • •

ACROSS

1 Play
6 "It is but a ___: and he shall. . .be clean" (Lev. 13:6)
10 "Is this house. . .become ___ ___ of robbers" (Jer. 7:11) (2 wds.)
14 Tiny amounts
15 Women's magazine
16 "Forty ___, and ten bulls" (Gen. 32:15)
17 Flying insects
18 "___ of the right ear" (Lev. 14:28) (pl.)
19 Surrender
20 Coiffed
22 Pout
24 "A full reward be given thee of the LORD ___ of Israel" (Ruth 2:12)
25 Toothbrush brand (2 wds.)
27 Nudge
29 Naomi came to live "in the ___ of Moab" (Ruth 1:1)
32 Precedes an alias
33 Reduced (abbr.)
34 "When Boaz had eaten and ___" Ruth came and lay at his feet (Ruth 3:7)
37 In the dove's mouth was "an olive ___" (Gen. 8:11)
41 Type of lily
43 This fell on all the congregation in Josh. 22:20 (var.)
44 Jesus' ___ was Mary (familiar)
45 The garden that God planted (Gen. 2:8)
46 Pimpled
48 Call for help
49 "He took ___ men of the elders of the city" (Ruth 4:2)
51 Most costly
54 "Let me. . .gather after the reapers ___ the sheaves (Ruth 2:7)
56 Treatment of something
57 "___ it for thee" (Ruth 4:8)
58 "Ye shall eat. . .the fallow ___" (Deut. 14:4–5)
60 Boaz to his servant: "Whose ___ is this?" (Ruth 2:5)
64 Goofs
66 Awkward person
68 Saudi Arabia citizen
69 Tropical edible root
70 Extremely long time periods
71 Makes music vocally
72 Colorless
73 "She told. . .all that the man had ___ to her" (Ruth 3:16)
74 Set in

DOWN

1 Fades
2 "He shall ___ up Israel out of this good land" (1 Kings 14:15)
3 Lawyer (abbr.)
4 Ruth's husband that died (Ruth 4:10)
5 Insist
6 The servant was ___ over the reapers (Ruth 2:6)
7 "___ up upon the rocks" (Jer. 4:29)
8 Dog food brand
9 Engage beforehand
10 Animal organization
11 San ___, CA
12 "He shall surely ___ her to be his wife" (Ex. 22:16)
13 "Lend him sufficient for his ___" (Deut. 15:8)
21 A group of Indic languages
23 Deer relative
26 Set to music
28 The Ishmeelites came "bearing spicery and ___" (Gen. 37:25)

29 "In any ___ thou shalt deliver him the pledge" (Deut. 24:13)
30 Ruth's son (Ruth 4:16–17)
31 "Began to ___ him" (Luke 11:53)
35 Urn
36 "This scripture must ___ have been fulfilled" (Acts 1:16)
38 "Trode them down with ___" (Judg. 20:43)
39 "___, O thou seer" (Amos 7:12)
40 "Abide here ___ by my maidens" (Ruth 2:8)
42 Upon
46 "They ___ him" (Ps. 106:32)
47 "Ruth. . .the wife of the ___" (Ruth 4:5)
50 "Thou hast shewed more kindness in the latter ___" (Ruth 3:10)

52 Tennis player Andre
53 "How shall we do for wives for them that ___?" (Judg. 21:16)
54 Distinctive qualities
55 "With oil of ___" (Est. 2:12)
56 Relating to a city
57 ___ carotene; found in carrots
59 European monetary unit
61 Phoenix's basketball team
62 Saul's army "destroyed all the people with the ___ of the sword" (1 Sam. 15:8)
63 Itemize
65 Chinese sauce
67 Compass direction

SAMSON: THE STRONG MAN BECOMES WEAK

84

by Tonya Vilhauer

• • • • • •

ACROSS

1 "He ___ the withs" (Judg. 16:9)
6 Saloon
9 "Puah, the son of ___" (Judg. 10:1)
13 Clark's partner
14 Flightless bird
15 "Samson's wife was ___ to his companion" (Judg. 14:20)
16 Their cattle will not ___ (Ps. 107:38) (var.)
17 TV station
18 "Samson our ___" (Judg 16:23)
19 "___ Iram" (Gen. 36:43)
20 The thread was ___ (Judg. 16:9)
22 Tyrannosaurus ___
23 Stretch to make do
24 Snakelike fish
25 Samson ___ a thousand men (Judg. 15:15)
27 Puffy
29 Russian Kathy
33 Verve
34 "That I may ___ Christ" (Phil. 3:8)
35 Chilled
36 "___ that I will cease" (Judg. 15:7)
39 "He shall be cast into the ___ of lions" (Dan. 6:7)
40 Soups
41 Samson about the pillars: "That I may ___ upon them" (Judg. 16:26)
42 Shirt protector
43 Garden tool
44 Jezebel wrote ___ in Ahab's name" (1 Kings 21:8)
46 No want in the ___ (Judg. 18:10)
49 "Samson ___ unto his father, Get her for me" (Judg. 14:3)

50 Samson took the ___ and all (Judg. 16:3)
51 Tap
53 Dismayed expression
56 "Because there. . .was he ___" (Deut. 33:21)
58 Card game
59 Gravy
61 Charged particle
62 Handgrips
63 Map collection
64 Not (prefix)
65 Mete out
66 "The house ___ upon the lords" (Judg. 16:30)
67 "The ___ is red" (Matt. 16:2)
68 Make ___ from cedar (Ezek. 27:5)

DOWN

1 "The haft. . .went in after the ___" (Judg. 3:22)
2 This is a day of ___ (2 Kings 19:3)
3 "He ___ out of his sleep" (Judg. 16:14)
4 "The vulture, and the ___" (Lev. 11:14)
5 Compass direction
6 "___ of great price" (Matt. 13:46)
7 Convex shape
8 Hunting prize
9 Obnoxious noises
10 "The Philistines had dominion ___ Israel" (Judg. 14:4)
11 Interbreeding population within a species
12 "___ stones" (Ex. 25:7)
15 Civet cat's cousin
20 Samson went away with the pin of the ___ (Judg. 16:14)
21 Eagerness

24 Native ruler in Asia
26 "The pen of the ___" (Judg. 5:14)
28 "One ___ to the righteous" (Eccl. 9:2) (pl.)
30 The waters are blackish "by reason of the ___" (Job 6:16)
31 Delilah used ___ ropes (Judg. 16:12)
32 Spots
34 Weave my locks with the ___ (Judg. 16:13)
36 Samson to Delilah "___ his heart" (Judg. 16:17)
37 "Will they not pay ___" (Ezra 4:13) (var.)
38 Slang for tattoo
39 Despises
40 Fly
42 Soft cheese

43 Not a razor has come upon my ___ (Judg. 16:17)
45 Comforts
47 Tracks
48 Samson "saw there an ___" (Judg. 16:1)
50 Joon's friend (movie character)
52 Samson took "the two ___" (Judg. 16:3)
53 Military division
54 Six hundred men "stood by the entering of the ___" (Judg. 18:16)
55 Structure Noah would have needed
57 Samson "___ firebrands" (Judg. 15:4)
58 Syllables used in songs (2 wds.)
60 State by Pacific Ocean (abbr.)
62 "Or for a ___" (Num. 15:6)

SAMUEL: GOD WAS CALLING

by Tonya Vilhauer

● ● ● ● ● ●

ACROSS

1 "Why make ye this ___" (Mark 5:39)
4 Yellow cabs
9 Heart rate measurement
12 David chose "__ smooth stones" (1 Sam. 17:40)
14 Samuel offered a ___ offering (1 Sam. 7:10)
15 Ladies' magazine
16 Hannah: "There abide for ___" (1 Sam. 1:22)
17 Japanese city
18 Existing
19 Buyer risk insurance
21 Samuel had his face to the ___ (1 Sam. 28:14)
23 Eli could not ___ (1 Sam. 3:2)
24 "The ark of ___" was in the Lord's temple (1 Sam. 3:3)
25 Hannah ___ a son (1 Sam. 1:20)
28 Sport assoc.
31 Angus
34 "Ruler of ___" (Neh. 3:19)
36 Slang for cool
38 Cc
40 Astringent
41 "They are without ___" (Rom. 1:20) (var.)
43 Settee
44 Denmark currency
45 New Jersey's neighbor (abbr.)
46 Haughty
48 Prophet (1 Sam. 9:9)
51 "___ the priest sat upon a seat" (1 Sam. 1:9)
53 The people refused to ___ Samuel (1 Sam. 8:19)
54 "___, my sons" (1 Sam. 2:24)
56 Samuel found favor with the ___ (1 Sam. 2:26)
58 Decadent

61 "The LORD ___ again in Shiloh" (1 Sam. 3:21)
66 Chowder ingredient
67 Muslim's God
69 "Go ye every man unto his ___" (1 Sam. 8:22)
70 "Vessels of the young men are ___" (1 Sam. 21:5)
71 2:1, e.g.
72 Cornbread
73 "I am like an ___ of the desert" (Ps. 102:6)
74 "Samuel said, As thy ___ hath made women childless" (1 Sam. 15:33)
75 Little bit

DOWN

1 "Borrow not ___ ___" (2 Kings 4:3) (2 wds.)
2 Prima donna
3 "My mouth is enlarged ___ min enemies" (1 Sam. 2:1)
4 Cut of beef
5 Author of *Sense and Sensibility*
6 Doctor's picture
7 "I wrote them with ___" (Jer. 36:18)
8 Canned chili brand
9 ___ cheese dressing
10 Method
11 Combine
13 Manasseh made. . .the inhabitants of "Jerusalem to ___" (2 Chron. 33:9)
15 Wear away
20 At sea
22 "___ not the poor" (Prov. 22:22)
25 Cheats
26 Blue
27 A tachometer measures this
29 Adornment

30 Scientist's office
32 Show emotions
33 Noah lived "nine hundred
   and ___ years: and he died"
   (Gen. 9:29)
34 David "feigned himself ___"
   (1 Sam. 21:13)
35 "Hannah ___ conceived" and
   bare a son (1 Sam. 1:20)
37 Insult (slang)
39 Samuel "went and ___ down"
   (1 Sam. 3:5)
42 Downwind
43 Bawl
47 "___ like him" (1 Sam. 10:24)
49 Samuel: "The LORD. . .is become
   thine ___?" (1 Sam. 28:16)
50 Rodent
52 Spoil

55 Eli was ninety eight ___ old
   (1 Sam. 4:15)
57 Samuel was girded with an ___
   (1 Sam. 2:18)
58 Reverberate
59 "His goods shall ___ away in the
   day of his wrath" (Job 20:28)
60 "Saul thought to make David
   ___" (1 Sam. 18:25)
61 Singing voice
62 Where doctors study
63 "To ___ in the day time"
   (2 Peter 2:13)
64 Volcano
65 "Who is this. . .with ___
   garments?" (Isa. 63:1)
68 "Glory is departed. . .because of
   her father in ___" (1 Sam. 4:21)

SARAH: THE MIRACLE MOM

by Tonya Vilhauer

• • • • • •

ACROSS

1 Florida City
6 "To the right!"
9 Tigers
13 Arrive at
14 Brat
15 Abram "Dwelt in the plain of ___" (Gen. 13:18)
16 "Make ready. . .___ measures of fine meal" (Gen. 18:6)
17 By way of
18 Advertiser
19 Tropical wood
20 "At the time appointed I will ___ unto thee" (Gen. 18:14)
22 "God shall ___ to place his name there" (Deut. 26:2) (var.)
23 ___ Lanka
24 Sarah will have a ___ (Gen. 18:10)
25 "He ___ unto him" (1 Kings 13:18)
27 Alters
29 The sun was risen when Lot ___ Zoar (Gen. 19:23)
33 "___; but thou didst laugh" (Gen. 18:15)
34 Type of partnership
35 Not any
36 Prepare
39 Old-fashioned fathers
40 Metric capacity unit
41 Recess
42 Israel "sat upon the ___" (Gen. 48:2)
43 "I will ___ his face" (Gen. 32:20)
44 Upset (2 wds.)
46 "A people ___ with iniquity" (Isa. 1:4)
49 Shina
50 Dit's partner
51 "Put a covering upon his upper ___" (Lev. 13:45)
53 Energy unit
56 Campanile
58 Sarah made cakes with "___ meal" (Gen. 18:6)
59 Jacket part
61 "And ___ the lamp of God went out in the temple" (1 Sam. 3:3)
62 "I am ___ old" (Gen. 18:12)
63 "I called him ___, and blessed him" (Isa. 51:2)
64 Arbiter (abbr.)
65 1996 Madonna movie
66 "The wicked ___ their bow" (Ps. 11:2)
67 Sarah conceived at the ___ time (Gen. 21:2)
68 Transparent gem

DOWN

1 Baseball gloves
2 Not in there! (2 wds.)
3 Sarah was ___ (Gen. 18:15)
4 "The ___ shall inherit the earth" (Ps. 37:11)
5 "His ___ was kindled" (Gen. 39:19) (var.)
6 "Hath he ___ all that he hath" (Gen. 24:36)
7 Discharge
8 Ornaments for military uniforms
9 Bounder
10 Ammunition, for short
11 "They set a ___" (Jer. 5:26)
12 The king ___ for Sarah (Gen. 20:2)
15 Impressionist painter
20 Pinkish
21 Orange peel
24 "Trust in the. . .Lord, and ___ upon his God" (Isa. 50:10)
26 Sarah ___ laughing (Gen. 18:15)

28 Sarah will bear a son ___ (Gen. 17:19)
30 Gnawer
31 "Thou made us to ___" (Isa. 63:17)
32 Change color
34 "God heard the voice of the ___" (Gen. 21:17)
36 "Abraham went and took the ___" (Gen. 22:13)
37 Environmental agency (abbr.)
38 Eleazar "shall ___ counsel for him. . .before the LORD" (Num. 27:21)
39 Mongers
40 "There I buried ___" (Gen. 49:31)
42 Sarah ___ Abraham a son (Gen. 21:2)

43 Abraham: "They will ___ me for my wife's sake" (Gen. 20:11)
45 Type of fur
47 Tonic
48 "Sarah, that is ___ years old" (Gen. 17:17)
50 Laundry detergent brand
52 Move a bike
53 Tell
54 "___ of the bricks" (Ex. 5:8)
55 "Abraham fell ___ his face, and laughed" (Gen. 17:17)
57 "The oppressed go ___" (Isa. 58:6)
58 Favorite for short
60 "One end of the borders. . .to the other ___" (Gen. 47:21)
62 "Weave the spider's ___" (Isa. 59:5)

SAUL: THE PEOPLE'S KING
by Patricia Mitchell

• • • • •

ACROSS

1 Cuban drum
6 Feature of Mount Lebanon
10 Damascus to Joppa (dir.)
13 O.T. trumpet sounds, often (Jer. 4:19)
15 Former monetary unit in Guinea
16 What David's men may have said when Saul entered their cave (1 Sam. 24:3–4)
17 Saul's kingdom, e.g.
18 Samuel to Saul: "Stay, and I will ___ thee" (1 Sam. 15:16)
19 Hearing David praised, "Saul ___ very wroth" (1 Sam. 18:8)
20 "Saul said, Cast ___ between me and Jonathan" (1 Sam. 14:42)
22 Samuel's assessment of Saul's behavior (1 Sam. 13:13)
24 Potter's tool
26 Goliath would ___ himself as invincible (1 Sam. 17:10)
28 Stake
29 Ziphites to Saul: "Doth not David ___ himself" (1 Sam 26:1)
30 David to Jonathan: "Thou shalt ___ kindly with thy servant" (1 Sam. 20:8)
31 Author Poe
32 ___ Jima
33 Regular church attender
34 Blvd.
35 Lager beer
37 Glimmered
41 What David and Jonathan may have done upon parting (1 Sam. 20:41)
42 "Saul took a sword, and ___ upon it" (1 Sam. 31:4)
43 Samuel's mentor (1 Sam. 3:1)
44 Groundcovers
47 Saul wanted to ___ David (1 Sam. 19:11)

48 Describes Saul (1 Sam. 9:2)
49 ___ qua non
50 Become less distinct
51 "Saul thought to ___ David fall by the hand of the Philistines" (1 Sam. 18:25)
52 What Jesus would do giving the Spirit" (John 20:22)
54 "Saul cast the javelin," intending to ___ David (1 Sam. 18:11)
56 Wiser than a sluggard (Prov. 6:6)
57 Samuel was one (1 Sam. 9:19)
59 Saul vented his ___ on the oxen (1 Sam. 11:6–7)
63 Joppa to Shechem (dir.)
64 Volcanic rock
65 Jonathan to David: "If it ___ my father" (1 Sam. 20:13)
66 300 men would do it (Judg. 7:6)
67 Eve's garden
68 Ahasuerus' new queen (Est. 2:17) (var.)

DOWN

1 Today's chariot
2 Arena cry in Spain
3 The brawling woman, perhaps (Prov. 21:9)
4 Ornamental screen grate
5 Saul fought "against the children of ___" (1 Sam. 14:47)
6 Los Angeles winter hour
7 Bathsheba gave David one as she bathed (2 Sam. 11:2)
8 God to Joshua: "___ the land by lot (Josh. 13:6)
9 Metric measure
10 Hiram's cedars needed this (1 Kings 5:10)
11 It has a 6 Across
12 Abigail offered to be this for David's servants (1 Sam. 25:41)
14 "It repenteth me that I have ___ up Saul" (1 Sam. 15:11)

21 Jonathan's words would ___ David away from Saul (1 Sam. 20:37)

23 Jesse sent "an ass ___ with ... wine" to Saul (1 Sam. 16:20)

24 Fruit

25 House where Saul's head would be displayed (1 Sam. 31:9)

27 Noah didn't need one

29 One among the dry bones, perhaps (Ezek. 37:4)

30 Saul's main servant (1 Sam. 22:9)

31 Nature of Saul's troubling spirit (1 Sam. 16:15)

33 African antelopes

34 Jonathan would ___ with David against Saul (1 Sam. 19:2)

36 Saul kept the best of these for himself (1 Sam. 15:9)

37 Mechanisms

38 Tropical wood

39 Women's magazine

40 1990 Hindi movie

42 Fever, chills indicator

44 Saul's kingdom (1 Sam. 13:1)

45 Austrian capital

46 Shoe part

47 Part of Joseph's coat, perhaps (Gen. 37:3)

48 God to Moses: "I will give thee ___ of stone" (Ex. 24:12)

50 Also on 23 Down

51 Tree noted for fall colors

53 Cyprus is one

55 Recipe measure (abbr.)

58 "As the lad ___" (1 Sam. 20:36)

60 Samuel to Saul: "Ye shall ___ with me to day" (1 Sam. 9:19)

61 Joppa to Jerusalem (dir.)

62 Saul's uncle (1 Sam. 14:50)

88 SHADRACH, MESHACH, AND ABEDNEGO: YOU'RE FIRED

by Tonya Vilhauer

• • • • • •

ACROSS

1 Cast into the ___ of a furnace (Dan. 3:6)
6 "None other that can shew it. . . except the ___" (Dan. 2:11)
10 Popular president's initials
13 Vinegar's acid
15 "Half ___ of land" (1 Sam. 14:14)
16 Downwind
17 South-Central Dravidian
18 "He shall ___ up his power. . . against the king" (Dan. 11:25)
19 Expert
20 Elizabeth's nickname
22 Jews were set over "the ___ of the province" in Dan. 3:12
24 Reduce (abbr.)
26 Market a product (abbr.)
28 Merriment
29 What waiters carry
30 "Flames of the ___ slew those men" (Dan. 3:22)
31 "That were under the ___" (Jer. 52:20)
32 "The king had ___ up" the image (Dan. 3:2)
33 "His rage and ___" (Dan. 3:13)
34 "The judgment shall ___" (Dan. 7:26)
35 Light colors
37 "A quiet and peaceful life in all godliness and ___" (1 Tim. 2:2)
41 "Destroy ___ the wise men" (Dan. 2:12)
42 They "changed the king's ___" in order to serve God (Dan. 3:28)
43 Before (poet.)
44 Spring mo.
47 ___ them into the furnace (Dan. 3:20)
48 African antelope
49 "An overflowing ___" (Ezek. 38:22)
50 The king "was ___ displeased" (Dan 6:14)
51 "___ it in a book" (Isa. 30:8)
52 The merchants were "in blue ___" (Ezek. 27:24)
54 Hit hard
56 Option (abbr.)
57 Writer Bombeck
59 Goat fur
63 Buck's mate
64 Car rental agency
65 "Worship the ___ image" the king set up (Dan. 3:5)
66 "Lies caused them to ___" (Amos 2:4)
67 Technical, for short
68 Run-down

DOWN

1 Entrance rug
2 He cast ___ like morsels (Ps. 147:17)
3 Northeastern state (abbr.)
4 Squat
5 Large striped cat
6 Vapor
7 Eight notes
8 Roam
9 "Is he a homeborn ___?" (Jer. 2:14) (var.)
10 Threshes
11 "___ went forth" (Dan. 2:13)
12 Peanut butter candy maker
14 "The stone was ___ out of the mountain without hands" (Dan. 2:45)
21 "Till his ___ were grown" like feathers (Dan. 4:33)
23 Merchant's wares "coral, and ___" (Ezek. 27:16)

24 Location

25 Cast idols to "the moles and to the ___" (Isa. 2:20)

27 "O ye ___ bones" (Ezek. 37:4)

29 Cooking measurement

30 "Three ___ weeks" (Dan. 10:2)

31 He commanded his army to ___ the boys (Dan. 3:20)

33 "There ___ a voice from heaven" (Dan. 4:31)

34 "No other God that can deliver after this ___" (Dan. 3:29)

36 Soil

37 Water carriers

38 "Blessed be the God. . .who hath ___ his angel" (Dan. 3:28)

39 "___, O king" (Dan. 3:24)

40 "___, Lord" (Mark 7:28)

42 "Unto the end of the ___" (Dan. 9:26)

44 Passageway between shops

45 Whiteness

46 Troublemaker

47 Vast

48 Gawk

50 "All people. . .should ___ him" (Dan. 7:14)

51 Taboos

53 ___ the furnace seven times hotter (Dan. 3:19)

55 Fall back

58 "Planteth an ___" (Isa. 44:14)

60 Lyric poem

61 "Riding upon a ___ horse" (Zech. 1:8)

62 Do not serve ___ other God (Dan. 3:28)

89 SOLOMON: THE WISEST MAN

by Tonya Vilhauer

• • • • • •

ACROSS

1 ___ hoop (child's toy)
5 Hook
9 "Will ___ them to be discharged" (1 Kings 5:9)
14 "Solomon did ___ in the sight of the LORD" (1 Kings 11:6)
15 Off-Broadway award
16 "LORD spake ___" (Mal. 3:16)
17 Ancient German character
18 Capital of Vanuatu
19 "He shall be king in my ___" (1 Kings 1:35)
20 "Servants came to ___ our lord king David" (1 Kings 1:47)
22 Poke holes in a lawn
24 ___ Francisco
25 "Two men more righteous and ___" (1 Kings 2:32)
27 Beast "had three ___" (Dan. 7:5)
31 Elizabeth's nickname
32 Metric unit
34 Camp bed
35 Santa call (2 wds.)
38 Wheeled vehicle
40 "There came ___ ___ out" (Lev. 9:24) (2 wds)
42 Imitative
44 Liquor
46 "The king shall ___ with his fathers" (1 Kings 1:21)
47 Poem
48 "The king bowed himself upon the ___" (1 Kings 1:47)
50 Goofs
51 Time period
52 "A spider's ___" (Job 8:14)
55 "It was ___ king Solomon that Joab was fled" (1 Kings 2:29)
57 "___ of the LORD" (1 Kings 8:17)
59 Selling again
61 Professional bookkeeper
64 Relating to spring
66 Spring flower
68 "Ahasuerus which reigned, from ___" (Est. 1:1)
71 Convexity
73 Pop
74 Violent public disorders
75 Groan
76 Solomon reigned ___ Israel (1 Kings 11:42)
77 Species of herring
78 "That ___ burdens" (1 Kings 5:15)
79 "Thou puttest thy ___ in a rock" (Num. 24:21)

DOWN

1 "Give me thy vineyard. . .for a garden of ___" (1 Kings 21:2)
2 Screamer's throat dangler
3 "David was clothed with a robe of fine ___" (1 Chron. 15:27)
4 Beers
5 "Amon the ___" (1 Kings 22:26) (abbr.)
6 "___ the priest" (1 Kings 2:22)
7 Net of square mesh
8 "Adonijah ___ because of Solomon" (1 Kings 1:50)
9 "Have we eaten at all of the king's ___?" (2 Sam. 19:42)
10 "Solomon thy son shall reign ___ me" (1 Kings 1:13)
11 North American Indian
12 Solomon's wisdom exceeded the sands "on the ___ shore" (1 Kings 4:29)
13 Solomon "made an ___ of building his own house" (1 Kings 3:1)
21 Compass point
23 Solomon "stood before the ___" (1 Kings 3:15)
26 And so forth

28 Colder

29 Hole maker

30 "The throne had six ___" (1 Kings 10:19)

31 Supervisor

33 Petrol

35 "He bringeth them unto their desired ___" (Ps. 107:30)

36 Musical production

37 Solomon's friend (1 Kings 5:2)

39 Wipe

41 "Joab was ___ unto the tabernacle" (1 Kings 2:29)

43 "Builders did ___ them" (1 Kings 5:18)

45 Ingot (2 wds.)

49 Pain measurement

53 "A people that do ___" (Ps. 95:10)

54 Make numb with cold

56 "___ king Solomon swear unto me today" (1 Kings 1:51)

58 1996 Madonna movie

60 Island country

61 "Solomon ___ unto these in love" (1 Kings 11:2)

62 "The people piped with ___" (1 Kings 1:40)

63 "Her that was set ___ for pollution" (Ezek. 22:10)

65 "Children of the ___ country" (1 Kings 4:30)

67 "He shall sit ___ my throne" (1 Kings 1:30)

68 Tax agency

69 Tweak

70 "Region of ___" (1 Kings 4:11)

72 "Solomon's provision for ___ day" (1 Kings 4:22)

STEPHEN: THE MARTYRED DEACON
by Tonya Vilhauer

• • • • • •

ACROSS

1 "Stand in the ___ before me" (Ezek. 22:30)
4 Island nation
9 "The saying pleased the ___ multitude" (Acts 6:5)
14 "Ye tithe mint and ___" (Luke 11:42)
15 Toothbrush brand (2 wds.)
16 Eagle's nest
17 "I have never eaten ___ thing. . . unclean" (Acts 10:14)
18 Ore digger
19 Tag
20 "They ___ Stephen" (Acts 7:59)
22 Men lamented ___ Stephen (Acts 8:2)
24 Bread
25 Central Thai
27 "Beware of ___" (Phil. 3:2)
31 Views
32 ___ Arabia
33 Simon Peter "drew the ___ to land" (John 21:11)
34 "They cast four anchors out of the ___" (Acts 27:29)
36 Muslim's religion
38 Pineapple (Gr.)
40 "The blood of thy ___ Stephen was shed" (Acts 22:20)
42 Dissension arose ___ Stephen (see Acts 6:9)
43 "Stephen, full of faith and ___, did great wonders" (Acts 6:8)
44 He lies in wait "as a lion in his ___" (Ps. 10:9)
45 "There ___ certain of the synagogue" (Acts 6:9)
47 Nourishes
51 "Kept the raiment of them that ___ him" (Acts 22:20)
53 Micah: "I will give thee. . .a ___ of apparel" (Judg. 17:10)
54 Synagogue of ___ (Acts 6:9)
55 Pixies
57 "A ___ came to hearken" (Acts 12:13)
59 "They ___ Stephen" (Acts 6:5)
62 Subject
65 "Who ___ thou, Lord?" (Acts 9:5)
66 Leaders
67 Put up
68 Out of the womb came the ___ (Job 38:29)
69 Domestic fish
70 "Consenting unto his ___" (Acts 22:20)
71 "He was ___ as a sheep to the slaughter" (Acts 8:32)

DOWN

1 Comprehends
2 Father's sister
3 Indian drug
4 "And ___ of them were men of Cyprus" (Acts 11:20)
5 Dry
6 "Stephen, a ___ full of faith" (Acts 6:5)
7 Bullfight cheer
8 They were scattered ___ (Acts 11:19)
9 Wheal
10 "We have ___ him say" Jesus will destroy this place (Acts 6:14)
11 Bolus
12 "Satan filled thine heart to ___ to the Holy Ghost" (Acts 5:3)
13 Lamprey
21 Bahamas' capital
23 Caesar's seven

25 Sticky black substances
26 European nomad
28 Preaching the word "unto the Jews ___" (Acts 11:19)
29 Camping equipment
30 Type of microscope
32 Simon's house is by the ___ side (Acts 10:6)
35 Trinitrotoluene, for short
36 Wrath
37 The ___ beat upon the house (Luke 6:48)
38 "By faith ___" offered God a sacrifice (Heb. 11:4)
39 Not any
40 "Blessed be the ___ high God" (Gen. 14:20)
41 "Stand in ___" (Ps. 4:4)

42 Spots
43 Luau dish
45 "The hole of the ___" (Isa. 11:8)
46 Corroded
48 Pelt
49 A third part
50 "Every one shall be ___ with fire" (Mark 9:49)
52 "God is ___ than men" (1 Cor. 1:25)
56 Land formation
57 Definer (abbr.)
58 Hormone
59 Midwest time zone
60 Color
61 Fall mo.
63 Mineral
64 Legume

THE BLIND MAN WHO SAID "I SEE"

by Tonya Vilhauer

● ● ● ● ● ●

ACROSS

1 Loose gown worn at church
4 "Both shall fall into the ___" (Matt. 15:14)
9 "Cleanse. . .that which is within the ___" (Matt. 23:26)
12 "Having faithful children not accused of ___" (Titus 1:6)
14 Take away
15 Comedian Jay
16 The people gathered "unto ___ the scribe" (Neh. 8:13)
17 ___ Rica
18 "For that which is put ___ fill it up" (Matt. 9:16) (2 wds.)
19 Sand hillside
21 "He is a ___!" (Matt. 23:16)
23 Boxer Muhammad
24 Cunning
25 Blemish
28 Children's safety org.
31 Drop
34 Tokens of honor
36 Jesus "led ___ out of the town" (Mark 8:23)
38 Aspire
40 "They ___ to Jericho" (Mark 10:46)
41 "Let them ___" (Matt. 15:14)
43 Austin novel
44 "Thine ___ be single" (Matt. 6:22)
45 "They are ___ with the showers of the mountains" (Job 24:8)
46 "A great ___ of people" went out of Jericho (Mark 10:46)
48 Sledge
51 Dab
53 Curse
54 Big truck
56 Movie 2001's talking computer
58 Capital of Lesotho
61 "They ___ from Jericho" and were followed by many (Matt. 20:29)

66 Little Mermaid's love
67 French city
69 Describes ointment that ran (Ps. 133:2)
70 "What ___ thou that I should do?" (Mark 10:51)
71 Ye shall be "as a tottering ___" (Ps. 62:3)
72 Writing table
73 Blind Bartimaeus ___ by the highway (Mark 10:46)
74 Wise men
75 The multitude wondered when they say "the blind to ___" (Matt. 15:31)

DOWN

1 Greek god of war
2 Ms. Minnelli
3 "Who did sin. . .that he was ___ blind?" (John 9:2)
4 Decorative sticker
5 Sarcastic
6 Chore
7 Midwestern time zone
8 "On their ___ crowns" (Rev. 4:4)
9 Penny
10 "God said ___ them, Be fruitful, and multiply" (Gen. 1:28)
11 "Preach the gospel to the ___" (Luke 4:18)
13 Small portion
15 "Persia, Ethiopia, and ___" (Ezek. 38:5)
20 Shakespeare's occupation
22 Pixy
25 Moves gently
26 "A ___ to go through a needle's eye" (Luke 18:25)
27 "The dead ___ raised up" (Matt. 11:5)
29 A camera takes one

30 You are made whole; "___ no more" (John 5:14)
32 Jesus told Peter to feed his ___ (John 21:15)
33 Citrus fruits
34 Genius
35 Jesus ___ a man that was blind (John 9:1)
37 "Two blind ___" (Matt. 20:30)
39 "After this manner will I ___ the pride of Judah" (Jer. 13:9)
42 Guided
43 Like an ostrich
47 California univ.
49 To build up
50 Listing (abbr.)
52 "Jesus departed ___" and was followed by two blind men (Matt. 9:27)

55 Bodies of water
57 Recesses
58 Cat cries
59 Opera solo
60 River sediment
61 Ding's partner
62 "Aaron's ___ that budded" was kept in the ark of the covenant (Heb. 9:4)
63 Binds
64 "Accusing or ___ excusing one another" (Rom. 2:15)
65 Dam
68 "They said unto him, ___ Lord" (Matt. 9:28)

THE CRIPPLE: HEALING AT THE GATE BEAUTIFUL

92

by Tonya Vilhauer

• • • • • •

ACROSS

1 Coalition
5 "We spend our years as ___ ___ that is told" (Ps. 90:9) (2 wds.)
10 Old-fashioned dads
13 Funny man Jay
14 Tie with a rope
15 "A man clothed in ___ raiment?" (Luke 7:25)
16 "A ___ of bees and honey (Judg. 14:8) (var.)
17 Synthetic fabric
18 Skirt
19 Flightless bird
21 Peter ___ the people (Acts 3:12)
23 North American nation
26 Fourth month (abbr.)
28 Office product company
29 Green olive insides
32 Sleigh
33 Mined metals
34 "Let me freely ___" (Acts 2:29)
36 "Unto the ___ day" (Acts 4:3)
37 "Unto you ___ God" (Acts 3:26)
38 "Barbarians saw the beast ___ on his hand" (Acts 28:4)
42 "His feet and ankle ___ received strength" (Acts 3:7)
43 Opera solo
44 Lifeless
46 Limited use of others' property
49 "A bow of ___ is broken by mine arms" (2 Sam. 22:35)
51 Chatter
52 This man "whom ye ___ and know" (Acts 3:16)
53 Canadian city
57 Kitten's cry
59 Give off
60 Adios (Fr.)
62 Whatever you ask I will give "unto the ___ of my kingdom" (Mark 6:23)

66 "Even the ___ of the cup of my fury" (Isa. 51:22) (var.)
67 Type of fur
68 Buckeye State
69 Acid
70 "Nor the ___ of fire had passed on them" (Dan. 3:27)
71 Peter: Why marvel as though "we had ___ this man to walk?" (Acts 3:12)

DOWN

1 Deli order
2 Downwind
3 "Ye denied the Holy ___" (Acts 3:14)
4 Refreshing shall ___ from the Lord (Acts 3:19)
5 Unceremonious
6 British drink
7 ___ mater
8 Angels sat where "the body of Jesus had ___" (John 20:12)
9 Peter fastened his ___ upon him (Acts 3:4)
10 The gift of the Holy Spirit was ___ out on the Gentiles (Acts 10:45)
11 "Those that follow ___" Samuel foretold of these days (Acts 3:24)
12 "___ to shew thyself approved unto God" (2 Tim. 2:15)
15 Actor McQueen
20 The lame ___ was healed (Acts 3:11)
22 "Rise up and ___" (Acts 3:6)
23 Peter looked ___ him with John (Acts 3:4)
24 Father offspring
25 Charge card, for short
27 Brittle resin
30 Georgia time zone

31 Shopping expedition
32 He ___ by the gate asking alms (Acts 3:10)
35 School assignment
37 Watch chain
38 Noah's son (Gen. 5:32)
39 Greek god of war
40 "Where are the ___?" (Luke 17:17)
41 The man sat at "the Beautiful ___ of the temple" (Acts 3:10)
42 Indonesian island
44 Refused
45 KJV's tears
47 Eli was mentor to ___ (1 Sam. 3:6)
48 Stretch to make do
49 "Neither did thy foot ___" (Deut. 8:4)

50 "Until the ___ of restitution" (Acts 3:21)
54 "It shall come to ___" (Acts 3:23)
55 Swiss-like cheese
56 Tease
58 "___ this miracle of healing was shewed" (Acts 4:22)
61 Building add-on
63 "___, our eye hath seen it" (Ps. 35:21)
64 "Bored a hole in the ___" (2 Kings 12:9)
65 Contender

THE LEPER: NO MORE SORES
by Tonya Vilhauer

• • • • • •

ACROSS

1 Abdominal muscles (abbr.)
4 "Mouth of the ___" (Nah. 3:12)
9 Winter mo.
12 His clothes shall be rent and "his ___ bare" (Lev. 13:45)
14 "Let him that ___ steal no more" (Eph. 4:28)
15 Deal with
16 Decorative needle case
17 Bump
18 "As small as the ___ frost on the ground" (Ex. 16:14)
19 Stag (2 wds.)
21 Uniformly
23 White-tailed sea eagle
24 "He shall be the ___ of the leper" (Lev. 14:2)
25 "We cry ___" (Rom. 8:15)
28 TV station
31 Despot
34 Took big steps
36 Wig (slang)
38 "The law of the leper in the ___ of cleansing" (Lev. 14:2)
40 Grand ___ race
41 Non ___ (not welcome)
43 "All that ___ in the waters" shall be an abomination (Lev. 11:10)
44 Succor
45 The angel "sat under an ___" (Judg. 6:11)
46 Frightens
48 Mexican money
51 Complex network
53 City in Yemen
54 The leper shall ___ unclean (Lev. 13:45)
56 Building add-on
58 Flashing light
61 "Command the ___ of Israel" (Num. 5:2)

66 They sold the poor "for a ___ of shoes" (Amos 2:6)
67 "The seed of ___ is a leper" (Lev. 22:4)
69 "Call on the ___ of the LORD" (2 Kings 5:11)
70 "The priest shall look ___ it" (Lev. 13:25)
71 Climb
72 The smith works it "with the strength of his ___" (Isa. 44:12)
73 God "hath compassed me with his ___" (Job 19:6)
74 Minds
75 "He shall not ___ of the holy things" (Lev. 22:4)

DOWN

1 Excuse me!
2 Second Greek letter
3 "Then said ___ to his servant" (1 Sam. 9:7)
4 Organic compound
5 Greek goddess
6 Visit places
7 Shade tree
8 Drive away
9 Evening, morning, and ___ (Ps. 55:17)
10 Opaque gem
11 The woman had a "box of ___ precious ointment" (Matt. 26:7)
13 "By our law he ought to ___" (John 19:7)
15 Chomps
20 "Whosoever is defiled by the ___" (Num. 5:2)
22 Large vessel
25 Vacation (2 wds.)
26 The bridegroom has his ___ (John 3:29)
27 Container

29 "She ___ the box" (Mark 14:3)
30 Uzziah "was ___ off" (2 Chron. 26:21)
32 Dote
33 Noah "sent forth a ___" (Gen. 8:7)
34 Resort hotel
35 Self-esteem
37 Vapor
39 "He saith, ___" (Matt. 17:25)
42 "Eat not of it ___" (Ex. 12:9)
43 "Thou art ___" (Acts 12:15)
47 Mary: "Generations shall ___ me blessed" (Luke 1:48)
49 "Laughed thee to ___" (2 Kings 19:21)
50 Bolus
52 "___, if the leprosy have covered all his flesh" (Lev. 13:13)

55 "They shall be baken with ___" (Lev. 23:17) (var.)
57 "With two ___ measured he to put to death" (2 Sam. 8:2)
58 "Wisdom ___ goats' hair" Ex. 35:26)
59 Sticky fastener
60 "Faithful children not accused of ___ or unruly" (Titus 1:6)
61 Ocean Spray's drink starters (abbr.)
62 Carries genetic info.
63 "It is a ___ thing that the king requireth" (Dan. 2:11)
64 Austin novel
65 "There shall the great owl make her ___" (Isa. 34:15)
68 Whiz

94 THE SHUNAMMITE WOMAN: SERVING THE MAN OF GOD

by Tonya Vilhauer

• • • • • •

ACROSS

1 "Take my ___ in thine hand" (2 Kings 4:29)
6 "The ___ is not to the swift" (Eccl. 9:11)
10 Compass point
14 Pergola
15 Aluminum, for short
16 Clip
17 Large stringed instrument
18 "Conceived, and ___ a son" (2 Kings 4:17)
19 Hawkeye State
20 Stagger
21 "Take this ___ of oil" (2 Kings 9:1) (var.)
22 Scolder
24 "Which ___ him an hundred pence" (Matt. 18:28)
26 "The king ___ with Gehazi" (2 Kings 8:4)
27 Blemished
30 "___ this Shunammite" (2 Kings 4:12)
31 Submit for consideration
32 He put his ___ on the child (2 Kings 4:34)
33 "And the lapwing, and the ___" (Deut. 14:18)
36 Dodge
37 Tax agency
38 "For the ___ of the house" (1 Kings 7:12)
40 In charge of (abbr.)
41 Fuss
43 Raging
44 "To ___ is better than sacrifice" (1 Sam. 15:22)
45 Scorch
46 "She ___ unto her husband" (2 Kings 4:22)
49 Run and ___ her (2 Kings 4:26)

50 Branch
51 "It is neither ___ moon nor sabbath" (2 Kings 4:23)
52 Giant
56 "And ___ with joy receiveth it" (Matt. 13:20)
57 Whim
59 "She constrained him to eat ___" (2 Kings 4:8)
60 Chinese secret society
61 "He sat on her knees till ___" (2 Kings 4:20)
62 Vassal
63 Sego lily's bulb
64 Chap
65 "It shall be for a ___ upon thine hand" (Ex. 13:16)

DOWN

1 "Every man's money was in the mouth of his ___" (Gen. 43:21)
2 "Shall fell every good ___" (2 Kings 3:19)
3 "All that were ___ to put on armour" (2 Kings 3:21)
4 "He arose, and ___ her" (2 Kings 4:30)
5 "Walked in the house to and ___" (2 Kings 4:35)
6 Fanatical
7 Actor Alda
8 Mongrel dog
9 "Like unto an ___" (Rev. 4:3)
10 "My wounds ___" (Ps. 38:5)
11 "Jehu ___ letters" (2 Kings 10:1)
12 "And ___ herself to the ground" (2 Kings 4:37)
13 "There shall come a ___ out of Jacob" (Num. 24:17)
21 "Laid him on the ___" (2 Kings 4:21)
23 Spice made from a berry

25 Silver bullet target
26 Bitter herb
27 ___ Astaire
28 "Therefore was his name called ___" (Gen. 29:34)
29 "The man of God saw her ___ off" (2 Kings 4:25)
30 "___ him to his mother" (2 Kings 4:19)
32 "The king of Israel hath ___ against us" (2 Kings 7:6)
33 Rascal
34 Adrenocorticotropic hormone
35 "What shall I do for ___?" (2 Kings 4:2)
39 Long, dramatic musical composition
42 "As in ___ the voice of the LORD?" (1 Sam. 15:22)

45 "A time to ___" (Eccl. 3:7)
46 Long, narrow boat
47 "I dwell ___ mine own people" (2 Kings 4:13)
48 Jargon
49 "God ___ it unto good" (Gen. 50:20)
50 Rodents
51 Symbol Ne and atomic number 10
53 Nerd
54 "He. . .went away in a ___" (2 Kings 5:12)
55 "The children of ___" (2 Kings 19:12)
58 Female deer
59 Sandwich

THOMAS: THE DOUBTER

95

by Tonya Vilhauer

• • • • • •

ACROSS

1 "He had found one ___ of great price" (Matt. 13:46)
6 "Thomas saith unto ___" (John 14:5)
9 Homeless child
13 Listlessness
14 "Come down ___ my child die" (John 4:49)
15 "Simon called ___" (Matt. 4:18)
16 "The Lord ___ to the church" (Acts 2:47)
17 Negative
18 "Where ___ both Peter" (Acts 1:13)
19 "She let them down by a ___" (Josh. 2:15)
20 Make tougher
22 Washington time zone
23 "Seven ___ lambs" (Gen. 21:30)
24 "The other ___ of the cherub" (1 Kings 6:24) (var.)
25 "I know that he shall ___ again" (John 11:24)
27 Mops
29 Pleasing and simple
33 Constellation
34 "Thomas, ___ of the twelve" (John 20:24)
35 Second letter of the Greek alphabet
36 Lukewarm
39 "___ not the poor" (Prov. 22:22) (var.)
40 "Whither thou ___" (John 14:5)
41 "___, and Dumah, and Eshean" (Josh. 15:52)
42 "___ us also go" (John 11:16)
43 "___ can we know the way?" (John 14:5)
44 "Cana in ___" (John 21:2)
46 Comforts

49 "God ___ not his Son" (John 3:17)
50 Plod
51 "Dragging the ___ with fishes" (John 21:8)
53 Ostrichlike bird
56 Spoken
58 "Blessed are they who have not seen, and yet ___ believed" (John 20:29)
59 "They shall hold the bow and the ___" (Jer. 50:42)
61 Doze
62 Promising beginner
63 "Between the ___ and the temple" (Luke 11:51)
64 Measure of national income/output
65 "The ___ being shut" (John 20:26)
66 Chemical element
67 "Verily, I ___ unto you" (John 1:51)
68 Revelry

DOWN

1 "___ be unto you" (John 20:26)
2 Endues
3 "And ___, and Philip" (Mark 3:18)
4 Regretted
5 Jehoiada bored "a hole in the ___" (2 Kings 12:9)
6 Dye
7 "Unto the ___ gate" (Acts 12:10)
8 Measuring metrically
9 Weave the "locks of my head with the ___" (Judg. 16:13)
10 On top
11 Roadside bombs (abbr.)
12 "___ not thyself because of evil men" (Prov. 24:19)

15 Aeneas "was sick of the ___"
   (Acts 9:33)
20 "Let us ___ go" (John 11:16)
21 Helper
24 "Lay on ___ at noon" (2 Sam.
   4:5) (2 wds.)
26 Nudges
28 Excuses
30 Downwind
31 "Groweth of ___ own accord"
   (Lev. 25:5)
32 Mouser
34 "They went ___ of the city"
   (John 4:30)
36 Chase
37 Time period
38 "Our ___ Lazarus sleepeth"
   (John 11:11) (var.)
39 Forums

40 "With an ox ___" (Judg. 3:31)
42 Comedian Jay
43 "Become the ___ of the corner"
   (Acts 4:11)
45 Crowbar
47 Inflame with love
48 Keen
50 Lively
52 Concise
53 Ardor
54 "God made them ___ and
   female" (Mark 10:6)
55 "Peace be ___ you" (John 20:26)
57 "___ in Galilee" (John 21:2)
58 Hula ___
60 "How ___ we know the way?"
   (John 14:5)
62 Discs

TIMOTHY: THE YOUNG PASTOR

96

by Tonya Vilhauer

● ● ● ● ● ●

ACROSS

1 WI airport (abbr.)
4 "Ten ___ of vineyard" (Isa. 5:10)
9 Female (abbr.)
12 Capital of Peru
14 Type of farm
15 Small particle
16 "We have not ___ this power" (1 Cor. 9:12)
17 More aged
18 Period of duty
19 Limber
21 Slanted font
23 "I will ___ you" (Heb. 13:23)
24 "With ___ the saints" (2 Cor. 1:1)
25 Pear-shaped instrument
28 "It shall be seven days under the ___" (Lev. 22:27)
31 Bluish green
34 Fatal
36 "Mightest ___" (1 Tim. 1:18)
38 "My own ___ in the faith" (1 Tim. 1:2)
40 Lawyer (abbr.)
41 "Grace, mercy, and ___" (2 Tim. 1:2)
43 American river
44 "He may exalt you in ___ time" (1 Peter 5:6)
45 "Be not ashamed. . .___ of me his prisoner" (2 Tim. 1:8)
46 "Ye were the ___ of all people" (Deut. 7:7)
48 Univ. instructor
51 "They passed through the Red ___ as by dry land" (Heb. 11:29)
53 Green Gables dweller
54 "Grace, mercy, and peace, from ___ our Father" (1 Tim. 1:2)
56 Music mediums

58 Crier
61 Foremost
66 Dueling sword
67 "By faith ___ blessed Jacob" (Heb. 11:20)
69 Adrenocorticotropic hormone
70 Defend
71 Uncanny
72 "Loose his ___ from off his foot" (Deut. 25:9)
73 Dynamite, for short
74 "We pray you in Christ's ___" (2 Cor. 5:20)
75 "___ no man any thing" (Rom. 13:8)

DOWN

1 Cudgel
2 "Professing themselves to be ___" (Rom. 1:22)
3 "Grace be with thee. ___" (1 Tim. 6:21)
4 Mud brick
5 "Oppositions of science falsely so ___" (1 Tim. 6:20)
6 "They ___ upon horses" (Jer. 6:23)
7 "But ___ the messenger came to him" (2 Kings 6:32)
8 "I came into the regions of ___ and Cilicia" (Gal. 1:21)
9 "Let no man think me a ___" (2 Cor. 11:16)
10 Decorative needle case
11 Artist Chagall
13 "___ to your faith virtue" (2 Peter 1:5)
15 Hebrews "of ___ salute you" (Heb. 13:24)
20 "There was ___ ___ of glass" (Rev. 4:6) (2 wds.)
22 Gentle

25 Rest
26 "I will ___ things" (Matt. 13:35)
27 "Make full proof of ___ ministry" (2 Tim. 4:5)
29 "Men that walk over them are not ___ of them" (Luke 11:44)
30 McDonald's Big ___
32 Wan
33 People were making a ___ in Matt. 9:23
34 Fellow
35 Medical assistant
37 Sport's official (abbr.)
39 "I suffer ___ a woman to teach" (1 Tim. 2:12)
42 Goddess
43 "Rule his ___ house" (1 Tim. 3:5)
47 "Take thine ___" (Luke 12:19)

49 Eyed
50 Enemy
52 The saints in ___ (2 Cor. 1:1)
55 Removes moisture
57 Chopped
58 Lift something heavy
59 "Some men's sins are ___" (1 Tim. 5:24)
60 "I ___ into Macedonia" (1 Tim. 1:3)
61 "Take ___ of the church" (1 Tim. 3:5)
62 A pattern of birth defects
63 Resound
64 Store
65 "I charge ___ before God" (1 Tim. 5:21)
68 "Lay hold upon the hope ___ before us" (Heb. 6:18)

97 WIDOW OF ZAREPHATH: GOD CARES FOR HIS OWN

by Tonya Vilhauer

• • • • • •

ACROSS

1 "Gather the wheat into my ___" (Matt. 13:30)
5 Experts
9 Abhors
14 Region
15 Scottish skirt
16 Make ashamed
17 Pointed ends
18 Opera solo
19 "Heard the ___ of Elijah" (1 Kings 17:22)
20 Religion of Muslims
22 "He ___ to her" (1 Kings 17:10)
24 "The ___ of the house of David" (Isa. 22:22)
25 Dishevel
27 "Jacob shall return, and be in rest and at ___" (Jer. 46:27)
31 "Brought ___ upon the widow" (1 Kings 17:20)
32 "Not ___ death" (Luke 2:26)
34 Bookkeeper
35 Won
38 "As soon as the ___ was gone, David arose" (1 Sam. 20:41)
40 "Ten ___ of vineyard" (Isa. 5:10)
42 "Jacob, whom he ___ Israel" (2 Kings 17:34)
44 Really cool (slang)
46 "Bring me. . .bread in ___ hand" (1 Kings 17:11)
47 Fetch me water "that I may ___" (1 Kings 17:10)
48 "He said, ___, I know it" (2 Kings 2:3)
50 Intensifies
51 Wing
52 Quip
55 Snare, and a ___" (Rom. 11:9)
57 Soybean
59 There was no ___ in him (1 Kings 17:17)

61 Very high wavelength
64 African vacation
66 "My ___ for the LORD" (2 Kings 10:16) (var.)
68 ___ la vista
71 Player's cards
73 "The burning ___" (Lev. 26:16)
74 The Lord "shall ___ them" (Josh 23:5)
75 "There was ___ ___ of glass" (Rev. 4:6) (2 wds.)
76 "They could not. . .strengthen their ___" (Isa. 33:23)
77 "There shall not be. . .rain these ___" (1 Kings 17:1)
78 "___ for repentance" (Matt. 3:8)
79 U.S. leader (abbr.)

DOWN

1 Dye by hand
2 "___, get thee to Zarephath" (1 Kings 17:9)
3 Retort
4 Rocket builders
5 Precedes an alias
6 Round
7 There were many widows "in the days of ___" (Luke 4:25)
8 "There shall be no herd in the ___" (Hab. 3:17)
9 "I ___ not a cake" (1 Kings 17:12)
10 "Where he ___" (1 Kings 17:19)
11 ___ chi
12 Escudo
13 "And ___ said unto Elijah" (1 Kings 17:18)
21 Cable subscription
23 Downwind
26 "___ in a cruse" (1 Kings 17:12)
28 Pungent
29 Paul "would not ___ the time in Asia" (Acts 20:16)

30 "Thy ___ delight my soul"
(Ps. 94:19) (var.)
31 "The children of ___"
(2 Kings 19:12)
33 "Did ___ many days"
(1 Kings 17:15)
35 Type of mint candy
36 Monte ___
37 Author Dickinson
39 The ___ the Lord sends rain
(1 Kings 17:14)
41 Put this ___ in the prison"
(1 Kings 22:27) (var.)
43 10 gram measurement
45 Prisoner
49 "Thou ___ a man of God"
(1 Kings 17:24)
53 Church group (abbr.)

54 Preacher Billy___
56 "Thou saidst, ___"
(Ezek. 25:3)
58 Flower
60 Rub out
61 Author Poe
62 "The mistress of the ___, fell
sick" (1 Kings 17:17)
63 Worries
65 Association of American Law
Schools (abbr.)
67 Incline
68 Attention-getting expression
69 "There was neither hammer nor
___ nor any tool" (1 Kings 6:7)
70 Whirlpool
72 Computer file extension

Woman at the Well: Taught by Jesus

by Tonya Vilhauer

• • • • • •

ACROSS

1 The sick man was "lying on a ___" (Matt. 9:2) (var.)
4 Small house
9 Bench
12 Sailors "hey"
14 Tylenol's competitor
15 "Had made a fire ___ of coals" (John 18:18)
16 "Everlasting ___" (John 4:14)
17 "Jesus made ___" (John 9:11) (pl.)
18 "I sent you to ___" (John 4:38)
19 "Our father worshiped in this ___" (John 4:20)
21 "Give me this water, that I ___ not" (John 4:15)
23 Garden tool
24 Jesus ___ on the well (John 4:6)
25 "___, the servant of Jesus Christ" (Jude 1:1)
28 Missile launched from land or sea
31 "Come ___, and heal" (John 4:47)
34 Disciples marveled Jesus "___ with the woman" (John 4:27)
36 Trained medical professional
38 "Touch the ___ of his garment" (Matt. 14:36)
40 Brad Pitt's job (abbr.)
41 North of the Beehive State
43 Plunge into water
44 "___ yet at Jerusalem" (John 4:21)
45 Abraham bought the sepulchre "for a ___ of money" (Acts 7:16)
46 Use bleach
48 "Who in presence am ___ among you" (2 Cor. 10:1)
51 "The gift of ___" (John 4:10)
53 A man told "all things that ___ I did" (John 4:29)

54 Chum
56 Monkey
58 Tropical vacation island
61 Are you greater than "his ___, and his cattle?" (John 4:12)
66 Great
67 "The water that I ___ give him" (John 4:14)
69 Metric weight unit
70 "The woman. . .went her way into the ___" (John 4:28)
71 Crippling disease
72 Green seedless plant
73 KJV's hast
74 What a dropped melon does
75 Ball holder

DOWN

1 "There was a ___" (Luke 8:24)
2 American state
3 Meat alternative
4 Chocolate tree
5 Jesus lays "down his life for his ___" (John 15:13) (var.)
6 Noodle
7 Wall plant
8 "Birds of the air have ___" (Luke 9:58)
9 "She became a ___ of salt" (Gen. 19:26) (var.)
10 Periods of time
11 "Jesus ___" (John 11:35)
13 Japanese money
15 Curly corn chip
20 "He would have given ___ living water" (John 4:10)
22 "Thou hast ___ five husbands" (John 4:18)
25 Isaac's son (Gen. 25:16)
26 Extreme
27 Dekagram
29 "Remember the ___"

30 Speed measurement
32 The fields "are ___ already to harvest" (John 4:35)
33 Drink the water of everlasting life and ___ thirst (John 4:14)
34 Sunbathe
35 Insult (slang)
37 "Whom thou ___ hast is not thy husband" (John 4:18)
39 "The woman. . .saith to the ___" (John 4:28)
42 Shoveled
43 Multiplication's opposite (abbr.)
47 "Lifted up his ___ against me" (John 13:18)
49 Zesty
50 "Master, ___" (John 4:31)
52 Showy flower

55 What a small child does when speaking
57 Aviate
58 High ___
59 Capital of Western Samoa
60 Strikes
61 "Go, ___ thy husband" (John 4:16)
62 Dam
63 "To ___ in the day time" (2 Peter 2:13)
64 "Or ___ be absent" (Phil. 1:27)
65 "They shall take away thy ___" (Ezek. 23:25)
68 "And ___ for joy" (Luke 6:23) (var.)

ZACCHAEUS: THE TREETOP OBSERVER

99

by Tonya Vilhauer

• • • • • •

ACROSS

1 Compass direction
4 The angel ___ Mary (Luke 1:28)
9 Cooking measurement
12 Hawaiian island
14 He shall not "shoot an ___" in the city (Isa. 37:33)
15 Snack cake
16 Rental car service
17 "Shall we ___ with sword?" (Luke 22:49)
18 Cookie
19 Boat races
21 "The kingdom of God should immediately ___" (Luke 19:11)
23 A storm is coming, for the sky is ___ (Matt. 16:3)
24 ___ de Janeiro
25 "Son of man is ___" (Luke 19:10)
28 "___, I am warm" (Isa. 44:16)
31 "Strain at a ___" (Matt. 23:24)
34 Videos
36 Curve
38 Be not as the horse "with ___ and bridle" (Ps. 32:9)
40 Actor Alda
41 Had
43 River of Egypt
44 Zacchaeus could ___ see Jesus (Luke 19:3)
45 Romance
46 Ice cream dessert
48 "Go up, ___ an altar unto the LORD" (2 Sam. 24:18)
51 Naught
53 "The Son of man is come to ___ and to save" (Luke 19:10)
54 "He was ___ at that saying" (Mark 10:22)
56 Lyric poem
58 Two-person U.S. spacecraft

61 "I restore him ___" (Luke 19:8)
66 Chilled
67 "He added and ___ a parable" (Luke 19:11)
69 Yes
70 A formal choice
71 "It is easier for a ___ to go though a needle's eye" (Luke 18:25)
72 Soft cheese
73 Compass direction
74 Used for winter fun
75 Commercials

DOWN

1 "He did ___ upon the wings" (Ps. 18:10) (var.)
2 Rescue
3 Liberal
4 "Zacchaeus, make ___" (Luke 19:5)
5 Fleet
6 Spring flower
7 "His ___ was to burn incense" (Luke 1:9)
8 "Neither shalt thou ___ by thy head" (Matt. 5:36)
9 "The king arose, and ___ his garments" (2 Sam. 13:31) (var.)
10 George Beverly ___
11 "I give to the ___" (Luke 19:8)
13 North American country
15 Get upon (2 wds.)
20 Zacchaeus sat in "a sycomore ___" (Luke 19:4)
22 "The ___ did eat" (Luke 15:16) (var.)
25 "His feet like in ___ to polished brass" (Dan. 10:6) (var.)
26 Egg-shaped
27 One-sixtieth of an hour (abbr.)
29 Vietnam capital

30 "They ___ hid from thine eyes" (Luke 19:42)
32 "Enter into, there ___" (Luke 9:4)
33 Hindu mark
34 "A ___ named Zacchaeus" (Luke 19:2)
35 "I did not ___" (Luke 19:22)
37 Investment options
39 Golf ___
42 "The word be ___" (1 Peter 3:1)
43 Greenland
47 Drug taker
49 Jesus and the apostles "went ___ privately" (Luke 9:10)
50 Zacchaeus ___ and climbed up a sycamore tree (Luke 19:4)
52 Jesus ___ up and saw Zacchaeus (Luke 19:5)

55 Phonograph records
57 Combats between two persons
58 "They should ___ him of the fruit" (Luke 20:10)
59 Study of material welfare of humankind (abbr.)
60 Dole out as in Luke 6:38
61 "The ___ of him went out" (Luke 4:37)
62 Watch chain
63 Pods used in soups and stews
64 "That I ___ not down" (Luke 19:22)
65 Colors
68 "Thou art not Caesar's ___" (John 19:12) (var.)

ZACHARIAS: THE FATHER OF JOHN THE BAPTIST

100

by Laura Lisle

• • • • •

ACROSS

1 "They made ___ to his father" (Luke 1:62)
6 The King of Edom's bones were burned into this (Amos 2:1)
10 Luke's second book
14 Thoughts
15 Food was sacrificed to this
16 In ___ of (instead of)
17 Dessert adornment
18 Heredity component
19 Odd's opposite
20 Zeus' sister
21 Expression of surprise
22 Open
24 Engrossed
26 "Hail, thou that art ___ favoured" (Luke 1:28)
27 Brie
30 "The wild beast shall ___ them" (Hos. 13:8)
31 Keeps
32 Approximate date
33 The Lord's is stretched out (Ex. 6:6)
36 "I am ___ and Omega" (Rev. 1:8)
37 Feline constellation
38 Radiuses
40 "Peace, good will toward ___" (Luke 2:14)
41 Anchor location (Acts 27:29)
43 Raging
44 Waters' name (Gen. 1:10)
45 "Elisabeth was ___" (Luke 1:7)
46 Roe
49 Literary Ms. Eyre
50 Spring birds
51 Droop
52 "Mighty men to ___ the waters" (2 Chron. 32:3)
56 Soon, as in Matt. 13:20
57 Dutch cheese
59 "The ___ which the builders rejected" (Luke 20:17)
60 Yield
61 "Should not perish, but have everlasting ___" (John 3:16)
62 "On earth ___, good will" (Luke 2:14)
63 "Mine ___ have seen thy salvation" (Luke 2:30)
64 What Simeon does (Luke 2:30)
65 It stings (Prov. 23:32)

DOWN

1 Exhaling sound
2 "An ___ soul shall suffer hunger" (Prov. 19:15)
3 May be park or drive
4 Christ's childhood home
5 Jerusalem to Bethlehem (dir.)
6 "The ___ shineth in darkness" (John 1:5)
7 Thought
8 First day of wk.
9 Sad
10 First Hebrew letter
11 Civic
12 Little
13 "And they ___ a new song" (Rev. 5:9)
21 One of Hiram's cargo (1 Kings 10:22)
23 Related to farming
25 Hired hit man
26 Unclean bird (Lev. 11:19)
27 Chowder ingredient
28 Drag, as in Luke 12:58
29 Sports channel
30 Layers
32 Describes crystal (Rev. 21:11)

33 12th Jewish month (Est. 3:7)
34 Ritual
35 Bearing
39 Nailed
42 Nap raisers
45 David's ammo holder
46 Cud-chewing animal (Lev. 11:5)
47 "The LORD ___ upon mount Sinai" (Ex. 24:16)
48 Foxes spoiled these (Song 2:15)
49 Brother of Jesus (Matt. 13:55)

50 "Run with patience the ___" (Heb. 12:1)
51 "Hold thou me up, and I shall be ___" (Ps. 119:117)
53 Cousin of 2nd plague (Ex. 8:2)
54 "Let us go up at ___" (Num. 13:30)
55 Look
58 "I shall not ___, but live" (Ps. 118:17)
59 Restful resort

PRISCILLA: BIBLE TEACHER
by Patricia Mitchell

• • • • • •

ACROSS

1 Priscilla would ___ 22 Across
6 The Israelite's trek across the desert, in a way
10 Goliath got more than simply this on the head! (1 Sam. 17:49)
13 Ezekiel's vision of the new temple included these (Ezek. 40:16)
15 "How much ___ he hath done to thy saints" (Acts 9:13)
16 "___ from the truth" (James 5:19)
17 Priscilla's ministry would ___ in many coming to faith
18 Describes John Mark, perhaps (Acts 13:13)
19 Paul was prepared "to ___ at Jerusalem" (Acts 21:13)
20 Priscilla and Aquila were expelled from here (Acts 18:2)
22 Priscilla and Aquila's student (Acts 18:24–26)
24 Priscilla had this not to correct 22 Across in public
26 The mother of Jesus
28 Harvard's rival
29 Sometimes before angels (Jude 1:9)
30 "Ye shall be baptized with the ___ Ghost" (Acts 1:5)
31 Celestial shooter
32 "He made a ___" (Ps. 7:15)
33 Pasta
34 Jesus' sacrifice would ___ salvation for us
35 Hair-growing product
37 22 Across was one, in a way
41 Subject of Priscilla's ministry
42 The heavens, perhaps
43 Priscilla lived long ___
44 Phenice was this (Acts 27:12)
47 "___ tidings" (Acts 13:32)
48 Priscilla was this to Paul
49 "My cry came before him, ___ into his ears" (Ps. 18:6)

50 Idol worshipped by the Israelites (2 Kings 17:16)
51 Priscilla to Aquila
52 Paul greets Priscilla in these (2 Tim. 4:19)
54 Lazarus had more than one of these (Luke 16:20)
56 Priscilla was one in ministry
57 First murderer (Gen. 4:8)
59 Hardly describes Priscilla
63 Rome to Corinth (dir.)
64 Record player
65 Dissimilar
66 Meaning of Esau's other name (Gen. 25:30)
67 Set in gold with beryl and jasper (Ex. 28:20)
68 Priscilla sailed here with Aquila and Paul (Acts 18:18)

DOWN

1 Pothole filler
2 Bard's before
3 Medical research org.
4 Priscilla had one in her home (1 Cor. 16:19)
5 Hagar or Onesimus, e.g.
6 Dorcas knew how to do this well (Acts 9:39)
7 Bird sanctuary
8 Describes the lame who came to Jesus for healing (Matt. 21:14)
9 Fido's food
10 God admonishes those who create this, as in 2 Peter 2:13
11 American songbird
12 Already fixed in place
14 Alzheimer's patients lose this
21 Priscilla remained calm, and did not do this (Acts 18:26)
23 French city
24 Priscilla, Aquila, and Paul
25 Temporary, as a person filling in (abbr.)

27 Boxer Muhammad
29 Easter mo., usually
30 "Naphtali is a ___" (Gen. 49:21)
31 Priscilla was this kind of girl (Acts 18:2)
33 "Holy hill of ___" (Ps. 2:6)
34 Priscilla shared God's ___
36 Ezra acted as Artaxerxes's in Jerusalem (Ezra 7:21)
37 God willingly does this to those who turn to Him (Acts 28:27)
38 God wants our whole heart, not just this (Matt. 22:37)
39 Priscilla probably would not have appreciated this kind of look
40 Never do this with God's commandments (Matt. 5:19)
42 Chicken ___ ___ king (2 wds.)
44 Priscilla to Paul (Rom. 16:3)

45 Priscilla was not ___ to travel
46 Paul did this to the idea of taking John Mark again (Acts 15:38)
47 Turn into gas
48 Priscilla, a serious person, would not act this way
50 The fool doesn't use his (Prov. 1:7)
51 Paul does this continually, with tears (Acts 20:31)
53 You might hear it in the joyful hills in Ps. 98:8
55 One might be on your desk (abbr.)
58 See 46 Down
60 "___, if thou have borne him hence, tell me where thou hast laid him" (John 20:15)
61 Aspen activity
62 KJV's yes

Puzzle 1. Aaron's Errands

```
BIAS█AQUA██WASP
IDLE█LUST█HALSA
RATE█BEAT█OTTER
CHANCEL█YALE███
HOR█OIL█MIRIAM█
█GMT█DAME█NBE██
ARGUE█SAGAS█URN
LION█LINEN█BRAD
PSI█ZINCS█POEMS
HEN█URGE█SLY███
ANGORA█BTU█ALA█
██RISE█ARMADAS█
ISAAC█SAME█BOTH
BERTH█ABBA█ERIE
MAKE██URIM█LENS
```

Puzzle 2. Amazing Abigail

```
NABAL█CPS██FOOL
EBONY█HAY█WORSE
ALONE█AIR█HEALS
TOTE█STRIFE█LOT
HOE█SOS█NOAH███
█MEALY█GOLIATH█
██CIA█LED█GLEE█
SHEEP█PAS█SHEAR
PORT█MEW█ATE███
█APRICOT█BURMA█
██CORN█EBB█EMU█
WPM█DEADLY█MAON
IRATE█MOO█TENET
FOUND█ESP█ALIBI
EMIT██SEE█IDEAL
```

Puzzle 3. Abraham:
Man of Faith and Action

```
ABS█HIKE█LESSOR
BIT█EDEN█EXHALE
ROE█LAND█EXITED
ATROPHY██SON███
MINI█OARS█NAHOR
█CALL█ELF█EMU██
██EOS█FAO█MAID█
SPURTER█BURETTE
LESS█EEL█LAX███
ORE█DIE█MIFF███
BURNT█NEBE█CORE
██OUR█IGNORED██
CATTLE█MAYO█MSG
ORACLE█ALPS█ACE
BETHEL█MYTH█LAD
```

Puzzle 4. Abraham:
Keeper of the Promise

```
BACH█TRIAL█TALC
AURA█WINCE█ICED
STARSOFTHESKIES
HONEY█LOO█LIDS█
███NNE█OUI████
APACE███SCOFFS█
ALAN█BABE█ECLAT
SANDSOFTHESHORE
STEEP█TUFT█RUMP
NELSON██USERS██
███USS█ZIP████
SASS█TAI█INDIA█
FATHEROFNATIONS
ALTO█ENACT█NOSH
STYE█VERSE█ARTY
```

Puzzle 5. Absalom:
A Monarch Wanna-Be

```
MAID█FAIR██DADA
ALSO█RARE█HATED
MULE█INKS█EVENS
BLESSED█THAI███
OAT█WNW██ELDERS
█CAD█THEE█DIN██
AMMON█FIELD█EGO
MEAN█PEERS█EMIR
ALI█BLARE█GLADE
SON█AARS█OAK███
ANEMIC█OPT█MST█
██OLEO█APELIKE█
HOUSE█PASO█OMEN
EASED█EGIS█REED
XRAY██NOSE█DOTS
```

Puzzle 6. Adam: The First Dude

```
BOBBY█SCAB█ARAB
ADORE█PURL█DALI
BONES█ERIE█STIR
AREA█UNEASE█END
███TEND█SNORES█
ETCHED██SEED███
AHA█LOGGED█DRAB
COLA██OUT██SOUL
HULL█MAYHEM█ATE
███ABEL█YARROW█
CURSED██SEMI███
EVE█TULIPS█THEM
DUST█SIDE█SUEDE
ALTO█AFEW█PARER
RASP█SEAS█ALONE
```

Puzzle 7. Amos Speaks God's Word

Puzzle 8. Andrew's Catch

Puzzle 9. Anna the Prophetess

Puzzle 10. Barnabas:
Bearer of God's Word

Puzzle 11. Bathsheba the Beautiful

Puzzle 12. Benjamin:
The Younger Brother

Puzzle 13. Cain: First Born

Puzzle 14. Daniel: The Lion Tamer

Puzzle 15. David: The Great King

Puzzle 16. Deborah: The Judge

Puzzle 17. Dorcas:
Full of Good Works

Puzzle 18. Eli: The Great Priest

Puzzle 19. Elijah Heard It

Puzzle 20. Elisha: Man of God

Puzzle 21. Elisabeth's Joy

Puzzle 22. Esau's Error

Puzzle 23. Esther: The Blessed Queen

Puzzle 24. Eve: The First Woman

```
Puzzle 25 grid:
BOP . . AMONG . . MAR
ARIA . FEMUR . HOME
LEND . FAENA . ADEN
MOTORINN . CLIENT
. . . AXE . EAT
. KING . RAD . WISP
BORNEO . NAP . POI
RAKE . LIGHT . BURR
ALE . ELI . AZORES
. ADAR . LOB . EATS
. . . DIV . EBB
SCRIBE . BEAUTIFY
OHIO . RIOTS . ACLU
PUPS . STOLE . MEAL
SBE . . ASKED . DYE
```

Puzzle 25. Ezra: The Scribe

```
Puzzle 26 grid:
SCRAM . CDS . . VA
NAACP . LEE . HOBOS
URGE . AGE . AARGH
BLESSEDARTTHOU
. . . PASS . REUSE
MASTIC . NU
ISWITHTHEE . BON
REAR . WAC . IRON
ATE . SILKSCREEN
. . IN . PAROLE
AMONG . AVIS
TAKINGPICTURES
ASIAN . LAX . NODE
KENYA . ACE . STAGE
CA . DEN . WOMEN
```

Puzzle 26. Gabriel: The Archangel

```
Puzzle 27 grid:
EBBS . RIGID . MST
SARI . IRONY . FETA
CRAG . PEACE . USER
. NAP . THRESHER
TSP . DEN . NEEDY
RAINDROP . ODDS
AUTO . LUCAS
PLAT . BARAK . FALA
. MINIM . EVIL
. ZEEB . MESHWORK
SNIPS . LIE . WAY
WITHHELD . SRI
ECHO . MOOSE . RUTH
DEED . MOWER . ASIA
ERR . APNEA . NAPS
```

Puzzle 27. Gideon:
God's Man of Valor

```
Puzzle 28 grid:
OMAHA . HEAR . WRAP
PARAN . EDGE . HALE
ANENT . AGES . OBOE
LEAD . PRY . ISRAEL
. MAID . ADULTS
STRAIT . FLUB
THEIR . ARIES . SRI
AANDW . DIE . ISAAC
BID . AVIAN . SLAVE
. VEER . STORED
MASERU . MUST
CURTSY . TEN . HITS
ARIA . BAIT . AFORE
LAST . IDLE . TUTOR
FLEE . GOLD . ELATE
```

Puzzle 28. Hagar: The Other Wife

```
Puzzle 29 grid:
NETS . CHUB . PEAL
EMIT . GRATA . ALMA
WINE . LINEN . CLEW
TREESEED . QUEENS
. . PEAS . HURL
CAREEN . REENACT
ADAR . SPENT . PARE
III . RAN . RUN
NOSE . NOMAD . FLED
. SEASONS . ERRORS
. GATE . SHOE
TEBETH . EPOWERED
HAIR . IDLER . DODO
USEL . NISAN . OMIT
DEFY . GEEK . METE
```

Puzzle 29. Haman Trades Places

```
Puzzle 30 grid:
SWAPS . AREA . SWBW
AIDES . DEAD . MALE
INANE . OATH . IRAN
DEMI . IBM . EATEST
. . NATO . PRIEST
PRINTS . BEER
RURAL . FLESH . WET
ALOHA . EAR . EPHAH
YEN . NEEDS . AROSE
. . TALE . IDEATE
. BEFITS . ROSE
SENECA . YIN . NASA
TIDE . BOWS . BISON
AGED . LACK . ONION
BEDS . ERAS . AGATE
```

Puzzle 30. Hannah's
Child of Promise

Puzzle 31. Herod the Tetrarch

Puzzle 32. Hezekiah:
Jehovah Follower

Puzzle 33. Hosea:
The Long-Suffering Spouse

Puzzle 34. Isaiah:
The Faithful Prophet

Puzzle 35. Ishmael: The Other Son

Puzzle 36. Jacob: The Usurper

```
A L A S   A G O R A   S E E
D E V I L   B R A U N   T N T
A F I R E   B U R N T   A S H
M T V   S N O B   I S S U E
    G I F T   B R O T H E R
S C H O O L   S A U C Y    
O R I O N   W I T H   M O B
F O R D   T E E T H   P I P E
A P E   M A T E   T O N A L
    M O U N T   T O K I L L
A T L A N T A   B O N Y    
H E I R S   C L E G   P S I
E R N   T A B L E   U P E N D
A R E   E L I A S   E E R I E
D A D   R E N D S   P U P A
```

Puzzle 37. James the Disciple

```
S T A R   T E S T   U N F E D
C O L A   O D O R   S I E V E
A W A Y   B E M A   E S T E E
R E M   M A N A M A   S E N D
F R O L I C       S K I    
      I N C   A C H E   T S P
    D I G I O R N O   G R A C E
N O S H   A G E   O M A N
B O L T S   R E D E E M E R
E R E   U S E R   F D A    
      P E A       F I N E S T
B A B A   D E S P O T   A T E
A L A R M   R E A R   P R O X
S O R T S   M A S T   E T N A
S E E S T   A M O S   T H E N
```

Puzzle 38. Jehovah:
The Great and Mighty One

```
F F A   A B L E   C U P F U L
L A D   B A I T   U N E A S E
E R R   E T N A   S C A R E D
S C O T T I E   S A C      
H E I R   K N E W   P E R C H
S T O P   Y E A   O U I
    U S A   E A R   I M P S
A L L T I M E   R A W N E S S
L I E S   E V E   B A T
A C V   N I P   C A L M
S E I S M   L A N D   C O A T
    P E A   O R A T O R Y
A F I E L D   F L U X   T I P
T O I L E D   B A N E   E N E
E X I L E S   I N K S   R E D
```

Puzzle 39. Jeremiah:
The Great Prophet

```
E R M A   Z I L C H   M A S S
R A I L   A D O R E   A L M A
I S L E   P O S E R   S T O P
C H E V R O L E T   K H A K I
      E A T   E W E   R E D
J O T   M E T E   B R A
E M U S   C H R O N I C L E S
H A R E   E O N   T I L L
U N F R I E N D L Y   H O S E
      F D R   E Y E S   N E W
S A C   E R E   A K A
C I R C A   G A R R I S O N S
A D A R   P Y L O N   K N E E
L E N O   A P P L E   E C O N
D R E W   S T O O D   R E N D
```

Puzzle 40. Jeroboam:
Mighty Man of Valor

```
S O A P   L Y N X   T H O R N
A U T O   L A N E   R A M I E
A C T S   A M E N   A S I D E
R H Y T H M S   O M I T T E D
    P E A   P I T Y      
    I D O L S   S H E   D E L
D R O N E   S T O N E   E S E
E A T E N   N A B   S A L T S
A T E   A F O R E   C R I E S
R E D   E W E   C U R S E
    C R E W   A D O
C H E R I T H   C L O G G E D
A U R A S   I D O L   A E R O
P L A N E   T A M E   N A I L
E A S E S   E Y E D   T R E E
```

Puzzle 41. Jezebel: The Evil Queen

```
L I F E   A M E B A   S B W
O S A K A   E A T E N   A L I
A L I E N   S T A G G   T E N
D E L   S P O T   U S I N G
      S W A P   F R I E N D S
H O S T E L   S O U S E
I N C U R   H I G H   B C G
R Y A N   H E E L S   B O I L
E X T   P E R O   A O R T A
      P E R I L   D R O N E D
Z A P O T E C   N E C K
E L A T E   R I C H   D Y E
S T Y   R A V E N   E N E M Y
T E E   E X I S T   D A N C E
A R E   D E A T H   P T A S
```

Puzzle 42. Job: Put to the Test

Puzzle 43. Joel: The Minor Prophet

Puzzle 44. John:
The Beloved Disciple

Puzzle 45. John the Baptist:
Forerunner of the Lord

Puzzle 46. Jonah:
In the Belly of the Whale

Puzzle 47. Jonathan:
Best Friend Forever

Puzzle 48. Joseph:
God's Man in Egypt

Puzzle 49. Joseph:
Father of Our Lord

Puzzle 50. Joshua: The Successor

Puzzle 51: Judah: Son of Praise

Puzzle 52: Judas Iscariot:
The Betrayer

Puzzle 53: Laban the Trickster

Puzzle 54: Lazarus:
A New Lease on Life

Puzzle 55: Leah: The Unloved Wife

Puzzle 56: Lot: The Nephew

Puzzle 57: Luke:
The Beloved Physician

Puzzle 58: Mark: The Evangelist

Puzzle 59: Martha the Server

Puzzle 60: Mary: The Virgin Mother

Puzzle 61: Mary Who Sat at Jesus' Feet

```
CHASM SANG  ASSN
AORTA OREO  THEE
SPEAR LORD  EELS
HEARTS SOLD BLT
  CHIME IOTAS
BETHANY KEY
APR GRAVE  PACT
LEAF RYE   ODOR
DEMO THEIR EMU
 UGH NOMINEE
 FUROR ASPEN
AIM DICT ESCORT
LOBE VASE CURIO
ANEW EVEN ABBOT
RARE DEAD LISTS
```

Puzzle 62: Mary Magdalene: The First at the Tomb

```
FIRST LSD  SAGS
ADIEU MOTE OLEO
LOSER UPON FINO
ALF RISEN FAGOT
  JERK FIM NAY
SCOOTER UGH
NOVA ABUT  AFAR
OMEN ATONE NEBE
WARN TSAR  KALE
 ADO ASPIRED
CEO KPH VILE
ANGEL OPERA BAD
IDLE EVIL TIARA
REEL LETS EMBER
ODDS FLY SPEAK
```

Puzzle 63: Matthew: The Tax Collector

```
GRACE JOKE JAMB
LOSER EVEN ODOR
ABIDE SENT BANE
DEAR AURORA PTA
  ODDS ORATED
HERNIA SPEW
APE DRIPPY ACTS
NEED CIA  YORE
DELI DEGREE RIB
 SLID WRONGS
FIGHTS HEAL
ONE MARTYR DEAF
AGES BORE PERIL
MOSS LAIN ASIDE
STEW ERMA STEED
```

Puzzle 64: Micah: The Younger Prophet

```
AREA HEAR  FAIL
PUNS YALE  MAFIA
ALES ERAS  ARCED
REMNANT TERM
TRY DAH MISSUS
  GAS MEAN PRE
ARMOR EERIE AGE
GOOD AVAIL EWER
ABS TRITE HANDS
TEE OILY NET
ESSAYS OIL PTA
 TOED LEPROUS
HELOT ERIC OWLS
ARENA LOVE MESA
GATE LEES PRAY
```

Puzzle 65: Miriam: The Watchful Sister

```
TAB SANG SCARAB
EPA AGUE CHOICE
RPM RARE AIRMEN
RABBITS BLT
ALOE EELS DACHA
 LORD EOS RED
 TIM OWN CORE
GODHEAD NOTOPEN
USES RAD WIN
ALA YIN PTSD
MODEM SAGA ACRE
 TOM LAOCOON
ACCUSE DARN TWO
SPADES IDOL INC
KADESH DENY ASH
```

Puzzle 66: Mordecai: Trusted Guardian

```
SAD FLEW RAISES
APE AIRS ELNINO
BLT SNOW PADRES
ROASTED SRI
EMIT NEXT MANES
 BLUE IRK AVE
 PSI III EMIR
SPLOTCH ONESELF
YOUR EEL GOT
NOT DAY SHED
CREPE RENT EYES
 LSD ARMREST
IDEATE ASIA LIE
TASSEL WALK ERR
SHIMEI ELLIE TEN
```

Puzzle 67: Naaman,
the Leprous Commander

Puzzle 68: Nathan:
Teacher of the Lord's Will

Puzzle 69: Nathanael Came and Saw

Puzzle 70: Nehemiah:
Builder of the Wall

Puzzle 71: Nicodemus:
Seeker of Salvation

Puzzle 72: Noah: The Great Builder

Puzzle 73: Obadiah:
Worshipper of Jehovah

Puzzle 74: Paul the Persecutor

Puzzle 75: Peter: The Rock

Puzzle 76: Pharaoh:
The Hard-Hearted Ruler

Puzzle 77: Philemon:
The Affectionate One

Puzzle 78: Philip: The Horse Lover

Puzzle 79: Pilate:
The Governor of Judaea

Puzzle 80: Rachel, the Beautiful Wife

Puzzle 81: Rahab's Scarlet Ribbon

Puzzle 82: Rebekah:
The Mother of Twins

Puzzle 83: Ruth:
The Faithful Daughter-in-Law

Puzzle 84: Samson:
The Strong Man Becomes Weak

Puzzle 85: Samuel: God Was Calling

```
ADO   TAXIS   BPM
FIVE  BURNT  ELLE
EVER  OSAKA  REAL
WARRANTY  GROUND
   SEE   GOD
 BARE  NFL  BEEF
MIZPAH  RAD  MIL
ALUM  ALIBI  SOFA
DKR  DEL  SNOTTY
 SEER  ELI  OBEY
   NAY    MEN
EFFETE  APPEARED
CLAM  ALLAH  CITY
HOLY  RATIO  PONE
OWL   SWORD   TAD
```

Puzzle 86: Sarah: The Miracle Mom

```
MIAMI  GEE  CATS
INFER  IMP  MAMRE
THREE  VIA  ADMAN
TEAK  RETURN  OPT
SRI  SON  LIED
 EDITS  ENTERED
 NAY  LTD  NARY
READY  PAS  LITRE
APSE  BED  SEE
MAKESAD  LADEN
 DARD  DAH  LIP
BTU  BELFRY  FINE
LAPEL  ERE  WAXED
ALONE  REF  EVITA
BEND  SET  BERYL
```

Puzzle 87: Saul: The People's King

```
CONGA  PEAK  SSW
ALARMS  SYLI  AHA
REGIME  TELL  WAS
 LOTS  FOOLISH
KILN  TOUT  ANTE
HIDE  DEAL  EDGAR
IWO  GOER  AVE
PILSNER  GLINTED
 HUG  FELL  ELI
IVIES  SLAY  TALL
SINE  BLUR  MAKE
RESPIRE  STAB
ANT  SEER  SPLEEN
ENE  LAVA  PLEASE
LAP  EDEN  ESTER
```

Puzzle 88: Shadrach, Meshach, and
Abednego: You're Fired

```
MIDST  GODS  FDR
ACETIC  ACRE  LEE
TELUGU  STIR  ACE
 BETH  AFFAIRS
ABBR  ADVT  GLEE
TRAY  FIRE  BASES
SET  FURY  SIT
PASTELS  HONESTY
 ALL  WORD  ERE
APRIL  CAST  GNUS
RAIN  SORE  NOTE
CLOTHES  SLOG
ALT  ERMA  ANGORA
DOE  AVIS  GOLDEN
ERR  TECH  SEEDY
```

Puzzle 89: Solomon: The Wisest Man

```
HULA  GAFF  CAUSE
EVIL  OBIE  OFTEN
RUNE  VILA  STEAD
BLESS  AERATE
SAN  BETTER  RIBS
 BETH  DKG  COT
HOHO  CAR  AFIRE
APISH  RUM  SLEEP
VERSE  BED  ERRS
ERA  WEB  TOLD
NAME  RESALE  CPA
 VERNAL  TULIP
INDIA  UMBO  PAPA
RIOTS  MOAN  OVER
SPRAT  BARE  NEST
```

Puzzle 90: Stephen:
The Martyred Deacon

```
GAP  SAMOA  WHOLE
RUE  ORALB  AERIE
ANY  MINER  LABEL
STONED  OVER
PITA  THAI  DOGS
SEES  SAUDI  NET
 STERN  ISLAM
ANANAS  MARTYR
ABOUT  POWER
DEN  AROSE  EATS
SLEW  SUIT  ASIA
 IMPS  DAMSEL
CHOSE  TOPIC  ART
DUCES  ERECT  ICE
TETRA  DEATH  LED
```

Puzzle 91: The Blind Man
Who Said I See

Puzzle 92: The Cripple:
Healing at the Gate Beautiful

Puzzle 93: The Leper: No More Sores

Puzzle 94: The Shunnamite Woman
Serving the Man of God

Puzzle 95: Thomas: The Doubter

Puzzle 96: Timothy:
The Young Pastor

Puzzle 97: Widow of Zarephath:
God Cares for His Own

Puzzle 98: Woman at the Well:
Taught by Jesus

Puzzle 99: Zacchaeus:
The Treetop Observer

Puzzle 100: Zacharias:
The Father of John the Baptist

Puzzle 101: Priscilla: Bible Teacher